Inside the Royal Court Theatre, 1956–1981

EDITED BY GRESDNA A. DOTY AND
BILLY J. HARBIN

Inside the Royal
Court Theatre,
1956–1981

ARTISTS TALK

Louisiana State University Press
Baton Rouge and London

Copyright © 1990 by Louisiana State University Press
All rights reserved
Manufactured in the United States of America
First printing
99 98 97 96 95 94 93 92 91 90   5 4 3 2 1

Designer: Diane Batten Didier
Typeface: Garamond #3
Typesetter: G & S Typesetters, Inc.
Printer and binder: Thomson-Shore, Inc.

All photographs reproduced herein are courtesy of LSU Public Relations, except for the photo of the Royal Court Theatre façade, courtesy of Otis Wheeler.

Library of Congress Cataloging-in-Publication Data

Inside the Royal Court Theatre, 1956–1981 : artists talk / edited by Gresdna A. Doty and Billy J. Harbin.
    p.   cm.
  Includes bibliographical references.
  ISBN 0-8071-1550-9 (alk. paper)
  1. Royal Court Theatre. I. Doty, Gresdna A. (Gresdna Ann), 1931–
  II. Harbin, Billy J., 1930–
PN2596.L7R5165 1990
792'.09421'09045—dc20   89-13477
                                                            CIP

The paper in this book meets the guidelines for permanence and durability of the Committee on Production Guidelines for Book Longevity of the Council on Library Resources. ♾

To
Oscar G. Brockett
Richard Moody
and the memory of Hubert C. Heffner

Contents

Illustrations

Preface

The editors of this volume organized a conference, "The English Stage Company at the Royal Court Theatre: Production Practices and Legacies, 1956–81," held at Louisiana State University, October 7–10, 1981. Both of us had carried out research on the English Stage Company (ESC), and, as the theatre operation neared its twenty-fifth anniversary, a conference to celebrate the event seemed appropriate in view of the company's impact on theatres all over the world. Under the exceptional, even visionary, leadership of its first artistic director, George Devine, the English Stage Company at the Royal Court became established as a writers' theatre, committed to the production of new and noncommercial works. It was a daring and courageous commitment at a time when virtually the only stages available to the writer were in the commercial West End, when the only dramatists being recognized and encouraged were traditional and marketable, and when government subsidies for noncommercial operations were practically nonexistent.

The ESC has had six successive managements: George Devine, 1956–1965; William Gaskill, 1965–1972; Oscar Lewenstein, 1972–1975; Nicholas Wright and Robert Kidd, 1975–1977; Stuart Burge, 1977–1979; and Max Stafford-Clark, 1979 to the present. Although each change of director inevitably resulted in subtle shifts of artistic priorities and goals, the company's commitment to the writer as the source and inspirer of its operation has remained unchanged through the years. The conference at Louisiana State University brought together all of the living past and present artistic directors except Oscar Lewenstein (who was unable to come because of illness) and writers, directors, designers, and critics associated with the Royal Court Theatre. American theatre figures, representing major professional noncommercial operations across the country, led the panel sessions and participated in the discussions. These included John Dillon, artistic director, Milwaukee Repertory Theater; Karl Eigsti, designer, New York; Gerald Freedman, artistic director, Great Lakes Theater Festival, Cleveland; Amlin Gray, resident dramatist, Milwaukee Repertory

Theater; Brooks Jones, artistic director, Center for the Arts, Purchase, New York; Michael Murray, producing director, Playhouse in the Park, Cincinnati; Joel Schechter, associate literary manager, Yale Repertory Theatre; and Alexander Speer, administrative director, Actors Theatre, Louisville. Other distinguished participants in the conference were Oscar G. Brockett, theatre historian; Martin Esslin, author and critic; and Irving Wardle, drama critic of *The Times* (London).

Through six sessions, the participants explored and assessed the ESC's artistic philosophy, operating policies, government subsidies, and production practices. A seventh session, "The Court 'Style' and Its Legacy: Acting and Directing," was canceled when Max Stafford-Clark argued convincingly that he would much rather conduct an acting workshop to demonstrate the process than talk about it. Both he and William Gaskill directed LSU students (and Court actor Antony Sher) in two separate meetings. Stafford-Clark led a two-hour session on improvisation, and Gaskill explored with actors a textual study of scenes from Edward Bond's *Saved.*

In the opening session of the conference, participants viewed a videotape of a performance presented in 1966 as a memorial to George Devine. The presentation contained scenes from plays of the Court's previous decade, featuring such stars as Joan Plowright, Laurence Olivier, Robert Stephens, Sybil Thorndike, Noel Coward, Nicol Williamson, Vanessa Redgrave, Maggie Smith, and John Osborne. Scenes were shown from John Arden's *The Happy Haven;* Ann Jellicoe's *The Sport of My Mad Mother;* John Osborne's *Look Back in Anger, The Entertainer,* and *Inadmissible Evidence;* N. F. Simpson's *One Way Pendulum;* and Arnold Wesker's *The Kitchen.* The videotape has never been shown publicly.

To preserve a record of the conference, we hired a stenographer to record the proceedings. In addition, all sessions were filmed on videotape. The tape was invaluable; the manuscript furnished by the stenographer proved unreliable because of her difficulty in understanding British accents and theatre terminology. From the videotape we retrieved more than twenty hours of discussions, transcribing the proceedings word by word. This volume is an edited account of those sessions.

We are grateful to the many people who made the conference possible. We especially thank Oscar Lewenstein, whose friendship and visits to Louisiana State University deepened our interest in and appreciation for the work of the ESC. We are also grateful to Harriet Cruickshank, who not only generously helped us in our independent research efforts but also coordinated our planning for the conference from her London base. We are indebted to Jocelyn Herbert for loaning us her videotape of the memorial performance for George Devine and to Herbert and Deirdre Clancy for allowing us to exhibit their costume and scenic designs created for the ESC at the Royal Court. Throughout the planning stages for the conference and the long period of editing the manuscript, Max Stafford-Clark's support and cooperation have been invaluable.

Without the support of the central administration of Louisiana State University, the conference could not have taken place. We are indebted to former chancellor Paul Murrill and former vice-chancellor Otis Wheeler for their early commitment to the project and to their successors, James H. Wharton and Carolyn H. Hargrave, for sustaining the university's financial support. Former assistant vice-chancellor for academic affairs Huel Perkins provided invaluable advice and support, and a gracious welcome for our conference guests. Henry Snyder, who served as dean of the College of Arts and Sciences at the time of the conference, likewise aided us enormously with his encouragement and generous hospitality to conference participants.

Equally significant was the funding from sources outside the university. We express our gratitude to the National Endowment for the Humanities, the Exxon Education Foundation, the late Ella V. Schwing, Russ Willis, Margaret Stones, and a generous friend of LSU Theatre who wishes to remain anonymous.

Elaine Pizzolato and Bryan Ortis patiently typed and retyped the manuscript, and we are grateful to them. We are also indebted to Catherine Landry, LSU Press editor, for her guidance in the publication of this book and to Trudie Calvert for providing invaluable editorial assistance. Warm thanks go to Beverly Jarrett, former associate director of LSU Press, for her encouragement and sustained interest in the book beginning with the first day of the Royal Court Conference.

Most of all, we offer thanks to the participants in the conference from both sides of the Atlantic. Our British participants generously juggled schedules and undertook long transoceanic flights to a place that must have seemed remote to most of them for no reward other than transportation expenses and the opportunity to join in a celebration and evaluation of the Royal Court's work. Months after the conference, many of them again gave their time to read the edited manuscript of this book.

Inside the Royal Court Theatre, 1956–1981

Introduction

The English Stage Company, a noncommercial organization devoted to new drama, has been in residence at the Royal Court Theatre in London's Sloane Square for over thirty years. Its remarkable longevity and persistent artistic vitality as a "writers' theatre" remain unequaled by any other professional theatre operation in Great Britain. The ESC narrowed the gap between art theatre and the commercial establishment, waged a historic court battle against stage censorship, and spearheaded the experimental alternative theatre movement. It provided a forum for the epic and absurdist drama of Germany and France and a training ground for a new generation of British playwrights, directors, actors, and designers, who, in turn, carried their art into the national theatres, the fringe, the West End, Broadway, and the founding of new companies. At the Royal Court, artists rose to prominence, became in demand by other venues, and moved into the mainstream. Others emerged to take their places and to continue the cycle. Despite artistic mistakes, management quarrels, personality clashes, box office failures, and financial crises, the Royal Court Theatre has kept its doors open and its stage alive. As William Gaskill notes in the discussion that follows, the value of any serious artistic organization lies not in the battles it fights but in the quality of the work it produces. The quality of the work at the Court over the past thirty years needs no defense; the record speaks for itself.

The opening production of the ESC on April 2, 1956, of Angus Wilson's *The Mulberry Bush,* a play long forgotten, gave little indication of the distinctive course the new company wished to pursue. George Devine (1910–1966), appointed as artistic director in 1955, and his associate, Tony Richardson, wanted above all for the Royal Court to be a house for new plays and, in addition, a venue for modern classic works that had influenced contemporary playwrights. Before accepting their posts with the ESC, Devine and Richardson had sought to establish a company of their own that "could become an essential part of London theatre life." For that purpose, Devine in 1953 drew up a proposal for "a modern theatre experi-

1

ment," which included a list of the kind of plays desired for his repertoire. In addition to "as many new plays as possible," he listed five categories of dramatic sources: 1) dramatists who "have had an important influence on contemporary theatre"; 2) significant plays "never performed in London"; 3) short plays from the art theatre presented as "double or triple bills"; 4) "one modern play each season of [an epic] nature"; and, 5) "adaptations from writers whose work seems apposite such as Charles Dickens."[1] Devine had a sort of European art theatre in mind for the Royal Court and thought that he "must find British writers who would somehow fall into this path." He therefore sought out poets and novelists (Angus Wilson and Nigel Dennis, among others) as possible sources to create a new body of drama.[2] But, unexpectedly, the third play produced by the ESC (on May 8), John Osborne's *Look Back in Anger,* came not from an established literary figure but from an unknown young writer with a lower-middle-class background. Its explosive success propelled the Royal Court Theatre into international prominence and altered the future course of the ESC.

Osborne's passion and indignation caught the imagination of a postwar generation frustrated and angered by the social and political conditions they had inherited. Although the form of the play, with its chronological, cause-and-effect structure of events, was thoroughly conventional, its cynical view of middle-class impotence, spun out in brilliant rhetoric through the character of Jimmy Porter, was unprecedented in British drama. According to Gaskill, the plays that Devine began receiving convinced him that the European art theatre repertoire that he had sought to emulate was not to be the primary mission of the Court, but that the emerging writers themselves "would dictate the character of the new theatre." On the heels of Osborne's success, writers, directors, actors, and designers began to come forth from a different social class and regional background than they traditionally had, and it was their work that gradually defined the unique nature and style of the English Stage Company at the Royal Court.[3]

New writers flooded the Court with scripts, not merely because it emerged as the only major noncommercial theatre in London but, above all, because George Devine created an environment that welcomed, nurtured,

1. Quoted in Gordon Bolar, "The Sunday Night Productions Without Decor at the Royal Court Theatre, 1957–1975" (Ph.D. dissertation, Louisiana State University, 1984), 19.
2. William Gaskill, Chap. I herein.
3. *Ibid.*

and supported them. Playwrights chosen for production found that a script accepted was a script trusted; remarkably, respect for the integrity of the text pervaded all areas of the production process. Success and failure were concepts redefined by Devine and Richardson: success had to do with the quality, not the marketability, of the script; it had to do with nurturing what one believed in. When Tony Richardson said that every writer has "the right to fail," he meant the right to fail at the box office or with the critics, which to the Court did not mean failure.[4]

"One splendid thing about George," Osborne has said, "was that he gave you the impression that whatever you did, whatever seemed to go wrong didn't really matter. He said, in effect, 'This is what we've decided to do. It's right and it's good and we're going ahead.' You always knew he was on the writer's side." William Gaskill tells with relish of his first directing experience in New York with Osborne and Anthony Creighton's *Epitaph for George Dillon.* Negative notices from the critics stopped the opening night party cold, and as the celebrants fled for the exits, Gaskill telephoned Devine in London with news of the failure: "Don't worry boy, there's a lot to do back here," said Devine. Ann Jellicoe found that Devine's trust in her talent never wavered, despite the rejection by critics and audiences of her first play, *The Sport of My Mad Mother.* As she recounts in the first chapter, on the opening night of her second play, *The Knack,* before the notices were in, Devine wanted her to know that the play's reception did not matter. "I want another play out of you," he said, "for which I am prepared to pay money." Osborne says that Devine offered "inspirational support"; his passionate enthusiasm for the individual artist and his or her talent "humanized the whole process" of getting one's work before the public.[5]

Because the ESC received more worthy scripts than the theatre's one stage could accommodate, Devine established a series called "Sunday night productions without decor," under the auspices of the English Stage Society, a group of supporters formed in late 1956. Because the society functioned as a private club, with audiences attending the productions as members, the Sunday night series could evade the censoring scrutiny of the Lord Chamberlain. Plays in the series were given a two-week rehearsal period and

---

4. Ann Jellicoe and Donald Howarth, Chap. I herein.

5. John Osborne, "On the Writer's Side," in Richard Findlater (ed.), *At the Royal Court: Twenty-five Years of the English Stage Company* (Ambergate, 1981), 22, 24; William Gaskill, "Glorious Riches Spring from Talents in Turmoil," *The Times,* January 13, 1986; Ann Jellicoe, Chap. I herein.

presented for one showing "with only indications of scenery and costumes." The playwrights were paid £5, the actors less; a play could be staged for as little as £100, compared to the £5,000 cost of a three-week run in the main bill.[6] The series provided an experimental stage for new work or revivals at a time when virtually no other experimental stages existed in London. Besides its main objective of permitting an author to see his or her work performed, the series served as an apprenticeship for directors. John Dexter, Lindsay Anderson, William Gaskill, and Anthony Page, all of whom were to figure prominently in the history of the Court, made their directorial debuts in the Sunday night series in the late 1950s.

As Irving Wardle emphasizes, Devine was by temperament a teacher who sought to make the Royal Court fully as much a training center as a producing theatre.[7] To this end, another of his innovative efforts was the Writers' Group, which began meeting weekly in 1958 and continued for two years. Devine and his mentor, Michel Saint-Denis, attended early meetings. Devine presented a series of lessons on the use of masks, which he had learned from Saint-Denis; he taught a "pure and mystical technique . . . by which the mask releases . . . a totally free and distinct personality." John Arden made use of this work in *The Happy Haven* (1960). Gaskill and Keith Johnstone guided many of the sessions, using exercises in improvisation to help free a writer's block or resolve script problems. "We tried to explore the nature of theatre," Jellicoe has said.[8] Arden, Arnold Wesker, Jellicoe, Wole Soyinka, Edward Bond, and David Cregan were among the members of the Writers' Group; others, including N. F. Simpson and Donald Howarth, disliked participating in group exercises and preferred to work alone.

For his vision of what a theatre should be, as well as his resourcefulness in trying to achieve it, Devine was indebted in large measure to John Gielgud (1904–), Theodore Komisarzhevsky (1882–1954), and especially Michel Saint-Denis (1897–1971). From the avant-garde movements in Russia and France, Komisarzhevsky and Saint-Denis brought to England in the two decades before World War II the first modern conception of a director. Gielgud, who came under the influence of both, sought to integrate their ideas into his own English tradition. Devine's absorption of these Russian, French, and English heritages deeply influenced the role he

6. "1957–1960," in Findlater (ed.), *At the Royal Court*, 42.
7. See Irving Wardle, *The Theatres of George Devine* (London, 1978).
8. Ann Jellicoe, "The Writers' Group," in Findlater (ed.), *At the Royal Court*, 56, 55.

found himself assuming at the Royal Court as the radical nurturer of a new wave of playwrights, directors, actors, and designers.

In 1932 Gielgud had directed *Romeo and Juliet* for the Oxford University Dramatic Society (OUDS) (of which Devine was then president); Peggy Ashcroft (then married to Komisarzhevsky) acted Juliet, Edith Evans, the Nurse, and Devine, Mercutio. Gielgud introduced Devine to the discipline of the profession, to new directions in Shakespearean staging (which Gielgud had gained from Harley Granville Barker and Harcourt Williams), and, most important for Devine's career, to Theodore Komisarzhevsky.[9] On the basis of Devine's performance of Mercutio, Komisarzhevsky offered him in the same year the opportunity of a professional London debut in *Le Cocu magnifique*. The event ended Devine's Oxford education (he quit, without degree) and marked the beginning of his tutelage under Komisarzhevsky and, eventually, Michel Saint-Denis.

For Devine and other actors of his generation, Komisarzhevsky "was an art theatre god."[10] He had studied architecture before becoming director of the Nezlobin Theatre and the Moscow Imperial Grand Opera. Emigrating to the West in 1919, he established his reputation in London in 1925–1926, in a small theatre in Barnes, with innovative productions of Chekhov, Gogol, and Andreyev. Komisarzhevsky had a particular interest in exploring ways in which scenic and lighting elements could help communicate the truths of the play, an interest Devine shared; by the time Devine came to the Court, he had become expert in these areas. From the Moscow Art Theatre tradition, Komisarzhevsky carried to London the conception of organic staging (which emerges from a detailed examination of the psychological elements of the text), and, from the work of Vsevelod Meyerhold, an irreverence for tradition and a bold commitment to experimentation.

Komisarzhevsky's efforts to establish an art theatre in Barnes lasted only one season; he spent the rest of his career in England without a theatre of his own, struggling as a free-lance artist against the pressures of an ingrained commercial stage tradition. "The work of a non-commercial producer," he said, "is somewhat similar to the man who tries to break a wall with his head." From Komisarzhevsky, Devine gained an understanding of the artistic potential of technical theatre and the crucial importance of the text as a

9. Devine himself was directed by Granville Barker only once, in a revival of Barker's *The Voysey Inheritance,* in 1934 (Wardle, *The Theatres of George Devine,* 21, 40).
10. *Ibid.,* 27.

guide to "an inner realist style." Furthermore, it was from Komisarzhevsky that Devine "began to learn the art of operating within prevailing theatrical conditions, without capitulating to them inside his own head." [11]

Devine met Michel Saint-Denis in 1935 in the London studio of Elizabeth Montgomery, Margaret Harris, and her sister Sophie, who operated the design firm called Motley. Saint-Denis, the nephew of Jacques Copeau (1879–1949), had been an actor in his uncle's troupe, Les Copiaus, which Copeau organized in 1924 upon his retirement from the Théâtre du Vieux Colombier. Saint-Denis had taught in the Vieux Colombier school and, during five years with Les Copiaus, worked at Copeau's side as actor, writer, and "general factotum." Copeau's work, which rejected the scenic effects and well-drilled stage behavior of the conventional theatre of illusion, followed the tradition of the traveling troupes of Molière; its emphasis was on simplicity, clarity, and imaginativeness in text and performance. It required artists willing to forgo career ambitions in the pursuit of ideals. When Copeau disbanded Les Copiaus in 1929, Saint-Denis, well schooled in the spirit of his uncle's work, regrouped the actors as La Compagnie des Quinze. He added a resident writer, André Obey, to build a repertoire and in 1931 brought the company to London. Their success was such that they returned for engagements in 1932 and 1933, leaving their mark on the history of the British stage; such joyous acting, combining vocal and physical expressiveness, acrobatics, and music, had not been seen in the English theatre. Wardle ranks the "long-term influence" of this troupe with that of the Berliner Ensemble's London engagement in 1956. [12]

In 1935 Saint-Denis returned to London to direct Gielgud in an English version of Obey's *Noah,* in which Devine acted two small roles. The event began Devine's professional association with Saint-Denis, which was to continue for the next twenty years and to affect him profoundly for the rest of his life. Saint-Denis' heritage extended beyond Copeau into the French avant-garde movements of the early part of the century; he possessed an astute understanding of the artistic significance of that heritage and a fanatical dedication to the perpetuation of its ideals. His impact on Devine was "akin to that of religious conversion." From him, Devine discovered a focus for his talents beyond acting, which had to do with the mission of founding an alternative theatre with a twofold purpose: ideally, it would

11. *Ibid.*
12. See David Bradby, *Modern French Drama, 1940–1980* (Cambridge, 1984), 1–7; also Wardle, *The Theatres of George Devine,* 44–46.

6

contain a school to train young artists and an acting company to carry the art to the public.[13]

In 1936 Devine and others persuaded Saint-Denis to become director of a new drama school, the London Theatre Studio. Devine assumed the title of assistant director and manager. The school's program emphasized the inter-relationship of the theatre arts, from curtain pulling to acting, and a training that fostered the harmonious alliance of all aspects of the work. Furthermore, Saint-Denis stressed the importance of the individual's artistic self-sufficiency in the community at large, apart from his professional commitment, and he recognized the responsibility of committed artists to infiltrate the conventional theatre establishment. Devine carried these tenets into the English Stage Company when he assumed its direction some twenty years later.[14]

The London Theatre Studio had as its ultimate goal the creation of an alternative theatre, with a school and company working side by side, an idea drawn from Copeau, which Saint-Denis and Devine sought to fulfill all their lives, with only partial success. A company at the London Theatre Studio never materialized. At the Royal Court, Devine was to have a company but not a school, although he always worked to incorporate schooling as an integral element in the Court's operation. The London Theatre Studio lasted four years, closing its doors in 1939 with the advent of World War II. Saint-Denis and Devine both participated in the war effort, and when the hostilities ended in 1945, they once again joined forces in another theatrical enterprise.

The Old Vic Theatre Centre opened on January 24, 1947, under three directors: Devine, Glen Byam Shaw, and Saint-Denis. The centre was to consist of three major programs: a school, a children's theatre, and an experimental stage, with Byam Shaw in charge of the first, Devine, the second, and Saint-Denis, the third. In addition, original plans called for two major acting companies. In the four years of its existence, however, a school and a theatre for the young was "as far as it ever went." There was the dream, too, of forging a national theatre. But for Devine and his associates, at least, that idea was aborted in 1951, when the Old Vic Theatre Centre's three directors resigned after many insoluble disputes with the governors.[15]

13. Wardle, *The Theatres of George Devine*, 50.
14. *Ibid.*, 51–56.
15. *Ibid.*, 207–36.

Devine's theatrical heritage helps explain the aims he held when he assumed his duties at the Royal Court Theatre. Schooled in the theory and practice of some of the major innovative artists of the era, he was well equipped to build on the foundation they had given him. His own genius emerged as he faced the daily challenges, artistic and otherwise, of running a noncommercial theatre. When Osborne came on the scene, striking a responsive chord in a new generation of artists, Devine recognized that the ESC's commitment must be to Osborne's contemporaries, the unestablished, young, and iconoclastic writers. None of Devine's mentors, from Gielgud to Saint-Denis, ever committed their theatres to such a risky and radical course.

In 1965, exhausted and in ill health, Devine resigned as artistic director of the ESC. During the nine years of his tenure, the Royal Court had produced about 150 plays, representing an extensive range of forms, styles, and visions. Nearly 100 of the plays were by new writers, indicating Devine's emphasis. But he recognized the value of examining new work in the context of a repertoire drawn from all ages and nations. Alongside unknown plays by Michael Hastings, Arden, Jellicoe, N. F. Simpson, Wesker, Soyinka, Bond, and Osborne appeared works of Aristophanes, Wycherly, Middleton, Ibsen, Chekhov, Brecht, Ionesco, Genet, and Beckett. Under Devine the Royal Court became not only a home for new British writers but an international center of theatrical learning for its audiences.

William Gaskill (1930–   ) took over the direction of the Royal Court in July, 1965; he was to hold the post for seven years, guiding the company through some of the most turbulent seasons in its history. Gaskill is the only artist who has remained close to the Court's inner workings throughout three decades, serving in advisory capacities when called upon and returning again and again to direct a new play or a revival, most recently *Women Beware Women* (1986) in a version by Howard Barker.

Gaskill had first come to the Royal Court in late 1957, a protégé of Tony Richardson; both were from Shipley in Yorkshire, and they had been together at Oxford. At about twenty-seven, they were twenty years younger than Devine, with none of his extensive experience among great British stars like Gielgud and Ashcroft or international gurus such as Komisarzhevsky and Saint-Denis. Ambitious, impatient with tradition, and literary, they had an arrogant self-assurance that comes with being both brilliant and young. In short, they were the first of a growing contingent of precocious, exceptionally talented artists who gave Devine a "link with the new generation." [16]

To test his skills, Gaskill was given a Sunday night production without decor, N. F. Simpson's example of English absurdism, *A Resounding Tinkle.* An "immediate success," it prompted Devine to offer Gaskill a staff position as an assistant to the artistic director at £15 a week. The job included running the script department and casting the plays. He shared an office with John Dexter, the only other such assistant; their tiny, windowless room became a gathering place for writers (Arden, Bond, Wesker, Soyinka, and others), "who were reading plays at five shillings a time." Devine always looked after the artists who warranted nurturing, financially and otherwise, a tradition he passed on to his successors. Evaluating scripts, assisting with casting, and planning the next season's repertoire were among the jobs parceled out as a means of providing fiscal and moral support. The jobs also involved the writers and directors in the inner operation of the theatre and kept them coming to the theatre daily, in effect, giving them an artistic home. If a job did not exist, one was created when the need arose. Gaskill, for example, wanting to support the talent of Christopher Hampton, made him resident dramatist in 1968, the first such post in the London theatre. [17]

Gaskill's success with *A Resounding Tinkle* led Devine to assign him the Osborne-Creighton play *Epitaph for George Dillon,* presented in the main bill in early 1958. The production transferred to the West End and to Broadway, giving further evidence of Gaskill's rising prominence as a major director at the Court. Its failure in New York bothered no one at the Court, and Devine beckoned Gaskill back to continue his work in Sloane Square. He was an imaginative and articulate interpreter of Simpson's fanciful pieces, and his production of *One Way Pendulum* (1959), together with previous mountings of the writer's works, brought Simpson international recognition; his plays were taken up by European and American theatres throughout the next decade.

The decade of the 1960s saw many of the talents developed at the Royal Court moving into other London theatres as their reputations created demands for their skills. In 1961 Gaskill departed to direct *Richard III* at

---

16. Bill Gaskill, "My Apprenticeship," in Findlater (ed.), *At the Royal Court,* 57.

17. *Ibid.;* Christopher Hampton, "Sloane Square Lessons," in Findlater (ed.), *At the Royal Court,* 116.

Stratford, taking Jocelyn Herbert with him as designer. Her designs at the Court for the plays of Beckett, Ionesco, and Wesker had quickly established her among the prominent scenic artists in the contemporary British theatre. Gaskill and Herbert became the first wave of artists to carry the Court influence into other venues, a move Devine encouraged. In 1963 Gaskill went to the newly formed National Theatre (then housed at the Old Vic), joined by a large number of Royal Court actors, including Colin Blakely, Frank Finlay, Robert Stephens, and Joan Plowright. Devine's company had begun its infiltration of the British theatre at large. In the 1960s, too, the ESC began to wield extensive influence in the film world when Oscar Lewenstein, John Osborne, Tony Richardson, and others became associated in the production of films under the Woodfall Films banner. Many of the films, such as *A Taste of Honey* (1961), *Tom Jones* (1963), *The Girl with Green Eyes* (1964), and *The Knack* (1965), relied on Royal Court writers, actors, and directors, who carried the Court's style of social realism to movie screens throughout the world.

Although Gaskill could certainly have marketed his directorial skills to make an exceptional commercial career, like Devine and Saint-Denis he has always been more interested in the work than in fame or money. Therefore, when Devine resigned and Gaskill was asked to consider taking over, "I realized that the continuity of George's work was more important than working at the National Theatre, and I told George I would do it." Olivier felt the loss and sent a telegram, "The Lord gave and the Lord has taken away."[18]

Gaskill's plan was to take the Court back to its original aim of presenting "new plays in repertoire with a resident company," an ideal that Devine had attempted in the beginning without success. Gaskill, too, soon had to abandon the plan as unrealistic and costly. In his first season, he directed Bond's *Saved*, which "unleashed the moral fury of the critics" and began a succession of struggles with the Lord Chamberlain, extending over three years. The embattled Court staff, led by Gaskill, drew strength from uniting against critics and censors. Upon the passing of the Theatres Act of 1968, Gaskill quickly presented a Bond season in the main bill, free finally of any censoring threats, although not free, of course, of attacks from the critics.[19] Gaskill's operation of the Court (abetted by the influence of Anthony Page and Lindsay Anderson, who became associate artistic directors

18. Gaskill, "My Apprenticeship," *ibid.*, 61.
19. Gaskill, "Glorious Riches Spring from Talents in Turmoil."

in 1969) was further distinguished by a number of important new plays and revivals: Arden's *Sergeant Musgrave's Dance;* Christopher Hampton's first play, *When Did You Last See My Mother?*; Alfred Jarry's *Ubu Roi* (designed by David Hockney); Bond's *Lear;* Soyinka's *The Lion and the Jewel;* Peter Gill's mounting of three D. H. Lawrence plays; and Gaskill's own innovative staging of *Macbeth.* Gaskill, Page, and Anderson also encouraged the partnership of the avant garde and the traditional stage by bringing in many stars in new ventures: Alec Guinness, John Gielgud, Ralph Richardson, Paul Scofield, and Peggy Ashcroft among them.

In 1969 Gaskill established the Theatre Upstairs, an experimental space on the second floor of the Royal Court Theatre. By his own admission, from this point on a split developed in the work that he could not resolve. In the same year, "tired after four years of struggle," he requested a six-month leave of absence, with a "stop-gap director" filling in for the period. The board rejected this request, but, to afford him relief from the sole burden of the Court's operation, countered with the proposal that his management be shared by Lindsay Anderson and Anthony Page. Although the arrangement was agreed upon, it further "accentuated the divergence of the Court's work."[20]

In his early days at the Court, Gaskill had been a rebel artist of the new generation, "deeply distrusting anything established," interested only in the new. But now at the age of about forty, he found that he was viewed by younger, radical artists like David Hare as a conservative guardian of a humanist tradition originated by Devine. Hare, Howard Brenton, and other emerging, stridently political playwrights had little interest in the crafts of the theatre or the niceties of style, and they found a great resistance to their work from the Court's directors. "I thought," Hare has said, "the political and social crisis in England in 1969 so grave that I had no patience for the question of how well written a play was. I was only concerned with how urgent its subject matter was, how it related to the world outside."[21] Although Hare had been appointed as resident dramatist, the directors continued to reject his work. And though the Theatre Upstairs was historically important as the first alternative stage established in a major theatre, it fostered divisiveness in the temptation it offered to relegate experimental works to its space, with the main stage saved for more accessible plays. In

---

20. *Ibid.;* Oscar Lewenstein, interview with Billy J. Harbin, July 29, 1978.
21. Jellicoe, "The Writers' Group," in Findlater (ed.), *At the Royal Court,* 53; David Hare, "Time of Unease," *ibid.,* 142.

his final years as artistic director, Gaskill wrestled with the dilemma posed by the political writers and the Theatre Upstairs:

> I made one last despairing effort to reconcile the outburst of experimental theatre with the main line in a vast festival in 1970, *Come Together*. We ripped the stalls out of the old house, built a new stage, put the audiences at the back . . . and every fringe group in existence was invited to appear. Stuart Brisley vomited from a scaffolding tower while the National Anthem was played backwards. Peter Dockley's *Foul Fowl* had creatures crawling through foam in hen-coops with live hens, miked over the whole building. On their first night *The People Show* threw oranges at the critics and a tethered rabbit upset a pot of paint on the new stage cloth. . . . The Theatre and I were approaching schizophrenia, [and] my inability to reconcile what I felt to be equally vital but different elements in the theatre eventually meant that I had to leave.[22]

Gaskill's seven-year management produced about 150 plays, of which more than half were new; 13 plays transferred to the West End. Income from transfers subsidized the nonmarketable plays by Beckett, Heathcote Williams, Ionesco, Brecht, and others. The Court had, in fact, become so dependent on transfers (and so confident of their continuance) that the income was built into the budget. After Gaskill's departure and during the tenures of succeeding directors, transfers to the West End greatly declined, bringing a series of financial crises and forcing the company into stringent economies.

Oscar Lewenstein (1917–   ), cofounder of the ESC and cochairman of its board after the death of Neville Blond in 1969, succeeded Gaskill in 1972. Unlike any of the previous or subsequent artistic directors of the ESC, Lewenstein had no acting or directing experience; he had spent some twenty-five years working in nonprofit and commercial theatre operations as a manager and independent producer. In 1946 he became the general manager of the Glasgow Unity Theatre but left in 1950 to begin an association of two years with Anthony Hawtrey. From 1952 to 1954 he served as general manager of the Royal Court Theatre, and in 1955 he cofounded the English Stage Company and began his career as a commercial impresario; at the same time, he served on the governing council of the ESC. During the

22. Gaskill, "Glorious Riches Spring from Talents in Turmoil."

next twenty-five years he produced over fifty plays, some in the West End and some in association with the ESC at the Royal Court. In the 1960s he became associated with Osborne, Richardson, and others in the production of films.

When Lewenstein assumed the reins of the ESC, Lindsay Anderson and Anthony Page remained as associate directors; Lewenstein invited Albert Finney to join the Court as a third associate. One of Lewenstein's major aims was to maintain all these directors in harmony at the Court; as a continuous member of the ESC Council since its inception, he had a thorough knowledge of the fiscal and artistic operation of the Royal Court and a familiarity with the myriad personalities and talents of the staff. When Gaskill resigned, "it seemed," Lewenstein has said, "that perhaps the only person who could hold these directors together to continue to work for the theatre was me, because I was on fairly good terms with them and there was a mutual respect." [23] Their continuance at the theatre meant, too, that established Court writers who looked to particular directors as interpreters of their work could still find them at the Court: Wesker had become artistically allied with John Dexter; David Storey with Lindsay Anderson; Osborne with Anthony Page; Bond with Gaskill; and Christopher Hampton with Robert Kidd. Each of these alliances produced new works during Lewenstein's directorship.

Lewenstein also wanted to extend the range of plays produced: "I felt that in the period preceding me the plays of the Court had become less plays on public issues than had been the situation under Devine; the plays seemed to have narrowed in focus." [24] During the three years of his regime, Lewenstein produced new plays by well-known Court writers (Wesker's *The Old Ones;* Osborne's *A Sense of Detachment;* Bond's *The Sea* and *Bingo;* Storey's *Cromwell, The Farm,* and *Life Class;* and Christopher Hampton's *Savages*); works that explored Irish, American, Australian, and Third World issues (Brian Friel's *Freedom of the City;* Edna O'Brien's *A Pagan Place;* Sam Shepard's *Tooth of Crime;* David Williamson's *The Removalists* and *Don's Party;* Mustapha Matura's *Play Mas*); a series of South African plays by Athol Fugard; a double bill of Samuel Beckett (*Not I* and *Krapp's Last Tape*); and new plays by unknown writers, including Caryl Churchill, David Edgar, Snoo Wilson, Howard Brenton, Richard O'Brien, Stephen Poliakoff, and David Lan.

The Fugard season in 1974 (*The Island, Sizwe Bansi Is Dead,* and *State-*

23. Lewenstein interview.
24. *Ibid.*

ments After an Arrest Under the Immorality Act) was undoubtedly one of Lewenstein's most important achievements.[25] Directed by Fugard, South African actors John Kani and Winston Ntshona (who were credited as coauthors) gave seventy-one performances of *The Island* and *Sizwe Bansi,* playing to 93 percent of capacity. The plays then transferred to the West End and later had engagements in the United States, bringing Fugard the recognition as a major artist that his earlier plays had promised.

Another distinctive contribution to the Court's history was Lewenstein's presentation in 1975 of a series of plays by Joe Orton: *Entertaining Mr. Sloane, Loot,* and *What the Butler Saw.* The first two had been produced in the West End with modest success in the mid-1960s, and Lewenstein had been working on arrangements to produce *What the Butler Saw* (also in the West End) at the time of Orton's sudden death in 1967, which halted the negotiations. But Lewenstein, loyal to the play, ultimately presented it at the Queen's Theatre in 1969, by which time the Theatres Act of 1968 had freed the play from censorship. The production failed; a faction in the gallery disrupted the performance with cries of outrage. It did not gain a fair appraisal from the critics or advance Orton's reputation as a dramatist. Lewenstein's post as artistic director at the Royal Court gave him the opportunity to bring Orton's major plays before the public again and to elicit from the critics a reassessment of Orton's place in English drama. *What the Butler Saw,* directed by Lindsay Anderson, and *Entertaining Mr. Sloane,* by Roger Croucher, were given outstanding productions; both transferred to the West End. *Loot,* directed by Albert Finney, although less well received, nevertheless contributed to the successful impact of the Orton season, which influenced a revival of interest in the playwright's works throughout Europe and abroad.[26]

At the completion of his term as artistic director in July, 1975, Lewenstein noted with some alarm, "Alas, the right to fail has become very expen-

25. Fugard later paid tribute to Lewenstein's significant role in bringing the plays to the Royal Court. See Athol Fugard, "The Gift of Freedom," in Findlater (ed.), *At the Royal Court,* 156–60.

26. Joe Orton was murdered by Kenneth Halliwell, who then committed suicide, on August 9, 1967. See John Lahr's biography of Orton, *Prick Up Your Ears* (London, 1978), and John Lahr (ed.), *The Orton Diaries* (London, 1986), 266, 256. Lewenstein later wrote: "To present a season of Joe Orton's three full-length plays was a happy way for me to end my term of office . . . the season was a great success, and, I think, established Joe's position in the British theatre. It was good to see *What the Butler Saw* given the recognition it deserved" ("Jubilee Memories," in Findlater [ed.], *At the Royal Court,* 168–69).

sive." For example, Peter Ramsay's *Runaway* (1974), Caryl Churchill's *Objections to Sex and Violence* (1975), and Ken Campbell's *The Great Caper* (1975) lost the Court £10,000, £9,500, and £12,000, respectively. They were plays "of interest and originality," which deserved to be seen "along side the work of our more established writers," but inflation and ever-increasing production costs meant that the Court's commitment to new writers was now made at great peril to the solvency of the theatre's operation. Lewenstein finished his three-year contract with a deficit of some £40,000, which was inherited by Nicholas Wright and Robert Kidd, who succeeded him. Nevertheless, Lewenstein had guided the theatre through a "conspicuously fertile period," presenting eighty productions, including fifty-two world premieres, ten English premieres, and nine transfers to the West End. His innovations included the appointment of Caryl Churchill as the Royal Court's first woman resident playwright and Ann Jellicoe as the first woman literary manager.[27]

Lindsay Anderson had been the ESC Council's choice to succeed Lewenstein, but he declined. The directorship was then opened up to applicants; forty-nine applied, and eight were interviewed. The two receiving the greatest number of votes were appointed joint artistic directors, "at their own suggestion."[28] Both Nicholas Wright (1941–   ) and Robert Kidd (1943–1980) had grown up professionally at the Royal Court, chiefly as directors. Gaskill hired Wright as casting director in 1967; he became assistant director in 1968 and the first director of the Theatre Upstairs in 1969. Kidd made his directing debut at the Court with the Sunday night production of Christopher Hampton's first play, *When Did You Last See My Mother?* Thereafter, he directed all of Hampton's plays at the Court: *Marya* (1967), Hampton's version of Isaac Babel's play; *Total Eclipse* (1968); *The Philanthropist* (1970); *Savages* (1973); and *Treats* (1976).

The Wright-Kidd direction of the ESC at the Royal Court was shaky from the start and became increasingly insecure. Personally and professionally incompatible, they became distrustful of each other's aims and artistic judgments and could not agree on a course of direction for the theatre. Wright, a protégé of Gaskill's regime, had more extensive experience in many phases of the Court's operation; Kidd had different loyalties

27. Oscar Lewenstein, Artistic Report to the ESC Council, July 22, 1975, pp. 1–2, in Lewenstein's personal collection, copies in possession of the editors; "1972–1975," in Findlater (ed.), *At the Royal Court,* 155, 149.

28. "1975–1980," in Findlater (ed.), *At the Royal Court,* 170.

and artistic interests. Their problems were compounded because their joint directorship came at a time when the financial liabilities of the ESC had reached crisis proportions. The council called an emergency meeting soon after the codirectors had been appointed "to discuss ways of clearing the Company's deficit." Various methods of raising funds were suggested. The list indicates the council's desperation: a pop concert benefit, possibly with Elton John ("Michael Codron said he would speak to his lawyer, who is also Elton John's"); a gala evening of excerpts from Court plays, with stars "who had been connected with the Court over the years"; an auction of memorabilia "donated by theatre people," combined with "a sale of scripts and authors' and directors' letters . . . from the files of the Court"; a sale of artists' works, "donated by sympathetic artists who have been connected with the work of the Court in some way"; a lottery "consisting of 200 tickets at £25 each," with total prizes of £2,000; and a benefit premiere of "Stanley Kubrick's new film." None of the fund-raising methods was realized. In the summer of 1976, however, Michael White, a member of the ESC Council, arranged for a benefit performance of *A Chorus Line,* which he was producing in the West End; the event realized £21,000 and enabled the Court to wipe out part of its deficit.[29]

Meanwhile, Wright and Kidd launched their directorship with David Hare's *Teeth 'n' Smiles* (September 2, 1975), directed by the author and designed by Jocelyn Herbert. Although not an enduring play, the production was a popular success, running to 87 percent of capacity and gaining a profit of about £12,000. But Howard Barker's *Stripwell,* which followed, lost several thousand pounds.[30] With financial pressures mounting, Wright and Kidd were forced to close the Theatre Upstairs from October, 1975, to May, 1976. Nevertheless, in November they produced one of the Court's finest productions, Bond's new play *The Fool* (directed by Peter Gill), a powerful depiction of the English peasant-poet John Clare and of the social conditions that fostered his mental breakdown. Other outstanding productions followed in April and May, 1976: Beckett's *Waiting for Godot* (in German, directed by the author originally at the Schiller Theatre, Berlin), *Endgame,* and a triple bill of *Play, That Time,* and *Footfalls.* Presented in

29. Nicholas Wright, interview with Billy J. Harbin, August 10, 1978; Minutes of a Meeting of the ESC Council, August 12, 1975, p. 1; Minutes of a Meeting of the ESC Management Committee, August 11, 1976; all minutes are in Lewenstein's personal collection, copies in possession of the editors.

30. Findlater (ed.), *At the Royal Court,* Appendix 2, Financial Tables for Year Ended March 27, 1976.

July was Peter Gill's play *Small Change,* a sensitive view of the social pressures on two working-class families in Cardiff.

Despite the artistic success of these productions, the financial plight of the Court became worse, bringing the Wright-Kidd partnership to the brink of ruin. *The Fool,* with a cast of twenty-two and seventy costumes, far exceeded the budget; at a cost of £18,650, it was then the most expensive production in the history of the Court. In thirty-eight performances, it played to little more than 60 percent of capacity and lost £20,000. *Small Change* played to only 26 percent in twenty-three performances, and Yemi Ajibade's *Parcel Post* fared worse, at 22 percent in fourteen performances. Richard O'Brien's *T-Zee* (on August 10) and David Storey's *Mother's Day* (September 22) flopped, with both the critics and the public. Although the Royal Court had always struggled with financial problems, the crisis now became so severe that the closing of the theatre seemed imminent. Wright, alarmed, had brought in *T-Zee,* hoping that it might duplicate the fiscal success of the author's *Rocky Horror Show.* Instead, it bombed. "It was a great mistake on my part," Wright said later. Storey's *Mother's Day* was presented in similar desperation; a play by Storey was surely worth doing and would surely draw audiences. But critics condemned the play, and audiences stayed away; the production lost over £11,000. "It was simply a bad play," Wright later acknowledged, and the author's name had made no difference at the box office.[31]

During the last nine months of 1976, the average box office income was only 35 percent of capacity, and the deficit had risen to nearly £30,000.[32] Transfers to the West End (a traditionally lucrative source of income) diminished during the joint directorship to only two productions, Hare's *Teeth 'n' Smiles* and Hampton's *Treats,* and both failed to draw audiences. Three major financial problems plagued the Wright-Kidd operation of the Royal Court: an inherited deficit, overexpenditure on production budgets, and failure to attain 55 percent of capacity, traditionally the figure necessary for solvency.[33] The Court's "salvation" would have to come from a much increased Arts Council subsidy, due in December. When it was announced that the Arts Council would provide no supplementary grant this year to reduce the deficit (as it had in the past), and that the grant to the Court for

---

31. "1975–1980," *ibid.,* 172–73; Minutes of a Meeting of the ESC Management Committee, December 30, 1975, November 17, 1976; Wright interview.

32. "1975–1980," in Findlater (ed.), *At the Royal Court,* 173.

33. Minutes of a Meeting of the ESC Management Committee, October 20, 1976.

1977–1978 would be raised by only 10 percent (amounting to £242,000), Robert Kidd resigned in a letter to the ESC Council chairman, Greville Poke, on January 10, 1977. He asked that his notice be "backdated to Wednesday, 8th December, 1976, when I first told you of my decision."[34] Since Wright's contract was linked to Kidd's, their directorship ended. The ESC Council could then have appointed Wright as sole director but determined instead that "a complete change" of artistic direction was needed; "discreet inquiries" for a successor were already being made.[35]

"It was a fatal weakness to think that Robert and I could work together," Wright later stated. "My interests were along the lines of emerging writers; whereas, Robert's interests were always of his own career. I suppose two people of such different interests *could* work together, but surely not in a position of parity running a complex organization like the Royal Court. It really takes a kind of benevolent despot."[36] Despite their travails and the brevity of their partnership (July, 1975, to December, 1976), they made notable contributions to the history of the Royal Court, which are sometimes overlooked because of the fiscal and artistic struggles that dominated their term. Their most important achievements were Bond's *The Fool,* Beckett's *Waiting for Godot,* and Gill's *Small Change.* Beckett's presence during the rehearsal of his play "was an inspiration throughout the theatre."[37] Wright also should be credited with persuading the ESC Council to raise the stipend for the commission of new plays from the traditional £200 to a maximum of £1,000, a cause for which he had argued throughout his term. The council approved the increase in April, 1976, noting that the Court was "in danger of losing authors due to being unable to pay them enough" and that "a flow of good plays is the life-blood of the company." Other innovations during the Wright-Kidd regime included raising the top salary for actors (the first increase in twenty years) from £50 to £75 (with minimum salary remaining at £39) and providing new contracts for directors, with £550 as a minimum stipend in the main theatre, £45 weekly in the Theatre Upstairs, and £39 weekly for assistant directors. Also, beginning in August, 1976, ticket prices were increased from a top of

34. Minutes of a Meeting of the ESC Council, October 20, 1976; Findlater (ed.), *At the Royal Court,* 175; Robert Kidd to Greville Poke, January 10, 1977, in Lewenstein's personal collection, copy in possession of the editors.
35. Minutes of a Meeting of the ESC Council, January 24, 1973.
36. Wright interview.
37. Minutes of a Meeting of the ESC Council, May 27, 1976.

£3 to £3.50, and from a low of 60*d.* to £1, giving the theatre a capacity of £6,622.[38]

The emergence in the 1970s of theatres producing new works, such as the Royal Shakespeare Company's Warehouse and the Other Place, the National's Cottesloe, and a number of fringe stages throughout London, "meant that the Court no longer had a monopoly of new plays." Indeed, some critics of the Court had begun questioning whether it had outlived its function as a writers' theatre because that function seemed to have been taken over by so many other venues. Stuart Burge (1918–), who succeeded the Wright-Kidd directorship, strongly felt, however, that the Royal Court was "still the only true writers' theatre" and "that there was still some need for the Court no matter how many new theatres had come along since Devine." This belief led him to accept the post at the Court (although he had just been appointed director of the Cottesloe Theatre at the National). He became the first "outsider" appointed as artistic director of the ESC. Although never a member of the Court's staff, he had come under the influence of George Devine just after the war as an actor in Devine's Young Vic company and later became one of Devine's assistants at the Old Vic Theatre School. In the long interval before coming to the Royal Court in 1977, he created Britain's first civic theatre (at Hornchurch in Essex), directed nearly a hundred plays for television, and assumed the artistic direction of the Nottingham Playhouse, retrieving it "from the chaos into which the theatre fell after John Neville's abrupt departure in 1968."[39]

Burge undertook the basic problem of "getting the theatre back on its feet" and "on some sort of coherent course." He began with the troubled ESC Council. It had lost several of its most informed and experienced members over the years and had been strongly criticized by Wright, Bond, Lewenstein, and others for its failure to enlist the Court's staff, who were intimate with the company's operation and cognizant of the current theatre scene. Sir Hugh Willatt was asked to form an independent subcommittee to examine the matter and to recommend changes in the ESC management structure. Eventually three ESC staff representatives were added to what Burge described as a "very limp Council . . . largely irrelevant to the

38. Minutes of a Meeting of the ESC Management Committee, April 22, May 5, January 15, June 8, 1976.

39. Sheridan Morley, "Stuart Burge's Loyalty to the Royal Court," *The Times,* April 15, 1981.

theatre's new problems." With the change, the board reflected "the reality of the theatre today."[40]

In his first year, Burge's initial productions of Tony Bicat's *Devil's Island* (February 24), Barrie Keeffe's *Gimme Shelter* (March 23), Sam Shepard's *Curse of the Starving Class* (April 21), and Howard Barker's *Fair Slaughter* (June 13) all lost money. The Court's ongoing financial struggles dominated the discussions at the council's monthly meetings. In June, 1977, it was noted that with a total grant from the Arts Council of £260,000 (nearly £20,000 had been added to wipe out the deficit left by Wright and Kidd) and a budgeted cost for the season of £220,000, the theatre "could only afford to lose £40,000 in the year." But apparently "this had already been lost and more." Greville Poke pointed out that Burge could hardly be blamed because in this transitional period he was "picking up the pieces and honouring . . . commitments made by the previous directors." Burge told the council that the crucial dilemma, as always, was that "we are expected to fulfill the function of presenting new work," which had a high cost and a very risky profit margin. Yet to offer commercial work "immediately lays us open to the charge of neglecting our function." The council discussed the £11,500 budget for Mary O'Malley's *Once a Catholic,* opening on August 10. If this production failed, it was noted, "we shall have to make up the deficit by having visitors [that is, bringing in guest productions] or going dark."[41]

Once a Catholic, however, was a great success, the first of a series of productions that changed the financial fortunes of the company and put the Royal Court back in the forefront of the British theatrical scene. Burge was initially opposed to presenting the play, considering it West End fare and not what the Court should be doing.[42] He was essentially correct, but the play did help bail the Court out of debt, and for that most of the staff, including Burge, were grateful. After thirty-eight performances at 90 percent of capacity, *Once a Catholic* transferred to the West End for a long and profitable run.

Meanwhile, Burge lined up other outstanding productions, several of which were financially successful and all artistically provocative in the best

40. *Ibid.;* "1975–1980," in Findlater (ed.), *At the Royal Court,* 175–76.

41. Minutes of a Meeting of the ESC Management Committee, May 16, June 27, 1977.

42. Wright interview. Wright and Jellicoe had commissioned O'Malley to write the play.

20

tradition of the Royal Court: Brecht's *The Good Woman of Setzuan* (78 percent of capacity), Nigel Williams' *Class Enemy* (66 percent), Bill Morrison's *Flying Blind* (39 percent), Leigh Jackson's *Eclipse* (17 percent), a revival of Osborne's *Inadmissible Evidence,* directed by the author (98 percent), David Edgar's *Mary Barnes* (91 percent), Caryl Churchill's *Cloud Nine* (92 percent), Martin Sherman's *Bent* (95 percent), and Edward Ravenscroft's long-neglected Restoration farce, *The London Cuckolds* (81 percent), brilliantly directed by Burge.

By the fall of 1979, Burge had succeeded in wiping out the company's sizable deficit. He demonstrated, too, that the Court could still attract and develop new writers of exceptional talent; its function as a writers' theatre remained viable and important. But the ever-increasing costs of a consistent production of new writing meant that the theatre's financial crises, if now and again happily resolved, would inevitably recur season after season.

The end of "the long era of subsidy by authors" contributed to the fiscal problems. Since its first season in 1956, the Royal Court had been subsidized by its playwrights, directors, and actors (as well as the staff behind the scenes) through their acceptance of low fees and wages. Over the years the subsidy diminished as artists and staff members had to demand higher pay (sometimes through their unions) to meet inflationary living costs. Pressure from the Writers' Guild and the Theatre Writers' Union, for example, forced Burge to increase commissioning fees for the main theatre to £2,000 and for the Theatre Upstairs to £1,500. Production costs, too, continued to mount. The record cost of £18,649 for Bond's *The Fool* during the Wright-Kidd term was soon surpassed in Burge's period: *The London Cuckolds* cost £21,186 and Sherman's *Bent,* £26,582. Burge was able to keep the Royal Court financially afloat through a notable number of profitable productions and increases in the Arts Council grants to £305,000 for 1978–1979 and to £385,000 for the following season.[43]

In the autumn of 1979, Stuart Burge was given a six-month leave of absence from the ESC to direct a television series of D. H. Lawrence's *Sons and Lovers.* Max Stafford-Clark, Burge's associate director, was asked to assume Burge's post until his return. (Jonathan Miller, Burge's second associate, apparently rarely came into the theatre.)[44] When Burge's tele-

43. "1975–1980," in Findlater (ed.), *At the Royal Court,* 177, 178, Appendix 2, Financial Tables, 1976, 1979, and 1980.
44. Anne Jenkins, ESC general manager, interview with Billy J. Harbin, August 12, 1978.

vision commitments made his return impossible, Stafford-Clark succeeded him as artistic director in early 1980.

The directing career of Max Stafford-Clark (1941–   ) had its origins in fringe companies. In 1968 he became artistic director of Edinburgh's Traverse; after two years he left (after having been impressed by the spirit and energy of touring American troupes) with the idea that "I never again wanted to have to manage a building as well as an acting company." [45] He made his directing debut at the Royal Court in 1971 with David Hare's *Slag* and over the next nine years directed fourteen productions for the Sloane Square house, six for the main stage, the others for the Theatre Upstairs. Meanwhile, in 1974 he cofounded (with David Hare and David Aukin) the Joint Stock Theatre Group, one of the most significant achievements in his career. His work in that company with Hare, and especially with William Gaskill, notably influenced his artistic direction of the Royal Court. Gaskill codirected (with Stafford-Clark) Joint Stock's first production, Heathcote Williams' *The Speakers,* and helped formulate the company's working methods.

Early in his directorship, Stafford-Clark issued a policy statement that affirmed his aims of committing the Royal Court anew to its traditional objective, "namely, to locate, develop and present the work of new writers." At the same time, he recognized, as had his predecessors, that the practice of that policy "is a hazardous and expensive business." From the outset Devine had sought to subsidize the production of new work by transferring plays into the West End and by reviving classical works as well as the Court's own successful plays, for "certainly, he did not believe that new work alone was a viable policy." [46] Since 1975, however, the number of plays moved into the West End had diminished as transfer costs escalated and commercial managements became less willing to take risks on Royal Court plays.

With West End revenue drying up, Stafford-Clark explored other means of supplementing grant monies. In 1982 he worked out an innovative scheme for exchanging productions with Joseph Papp's Public Theatre, an arrangement from which the Court profited, primarily in ways other than financial. To Papp's New York theatre Stafford-Clark took Caryl Churchill's *Top Girls* (1982) and *Fen* (1983), Michael Hastings' *Tom and Viv* (1984), and Ron Hutchinson's *Rat in the Skull* (1984). Papp sent to the Royal Court

45. Sheridan Morley, "Transatlantic Tributes," *The Times,* August 15, 1985.
46. Max Stafford-Clark, Royal Court Policy Statement, March 18, 1980, in Lewenstein's personal collection, copy in possession of the editors.

Thomas Babe's *Buried Inside Extra* (1984), the Vietnam Veterans Ensemble production of *Tracers* (1985), and Wallace Shawn's *Aunt Dan and Lemon* (1985). "I started the exchange out of financial necessity," Stafford-Clark said in 1985. Papp "promised to give us fifty thousand dollars as a challenge grant, provided we could match it from private donations here." Papp made good his promise within a year, after the Court managed to raise the matching funds.[47]

Aside from Papp's grant, however, the ESC made no money from the exchange, despite the success of the venture, because of the enormous costs of sending the productions overseas. But the exchange spurred a revival of critical and public recognition of the Royal Court's work, in both America and Great Britain. When *Top Girls* and *Tom and Viv* were brought back to the Court after their New York runs, Stafford-Clark was "able to stage them for another season and do very well with them as 'New York hits.'"[48]

Stafford-Clark brought other new thrusts to the Court's work, especially in his use of Joint Stock methods for developing plays, in his focus on female writers, and in his aggressive nurturing of talent through the Young Writers' Festival. The Joint Stock process involves a workshop period of three to four weeks during which the playwright, director, and actors collaboratively explore a given topic or theme through improvisation, investigation (research of documents or of individual experiences), and rehearsed readings. Over the next two months following the workshop exploration, the writer creates the script and then the group reassembles for an extended rehearsal period to refine the text and produce the finished play.[49] Most of Caryl Churchill's plays of the last decade (which are among Stafford-Clark's finest productions at the Court) have been developed through Joint Stock work methods: *Cloud Nine* (1979), *Top Girls* (1982), *Fen* (1983), and *Serious Money* (1987).

Hanif Kureishi's *Borderline* (1981), commissioned by Stafford-Clark in 1980, exemplifies the artistic director's special interest in developing new work based on public issues through extensive research and a workshop collaboration of artists. "I wasn't keen on the idea of a project about Asian

47. Morley, "Transatlantic Tributes"; Steve Lohr, "Cash Woes of Britain's Theaters," New York *Times,* November 10, 1986.

48. Morley, "Transatlantic Tributes."

49. Judith Kelly, "About Joint Stock Theatre Group," program notes for the Joint Stock production of Nicholas Wright's *The Crimes of Vautrin* (adapted from Balzac), 1983.

immigrants in Britain," Kureishi has written, "but Max Stafford-Clark preferred subjects that he [and the public] had no previous knowledge of; he liked to learn." Kureishi became more interested in the idea when he began to realize that, "like the refugee and the political prisoner, the immigrant is a kind of modern Everyman, a representative of movements and the aspirations of millions of people." The cast was composed of "two Asian, three English and one South African actors," and "the idea was that, as with other Joint Stock plays, everyone would play everything," women would play men, men play women, adults play children, whites play blacks, blacks play whites, and so on. During the workshop, the artists met and interviewed Asian people, improvised, and spent time in London's Southall area, where the play was set. "We were like journalists," Kureishi said, with Stafford-Clark continually "reminding me how little English people know about Asians living amongst them and that the theatre can . . . educate people." [50]

Stafford-Clark also turned the focus of the Court on female writers, which he considers one of his most important challenges. "Women are now writing the most interesting plays about human territory," he believes. [51] Besides the plays of Churchill, he presented Gilly Fraser's *I Can Give You a Good Time* (1981), Natasha Morgan's *Room* (1981), Carol Bunyan's *To Come Home to This* (1981), Sue Townsend's *Bazaar and Rummage* (1982), and Louise Page's *Salonika* (1982), among others. Some of the most remarkable new talents emerged through the Court's annual Young Writers' Festival (in its thirteenth year in 1986), to which Stafford-Clark has given serious attention and strong support. Andrea Dunbar is one of the exceptional female writers to be discovered through the festival. Stafford-Clark helped develop and directed for the main stage her play *The Arbor* (1981), after its initial promising run in the Theatre Upstairs. Her second play, *Rita, Sue, and Bob Too,* produced at the Court in 1982, justified Stafford-Clark's trust in her work. [52]

To help subsidize his production of new works, Stafford-Clark presented revivals of classics and successful Court plays, the most important of which were Thomas Kilroy's Irish version of Chekhov's *The Seagull* (1981); Jonathan Pryce's innovative interpretation of *Hamlet* (1984); the Edward

50. Hanif Kureishi, "Author's Note," *Borderline* (London, 1981), 4.
51. Morley, "Transatlantic Tributes."
52. In 1986–87 Oscar Lewenstein produced the film *Rita, Sue and Bob Too,* based on Dunbar's two plays. She wrote the screenplay.

24

Bond season, *The Pope's Wedding* and *Saved* (1984); and Howard Barker's version of Middleton's *Women Beware Women* (1986).

In 1985 Stafford-Clark's contract with the ESC was renewed for another five years, by which time he will have been the longest serving of all its directors. Like his predecessors, he has constantly struggled with the dilemma of keeping the theatre afloat without sacrificing the principle upon which it was founded, a commitment to new writing. All of the Court's directors have in times of crisis tended to become "entrenched and beleaguered" by critical disapproval of revolutionary new works and, especially, by the theatre's financial struggles for survival.[53] These battles can result in an artistic paralysis. They have led some directors to make decisions that seemed financially necessary but became artistically insupportable. The dilemma may be commonplace with any noncommercial theatre operation, but what sets the Royal Court apart is that it has survived for over thirty years still adhering to Devine's original mission, despite artistic setbacks, critical and public rejection, financial travails, and threats of imminent foreclosure. Stafford-Clark's pledge when he began his directorship of the Royal Court in 1980 remains his pledge now: "We will continue to present and champion contemporary writing to the limits that our abilities and our subsidy allow."[54]

B.J.H.

53. Morley, "Transatlantic Tributes."
54. Stafford-Clark, Royal Court Policy Statement.

I

Artists Talk: George Devine, "the Great Inspirer"

MODERATOR: *Michael Murray, producing director, Playhouse in*
                  the Park, Cincinnati

PARTICIPANTS: *William Gaskill, artistic director, 1965–1972*
                  Michael Hallifax, general stage manager of ESC, 1956–
                  1959
                  Donald Howarth, playwright, literary manager
                  Ann Jellicoe, playwright
                  Irving Wardle, biographer of George Devine, drama critic for
                  The Times

SPEAKING FROM THE AUDIENCE:
                  Oscar Brockett
                  Stuart Burge
                  Martin Esslin
                  Christopher Hampton
                  David Hare
                  and conference observers

MR. MURRAY: It seems important that I and other Americans are here as moderators to bring American questions and responses to this discussion of George Devine's legacy to the English Stage Company. We are trying to understand what the Royal Court was, and not only that, but what that means to those of us who are still working in the theatre on both sides of the Atlantic.

To put it in a historical context, in 1956 when the English Stage Company began operating at the Royal Court Theatre, I was a stage manager in New York City for the off-Broadway production of *The Iceman Cometh* at the Circle in the Square Theatre. A landmark production, it helped re-establish the artistic reputation of Eugene O'Neill. It brought professional recognition to several actors, such as

26

Jason Robards and Peter Falk, and established José Quintero as a director. The production also revitalized off-Broadway, which had been limping along until that time. What's interesting are the differences between the British and American theatre in 1956. When the Circle in the Square was being established here, the ESC at the Royal Court Theatre was being established in London. Why hasn't an institution like the Royal Court taken root in this country as it did there? Certainly, American theatres devoted to the writer were virtually nonexistent at that time. In San Francisco the Actors' Workshop was doing new plays, but usually European ones.[1] Actually, it was not until the early 1960s that writers began to have forums through Ellen Stewart's La Mama Experimental Theatre Club[2] and the many other off-off-Broadway houses that began to emerge.

To get to our specific topic, I believe that Mr. Wardle has written that George Devine, or the Court itself, was a cryptically English institution. Do you remember saying that?

MR. WARDLE: I meant that it worked pragmatically and didn't have laid-down manifestos and that what continuity it possessed in retrospect was a result of practical decisions made according to the passing contingency. Incidentally, anything I say about George Devine is a result of having spoken to people who knew him, such as these authorities on the panel. I don't have the authority of any of them; everything I say is at second hand.[3]

MR. MURRAY: I should point out how all of these people are authorities in this case. Mr. Gaskill was involved in the Court from the beginning, becoming in 1965 the second artistic director after George Devine. Mr. Wardle wrote *The Theatres of George Devine* and is critic for *The Times*. Ann Jellicoe was a member of a group of writers attached to the Court in the very beginning. Michael Hallifax served as general stage manager of the English Stage Company under George Devine be-

1. The Actors' Workshop was established in 1952 by Jules Irving and Herbert Blau, who gave up their operation in San Francisco in 1965 to become directors of a repertoire company at the Vivian Beaumont Theatre in New York. Blau resigned from this theatre in 1967 and Irving in 1973. Irving died in 1980.

2. Ellen Stewart created the La Mama Experimental Theatre Club in 1961. By 1967 she had produced 175 plays by 130 writers.

3. For his book *The Theatres of George Devine,* Irving Wardle interviewed Gaskill, Hallifax, Howarth, and Jellicoe, as well as many others associated with the ESC in the past and present.

tween 1956 and 1959. Mr. Howarth had his first play, *Sugar in the Morning,* produced in 1959 at the Royal Court, where he subsequently served as literary manager for two years. The English Stage Company at the Royal Court was a thing that was particularly English, was it not?

MR. HOWARTH: Yes, the Court was started off by some eccentric Englishmen getting together and forming a committee or council. At first there were two, Oscar Lewenstein, a theatrical producer and entrepreneur, and Ronald Duncan, a poet and playwright. They met at an arts and drama festival in Devon. Their aim was to form a company which would take plays performed at festivals to London, so raising the quality and artistic standards of theatre in general. The "Englishness" of it is that they then contacted influential people like the Earl of Harewood, who had really nothing to do with theatre, except that he had always been active in supporting the arts, especially opera. To form the ESC Council, they got together a group of people who they thought would be supportive and socially influential. This group then decided they would have to have an artistic director to run it, and Oscar Lewenstein suggested, and the council chose, George Devine. And from that moment the organization started to formulate itself into a theatre.[4]

4. The first council of the ESC at the Royal Court Theatre consisted of the following members under the chairmanship of Neville Blond: Ronald Duncan, Lord Harewood, James Edward Blacksell, Greville Poke, Oscar Lewenstein, Viscount Duncannon, Lord Bessborough, and Sir Reginald Kennedy-Cox. The story of the founding of the ESC varies a little among the principals involved (Duncan, Harewood, Blacksell, and Lewenstein). It has been told in Terry Browne's *Playwrights' Theatre* (London, 1975), in Wardle's *The Theatres of George Devine,* and in Richard Findlater's *At the Royal Court.* Lewenstein's version, given to the present editors in interviews in 1978 and 1983, is briefly as follows: The formation of the English Stage Company grew out of the Taw and Torridge Festival in Devon, which began in 1953, and which had been founded by Ronald Duncan, Blacksell, Harewood, and Benjamin Britten. Lewenstein produced a season of plays directed by Joan Littlewood for the festival through arrangements with Duncan. Lewenstein says:

> I got to know Ronald Duncan quite well, and in talking to him, we decided that we wanted to set up a nonprofit theatre to present serious noncommercial modern work. We formed the English Stage Company in 1954 and invited Lord Harewood, Blacksell, and Alfred Esdaile (who owned the Royal Court Theatre) to join us. We then met Neville Blond, a wealthy Manchester businessman, who agreed to become the chairman of the ESC Council and who acquired the Royal Court Theatre for us. We invited George Devine to be our artistic director: he accepted and brought in Tony Rich-

MR. MURRAY: Were they surprised then when George Devine's own personality moved in on the situation?

MR. HOWARTH: Yes, I think they were. George Devine had already tried to start a theatre with Tony Richardson prior to this group's forming. They had even drawn up a policy statement for a theatre company. So that when they were approached a couple of years later, the opportunity was there for the fulfillment of their earlier plans.

MR. MURRAY: George Devine was obviously the center of the Royal Court Theatre and, perhaps, one of the reasons it is still here today, because of the thrust he gave it in the first years. It is not easy for a person who wasn't there to understand what George Devine was.

MR. WARDLE: George Devine had quite a long background in the orthodox English theatre. He began as president of the OUDS, that is, the Oxford University Dramatic Society. He came down to London and acted with the Old Vic Company in the early 1930s; he then underwent what you might call a Pauline conversion when he met Michel Saint-Denis. They formed an outfit called the London Theatre Studio, which was a teaching continuation of the work of Jacques Copeau of the Vieux Colombier and the touring company of the Compagnie des Quinze during the late 1920s and early 1930s. And there was an elaborate aesthetic which I will not attempt to go into.

One of its tenets, one of its ideals, was that a school be attached to a production organization. This proved to be an elusive dream which Saint-Denis and Devine both were to pursue for the rest of their careers, because originally Saint-Denis had a company but not a school. In the 1930s he had a school but no company. After the war ended in 1945 they reformed, and the Old Vic Theatre Centre began with a school and a touring junior company but not a main house group. And then that went up in flames.

Now, when we get to Devine in 1956, his career was in the teaching of acting—he acted also—and with attempting to bring

---

ardson as his associate. Devine and Richardson had been trying to set up a similar organization earlier. We had part of Devine's first season already secured, which we turned over to him: Duncan's *Don Juan* and *The Death of Satan,* Miller's *The Crucible,* and Brecht's *The Threepenny Opera.* But Devine decided the Brecht piece did not fit in with his season and the rights were returned to me. I presented it, in fact, at the Royal Court Theatre just before April 2, 1956, which is the date that the ESC commenced operations with Angus Wilson's *The Mulberry Bush.*

about reforms in the practice of stage performance. His career begins again with the formation of the English Stage Company, with a concentration mainly on writing, from that point on. I don't know if this is the case, but it does seem as if he had attempted to bring about reforms—he and Saint-Denis jointly—in the acting-production sphere; these had repeatedly failed for one reason or another, so he then turned his attention to writing as an alternative, to which he had not previously given first priority.

MR. MURRAY: What did he want to reform?

MR. GASKILL: I believe that he wanted to make an art theatre. It is difficult to think of this now, because it's a concept which is no longer strong, but at that time there was no fringe theatre of any kind, virtually none. There were commercial theatres, such as those in the West End; also, theatres doing the traditional classics, such as the Shakespeare Memorial Company at Stratford (a forerunner of the Royal Shakespeare Company), which then didn't have a London theatre. But there was no serious, noncommercial art theatre, in the sense that Stanislavski used the word.

I think they all used to draw up schedules of the kind of plays that they would like to do; they were the sort of plays that Eric Bentley translates—Sternheim, Wedekind, Lorca, Pirandello—a whole body of European work, which represents a kind of ideal of theatre which is noncommercial. And so the movement, what little movement there was, was toward a kind of poetic drama, of which I suppose T. S. Eliot and Christopher Fry were the most obvious exponents. And there was the sense that we must find British writers who would somehow fall into this path.

That's an impression of the pre-1956 era as far as I could tell. At that time I knew Tony Richardson, who was George's associate for most of George's life at the Court and a very strong influence. An art theatre of some kind was certainly in their minds in the preparation stage. They didn't know quite what sort of theatre it was going to be, but they knew there was a need for new writers. There was no knowledge of what that new writing would be. So they approached novelists and poets, anyone they could think of as a possible source of drama.[5]

5. As Lewenstein has said, part of the first season had already been contracted before Devine accepted the position of artistic director. Devine therefore inherited the Duncan plays, *Don Juan* and *The Death of Satan*. Duncan's poetic drama and his conservative views of

But what in fact happened was that the play which made the name of the Court, *Look Back in Anger,* came from a quite different area than the poetic kind of art theatre vaguely envisioned, and once that had happened, it swung the whole movement in a completely different direction. Immediately, everyone realized that what they had been dreaming of, this European art theatre, was no longer the kind of theatre that would be realized, but that the writers themselves would dictate the character of the new theatre. The writing, directing, acting, and design talent began to come from a rather different social class and a regional background different from what was usual at the time.

So that the greatness of George, I think, was really to turn his back on Saint-Denis and that whole European art theatre influence and to say, "This IS the new theatre, and I will go along with this as I see it is the right moment for it," instead of pursuing something which had nothing to do with reality. He pragmatically saw what was actually going to work and that conditioned, and I think has continued to condition, the life of the Court.

I think, underneath, all his life Devine had a sneaking desire to go back to an art theatre. He was always sending memos out saying, "Perhaps we should study the work of the Noh theatre. I think writers could learn a lot if they watched the Kabuki." We set up workshops (we used to call them studios in those days) in which all the writers would study the work of foreign theatres. I think deep down he still very much wanted that kind of theatre. Certainly, in his later years, he concentrated mainly on Beckett and Ionesco, both of whom he was very close to and related to.

MR. MURRAY: Was there at the beginning a struggle to arrive at this new direction? In the first season or two along with the Osborne play appeared some of Ronald Duncan's poetic work.

MR. GASKILL: One has to understand that the work of Saint-Denis of the Old Vic school was based on the idea of a craft theatre; everyone

---

the theatre's mission had little or no support from Devine, who directed the Duncan plays in the initial season out of a sense of duty. The plays failed and were withdrawn after only eight performances. Duncan was never again produced at the Court, although his drama *The Catalyst* was produced in association with the ESC at the Arts Theatre Club in 1958 (Wardle, *The Theatres of George Devine,* 182–83 and 213; also see Ronald Duncan, *How to Make Enemies* [London, 1968]).

should know all the crafts. The actors, for example, used to study design and do the scene painting; everyone was involved. George himself was married to one designer and lived for a long time with another and was himself considered a craftsman.[6]

He knew much about lighting and carpentry and that side of the theatre. In the beginning of the Court, there was really a sense of an organic unit, consisting not only of writers and directors, but an acting company and a design workshop; a complete balance of talent. I think that held the Court together through that early period in which they didn't know whether they were going to do poetic drama, or novelist's drama, or whatever. Their aims became formulated very quickly; they were held together by theatre craft, which is what often holds us together; we're held together by the work of craftsmen.

MR. WARDLE: That's the direction in which Saint-Denis did not go—that having to do with all the practical side of theatre, irrespective of where the texts were taking them.

MS. JELLICOE: George once wrote, "Have we not seen six million Jews murdered"—I'm quoting from memory—"There have been drastic political and social changes all around us, and the best the theatre can give us is *The Mousetrap*. We want a theatre which will reflect what is happening."[7]

Ronald Duncan was wished on him. And I go on record saying this. Ronald Duncan was a poetic playwright. George did his plays, *Don Juan* and *The Death of Satan,* and he did a play by Angus Wilson, a novelist he hoped could make the jump to a playwright. But it wasn't until *Look Back in Anger* that suddenly he found his focus. And yet somehow he did know what he wanted. He wanted a theatre which should be relevant to life as it was then.

MR. HALLIFAX: I don't quite agree with Bill that we weren't sure of which way we were going. In the first season, we had *The Mulberry Bush,* by Angus Wilson, the novelist, which didn't entirely work. Also, there was *The Crucible,* which George was very, very eager to do. In fact, Sophie Devine's whole design concept for the season was based on *The*

6. Devine's wife, Sophie Harris, had designed professionally since the early 1930s. From the late 1950s until his death in January, 1966, Devine lived with Jocelyn Herbert, who began designing for the Royal Court Theatre in 1957.

7. Wardle quotes the passage at greater length in *The Theatres of George Devine,* 169. Wardle found the essay among Devine's papers (Irving Wardle to Billy J. Harbin, March 4, 1984, in possession of the editors).

Crucible, because originally, not only were we to have a permanent setting for the season, but all of the actors were going to have a form of permanent costumes; the costumes were based on and first used for *The Crucible.* Next, we had John Osborne's play, which had been chosen since July or August of 1955. So Osborne knew early that his play was going to be done, although he didn't know where it was going to be done because there wasn't a theatre at that time. Also, we had the Ronald Duncan plays, which, as Ann says, had been wished on George because Ronald was cofounder of this new company. So it was necessary that his poetic works be put on this stage. And, finally, there was to be Nigel Dennis' play. He was an author who had adapted one of his novels called *Cards of Identity.* So it was a varied and, in fact, very writer-oriented group of productions.

Somewhere in the background, George was always working. He talked about doing Sartre's *Le Diable et le Bon Dieu* but instead did Brecht's *The Good Woman of Setzuan,* because Peggy Ashcroft, who had just been made a Dame, would star in it and be a money puller. George was very caught up with the whole Brecht influence.

I was with two productions of George's, one he was in and one he directed and also acted in, when we were with the Shakespeare Memorial Company (which in 1961 became the Royal Shakespeare Company), based at Stratford-upon-Avon.[8] They sent us out on a huge tour—a Continental, Scandinavian, and United Kingdom tour. When we reached Berlin in July, 1955, George said, "I think it is absolutely essential that we all go across to Brecht's theatre." We did, and I was absolutely stunned by the presentation. We saw first *Mother Courage,* which was simply amazing.

The theatre had a permanent surround, a huge revolving stage, and quite a wide entrance upstage center. This was masked a bit further down the stage by a permanent masking piece, a huge flown piece. The production was fascinating, because if a little bush were needed, it was popped on by the property people (from out of our sight) onto the revolving stage. Round it came, and when it was no longer needed, it disappeared and something else took its place. It was really because of the Brecht influence that Margaret Harris designed the

8. Devine codirected *Much Ado About Nothing* and played Dogberry; he directed Gielgud in *King Lear* and played Gloucester. Both productions were sent on a six-month tour in 1955.

permanent setting for the Royal Court; that's another story, but that is really where the idea came from.[9]

MR. MURRAY: What was the character of George Devine to get this writers' theatre established, whereas other people here and abroad could not? Beckett, for example, has called him "the great inspirer."[10] What does that mean?

MR. WARDLE: In one of his letters to an irascible Neville Blond, Devine said, "The thing is difficult to do, otherwise someone would have done it before us." In that sense, one of the important claims to be made for him, is, first of all, an obsession with needing to make this theatre work; and second, an equal readiness to undergo any humiliation, hard work, wire pulling, administrative juggling, to keep the thing alive. I think from his point of view there always seemed to be two elements: the long-distance vision of what he wanted, plus the day-to-day politics of keeping the thing afloat.

MR. HOWARTH: Also, I think in his early years at the Court, the importance of Tony Richardson should not be underestimated. He was George's closest, dearest friend. And a lot of their talking and policy making came out of Tony's ambition; George recognized Tony's energy and talent; they were a team; they did it together.

Tony was only twenty-seven, and he had worked with George Devine in television in about 1953 or 1954. Tony had taken a BBC course in how to be a director for television, and he used George Devine as an actor in some of his demonstration half-hour programs. They presented a Chekhov half-hour short story. Tony cast George in the main part, and that's when the friendship started and their discussions about the future of the theatre.[11] George had been the presi-

---

9. Margaret ("Percy") Harris; her sister Sophie (who married Devine in 1940) and Elizabeth Montgomery made up the design firm known as Motley, which became established when Gielgud engaged them to design *Romeo and Juliet* in 1932. By 1956 the Motley firm was reduced to two, Margaret and Sophie.

10. Samuel Beckett, quoted in Findlater (ed.), *At the Royal Court*, 62.

11. In 1952 Devine appeared in Richardson's production of Chekhov's *Curtain Down*. Like Devine's earlier, Richardson's college at Oxford was Wadham. As youths in Shipley, Richardson and William Gaskill had run an amateur theatre together. When Devine and Richardson met, it was, says Wardle, "an attraction of opposites": Devine admired Richardson's youthful "fire," intelligence, and energy; Richardson respected Devine as "an experienced man of the theatre" (Wardle, *The Theatres of George Devine*, 160. See also Humphrey Carpenter, *O.U.D.S.* [Oxford, 1985], 121–26).

dent of the Oxford University Dramatic Society in 1935, and Tony Richardson had been the director of the OUDS in 1950. So they had that in common as well.

MR. HALLIFAX: My view is that of one of the work slaves at the Court, and the person to whom we looked with awe and admiration and indeed love, was George himself because he was the one who really knew about everything. We had absolutely total faith in him because we could go to him and he would help us solve a problem, and we simply went away and did it. Tony was much more mercurial, and he was not the one to whom we actually would turn because we knew George would come up with the answers. George was one of those old-fashioned actor-manager types who had been in every department and certainly had an answer to all of our technical problems. Tony was one who directed an enormous number of the plays wonderfully, but he wasn't the one to whom we would have turned in times of trouble.

MR. WARDLE: The subject of this discussion is the legacy of George Devine. One idea that occurs to me is that perhaps more than any other single person, he began defining what it meant to be the artistic director of a theatre at a time when subsidy was still a relative novelty. And a lot of his own fighting had to do with determining what the limits of power at the Royal Court were to a man in that position.

MR. GASKILL: I think it is important to have an image of him for those who perhaps didn't know him, nor have seen a photo. He was a large man, but not as large as he had been when he was young, and his hair had gone white during the war. But, in fact, he was only about forty-five when he took over the theatre. He was still quite young but looked like a father figure. He smoked a pipe, and he said, "If I didn't have white hair and didn't smoke a pipe, people wouldn't take any notice of me." He was a man of tremendous humility and self-knowledge.

Tony was tall and thin and came from Yorkshire; he was much younger, and he had, or has, an enormously, quick, fertile mind—a very, very fast thinker. So they had this combination. Then, of course, later on, George surrounded himself with younger directors, like me, John Dexter, Lindsay Anderson, and Anthony Page, who became, as it were, his children. And we had (and I think most people had) a relationship with him as a father figure. But in some ways, and he would be the first to say so, that was an artificially created image. It was an absolutely real relationship in which we loved and trusted him and often criticized him; we gave him a very hard time.

But he surrounded himself with a group of people whom he trusted, which is very unusual for directors, because most of us directors are envious of other people's talent, particularly younger people's talent, and will do nothing to encourage them in theatre.

George was not at all like that. He was in no way an envious man. He was very happy to have around younger people, and I think that this was certainly his immediate legacy, that he left a whole group of people whom he had schooled in the way of theatre, who could carry on what he had done.

MR. MURRAY: Did he teach you as a director? That is, did you and the others learn about directing from him?

MR. GASKILL: No, he used to do the lighting. I remember during Donald Howarth's first play, he said, "There's this boy who has written this play, which requires that we assemble a whole glass chandelier on stage. He ought to know better than that."[12] An impossible problem; then, he would see that it was possible. But that was typical of him. He saw everything through the practical and very rarely through the artistic. He would say, "I don't like the way that prop is made," or "That's got to be well lit for it to work." He never got into theoretical problems about ideas in theatre, but always about the craft of theatre.

MS. JELLICOE: He was terribly supportive, wasn't he? He was always enthusiastic about the next new idea, and I remember on many occasions extraordinary, sensitive support, because he had been through so much himself and understood problems of writers and directors.

First of all, he let me direct *The Sport of My Mad Mother*. He put his name with mine to protect me, but he only came in to about one rehearsal in five. By putting his name there, he made it possible for me to direct that play. One day, during a rehearsal, a note came onto my desk from the stage manager. It said, "Ann Jellicoe. Not to be given to Ann till after the rehearsal is over." So, I looked at it, in George's handwriting, and I thought, "No, no, I'll leave it. I know he doesn't want me to read it until after rehearsal."

12. Howarth's *Sugar in the Morning* opened April 9, 1959; it had previously appeared as a Sunday night production without decor (September 14, 1958) as *Lady on the Barometer*.

36

When I opened it, the note said, "You must not call the theatre doctor to see Philip Locke. Too much money has been spent already." [13] But he knew if it came in the middle of rehearsal it would distract my attention. And again, the night before the first night, Philip Locke lost his voice. George said, "Nobody is to tell Ann this. I will tell her myself." You felt surrounded by this sort of care.

About this image building, he once said to me, "I regard myself as your mad uncle." Also, he had a constant willingness to put up with things for the sake of the theatre. He once said, "If you knew how much shit I had to eat to get what I wanted." It has stayed in my mind ever since. But it was true, he was not afraid to be humble. He was not afraid to go very close to the ground to get what he wanted from people like Neville Blond. But he did it because he had a constant sense of what was ahead of him.

MR. WARDLE: I think that was partly a reflex of the Old Vic Theatre School when everybody took a stand on principle; if they were going to be criticized they would all resign. And in fact they all did resign, and the enterprise collapsed, after which George had this motto, "Never resign. Better to eat shit than to resign." [14]

MR. MURRAY: There was a group of writers that became attached to the Royal Court Theatre fairly early on.

MS. JELLICOE: Yes, there was a Writers' Group. I'll tell you what I think his great legacy was to the theatre. He trained others in his own respect for writers. George trained a whole generation of people. I don't think he directly taught them, he inspired them with that respect for the writer. And those people are now in positions of authority in the National Theatre, the Royal Shakespeare Company, and many other leading theatres. That's perhaps his greatest legacy, training those people in that attitude.

MR. WARDLE: If we're talking about legacy, this present conference at Louisiana State University is part of his legacy—given his continued interest in making contact with universities, in the belief that it was always necessary for those with the skills and background and the professional knowledge to keep on investing in those who haven't got

13. The play opened February 25, 1958; Philip Locke acted a leading role.

14. The resignations of George Devine, Glen Byam Shaw, and Michel Saint-Denis were accepted by Lord Esher, chairman of the Old Vic governors, on May 7, 1951.

there yet, because they were the ones who were going to do it next, the youth. I think he was doing this right up to the end of his life, going out and talking to youth conferences. Also, he was taking university trips to Brazil, America, and around England, with the proviso that he talk about youth. I think he was obliged to believe in youth, because he had this conviction that the theatre had a power to alter people for the better, and one thing's sure, it's not going to alter hardened, leathery, middle-aged playgoers. If it's going to change anybody, it's going to change the young.

MR. HALLIFAX: I'd better not go into the history of *Look Back in Anger,* because it's been mulled over. But the production of it really didn't take off until toward the end of October in 1956, as a result of the eighteen-minute excerpt on the BBC Television.[15] But after that, immediately the box office started ticking over and amazingly the theatre became filled with poeple, young people—in their later teens or early twenties—who, from the way they were behaving, hadn't been to the theatre at all before.

MR. WARDLE: At that time, young people had virtually no relationship with the theatre. So it was an original thing for George to think of at that time.

MR. MURRAY: Bill Gaskill has said that the artists, in the beginning, began to be more and more a part of a group of people from different regions and different classes than previously in the established theatre. Was this a conscious thing, or did it just happen?

MR. GASKILL: It was one of those things. A lot of us, like Donald Howarth and myself, came from the west side of Yorkshire, or Lancashire, or later from the Midlands. There was that whole movement of people who had not had those opportunities before. One has to set it straight here; it is true that having a regional accent had been a bar to working in the theatre. The working class could only appear on the stage if it was comic. And that changed. I don't think it was a class crusade in any sense. I think it just happened that the talented people had an opening at the Court. The doors were open to talented people regardless of where they came from or how they sounded. We were the first theatre to do a West Indian play, for instance, by Barry Reckord, very early on.[16] The whole class thing became a joke; actors of good

15. The excerpt was first broadcast on October 16, 1956.
16. *Flesh to a Tiger,* directed by Tony Richardson, May 21, 1958.

background would come pretending to be from the working class, for the benefit of those directors who would be deceived by them. Their eyes would sparkle, and they'd say, "I left school when I was fourteen," and they were lying. They had been to Oxford and Cambridge.

There were trends, too; for example, there was certainly a movement after that for writers to come from London and to write in the London idiom. The Bond-Orton generation had a London voice and not a regional voice. I don't think those things are really set up. I think it just happens—if the talent is there it must come out and be shown.

For about the first four years, in the beginning, before the Royal Shakespeare Company had come to London, and before the National had got going in the Old Vic, the Court was the only theatre where a new writer could have his play done. So everyone wanted to work at the Court or have his play done at the Court, and the talent just poured in through those doors into this tiny theatre. And that theatre had on its staff the strongest group of talented directors that theatre's had since I don't know when. But a kind of historical circumstance dictated that. Later, other theatres opened, and eventually the fringe started; so, the dissemination of the talent got wider and wider. But for those first four years, the concentration of talent at the Royal Court was remarkable.

MR. HALLIFAX: May I add my legacy for George? I think this is a technical one. I don't think everyone knows what he did. When we first went into this Victorian playhouse, it had house tabs, a house border, and all the rest of it.[17] And one of the first things we did was to prepare the floor, because George said, "We haven't got any money for the stage cloth," a stage covering which everybody used up to that time over the original floor. Luckily, we found underneath the dirt a splendid wooden floor, which was well worth playing on. Also, we covered over the orchestra pit and added a forestage with flanking doors.[18] This was really a copy of the theatre at Stratford-upon-Avon, so that we were able to permit actors to have a lower, downstage entrance,

17. The Royal Court Theatre was built in 1888.

18. Wardle reports that for Devine "a vital preliminary as one all-important feature of the new stage was its capacity to suspend the actor in a void with scenic statements made by lighting alone." Devine began by doing away with the Court's old house curtain (Wardle, *The Theatres of George Devine*, 172).

below the proscenium arch. In other words, actors came through where the stage boxes used to be. But one thing I remember clearly. We had a look at the house border, and we commented on how dirty it was, and George said, "Well, that will have to come down. We don't want the border." It destroyed the proportions of the theatre, of the actual proscenium arch, because it was incredibly tall and thin and emphasized that. The border came down, and we all suffered for weeks with hay fever because of the dust.

We experimented in *The Good Woman of Setzuan;* we didn't use the house curtain. We looked around and found pinoleum; it was made of tiny thin reeds, a very good material, because when you lit it from the front, it was just like gauze. It was transformable: when the audience came in, they saw this pale coffee-colored reeded screen in front of them, and then once the first scene started and the lights came up behind it, one was seeing through it. So we took away the house curtain; we used the "new" curtain quite a lot.

But we also didn't have any borders, because it meant more money, and George said, "Well, everybody can see there are lights coming from somewhere so the fact that we actually can see the source of the lights does not matter at all." And I think that the exposed lighting equipment incorporated into the total stage design is an important legacy that's been passed on.

MR. HOWARTH: And there's also a negative legacy left by George: the feeling in the acting profession that you couldn't get a part unless you had a proletarian accent, that if you had worked for Binkie Beaumont or the boulevard theatre before the Court, then you were already tainted with commercialism and conservative ways.[19] You weren't in the new forward generation. It produced the opinion that you couldn't get into the Court, that it was exclusive. So that is another legacy, a negative one. Perhaps even Max Stafford-Clark, who runs the Court now, is suffering from that. To embrace each new generation and to keep your theatre alive and contemporary is not an easy task, is it? Actors would say of the Court that in addition to the usual mask of tragedy and comedy there was a third mask which wore a sneer, the Royal Court sneer. And if you weren't one of them, you got that, you know. That's a legacy I think the Court has suffered from, that ex-

19. Hugh Beaumont, West End producer.

40

clusivity. Perhaps that is always true of a very successful or coterie-type theatre. The fringe also produces that kind of thing.

MR. GASKILL: Scripts were constantly being sent to John Gielgud. And he would say, "I don't want to appear in this Beckett-man's plays." But I don't remember George ever having an attitude of exclusiveness. Perhaps that accusation arose because of his close connection to the old, traditional theatre. He was so very close to all those famous actors, wasn't he?

MR. HOWARTH: Yes, they were his friends. But I wasn't thinking of the actors of the stature of Gielgud; I was thinking more of the average Equity member.

MR. HALLIFAX: I think a lot of that, incidentally, sounds rather like people who say, "I'm terribly sorry I haven't been to see your play. I haven't been able to get in," no matter whether they've tried. I think that's the way it was with a lot of actors; they weren't quite good enough to get in the Court.

MR. MURRAY: Going back to the theatre building itself, the Court has a proscenium stage. Did the theatre itself influence the work that was done there?

MR. WARDLE: Well, I think one point that was important to Devine himself was that this was not going to be a direct continuation of the little theatre clubs of the 1930s. It wasn't going to be playing to ghetto audiences, or to the people who were keen in following what Bill described as the Eric Bentley list of plays. It was going to be an ordinary proscenium house; it's not in the middle of London, but it's all we can get, and it's large enough, and it's for the middle-class theatre population. If anyone else wants to support it, fine. And, importantly, it still remains the only proscenium theatre in London continuously dedicated to new writing. Obviously, new work appears on other stages, subsidized and nonsubsidized, but only in the Court's proscenium house is it the daily bread and butter of the theatre's existence. That has been a very significant factor from the beginning to this day.

MR. GASKILL: There was really a deep ambiguity, I think, in the Court from the very beginning, perhaps between George and Tony Richardson. But it would be unfair to personalize it in that way. Success was always a possibility, and it became a reality very quickly. *Look Back in Anger,* although it didn't transfer to the West End, was a success, and it came to Broadway in the next season. It was followed by *The Entertainer*, which, because it had Laurence Olivier, was an absolute smash, and also came to Broadway. So within two years of the Court's starting, three Royal Court shows ran on Broadway.[20]

I joined the Royal Court in the end of 1957. The first play I did in the main house was John Osborne's *Epitaph for George Dillon*, and within six months I, a completely unknown director, actually whizzed over the Atlantic and was having to cope with David Merrick and Josh Logan. And that shouldn't happen to a dog! That is one of the most extraordinary experiences of my life. We opened out of town, in Atlantic City, I think, of all places.

In fact, *George Dillon* had one of those extraordinary openings that you all know so well, where it was wonderfully received and Josh Logan said, "This is the greatest; it will run forever," and all that. And one of those huge parties was thrown for the whole world of American theatre. And we were all there having a really good time when suddenly people were fighting to get out through the door, like water running out of a bathtub. There was an exodus of hundreds of people, and I said, "What's happened?" And they said, "The notices have come out!" The room was empty, and there was a pathetic group of six English actors who had come all this way from our theatre in Sloane Square, and we all fell about laughing. We thought it was terribly funny, because, of course, our livelihood didn't really depend on being a success on Broadway. We could always go back home. Finally, I rang George up in the middle of the night and said, "George, we failed in this place." He said, "Never mind, what's the next show?" And we knew that *that* life was going to go on. There were two worlds, one in which there was a little theatre in which a man was saying that we must do what we want to do at any cost, and the other, these commercial shows on Broadway.

The Court was an exciting place, but it would be difficult to say that it was a theatre of single vision, because it wasn't. I remember thinking about *The Sport of My Mad Mother* (which bombed, you know, in the American sense) that perhaps it might be a success; it's an exciting play, perhaps it might catch on. But it was far too innovative; nevertheless, at the time we actually thought it might. There's

20. *Look Back in Anger* opened in New York on October 10, 1956; *The Entertainer*, February 12, 1958; and *Epitaph for George Dillon*, November 4, 1958.

always that possibility; perhaps the audience will move with us. Perhaps this will be a new thing, and perhaps we'll even make money out of it, because it was really important. But you accept rejections, and you just go on doing good work.

MS. JELLICOE: *The Sport of My Mad Mother* was an awful experience in a sense.[21] In any other theatre the author would have been made to feel not wanted. I mean, one daren't put his face in the theatre after that kind of flop; but not at the Court. I had come, as it were, almost from nowhere, and so I had no previous experience of what one might expect. But it was through George that I went into the Royal Court Theatre almost every day for one reason or another and kept on going in, and the contact was kept. One kept on writing, and there was never any sense that you weren't welcome because your play had failed.

This is truly remarkable, I think. People normally don't want to be associated with failure. But by this means, I wrote *The Knack,* a comedy for four people, in one set, about sex, which was put on by that theatre, and it was a success. It wouldn't have happened had that support not come from George. On the first night of *The Knack,* before we knew what was going to happen, in the first interval, George said to me, "No matter what happens tonight, I want another play out of you for which I am prepared to pay money."[22] It is the gesture which matters. Writers are insecure and paranoid, and I don't think that sort of support exists now. Theatres do not nurse their writers now as George did. And as a result, the other people in the theatre nursed them, too. It was an extraordinary feeling of support and warmth.

MR. HOWARTH: If you were chosen, of course. I mean, there were a lot of writers who were rejected. For everyone who was accepted and was lucky enough, as some of us were, to get his play done, there were five hundred who got the rejection letter, "I am sorry, but that is not what we want to do."

MS. JELLICOE: They can't be expected to nurse everyone; they only looked after writers they did have faith in. But my point is that they did have faith in me, although my play failed fantastically.

21. *The Sport of My Mad Mother* was withdrawn after fourteen performances in March, 1958.
22. *The Knack* opened March 27, 1962.

MR. HOWARTH: Oh, surely. There's a loyalty to the chosen. We're lucky we benefited from that.

MS. JELLICOE: I don't see the point you're trying to make.

MR. HOWARTH: I was trying to say that just as there were actors who never got parts at the Court, so there were writers who never got their plays on at the Court, who subsequently got their plays on in other theatres, such as the Hampstead Theatre Club, and they were perfectly good writers and sometimes the Court wished it had done their plays.

MS. JELLICOE: Yes, but that's not what I am talking about. I mean, take the case of Edward Bond. Edward's play *Klaxon in Atreus Place* came into the Court in 1958, and it was spotted by Keith Johnstone and Edward was asked to join the Writers' Group. And then in 1962 they did a Sunday play of his, *The Pope's Wedding,* three years before *Saved.* They kept the links with Bond going by making him part of the Writers' Group. He formed friendships with various writers, which kept him coming into the Court, kept him feeling that he was part of something, and then finally he wrote *Saved* and became, I think, one of the best playwrights of our time. The other theatres took up other writers, but my point is that if you wanted to be stuck by, they stuck by you.

MR. GASKILL: I agree with Donald in the sense that I think that the Court was run—and this is one of the legacies, certainly through my time—by the personal taste of the artistic director and his associates.

MS. JELLICOE: But why shouldn't it?

MR. GASKILL: Exactly. I think the converse is to have a cynical theatre, such as I would take the National Theatre to be, which sees everything as equally acceptable and makes no judgment other than in terms of the potential success. I never have felt that Peter Hall has any personal taste at all. He'll buy anything. And it's very disturbing. It's very difficult to work for someone who has no personal taste because you don't know how to talk to him. When he says, "Oh, I like *Amadeus.*" And then he says, "But, also, I like this new play of Howard Brenton's," I say "What? How can you possibly like them both? It's not possible. You can't."

I think a theatre like the Royal Court has its dangers, unquestionably. It can become narrow, it can become elitist, and all those things. But if you have a basis of genuine positive enthusiasm for the work, I think that it will always be productive; and it will encourage the development of new work, rather than merely provide something which is put in the shop window and then is replaced by something else.

MR. MURRAY: Was there pressure in terms of needing to make money from these plays? Was it ever a question of, "We'll do this play because it looks like it might transfer to the West End for a profitable run?"

MR. GASKILL: There were instances of cynicism.

MS. JELLICOE: *Look After Lulu,* an adaptation by Noel Coward of a farce by Feydeau was cynical, I think. But there were very few instances of that.[23]

MR. MURRAY: Given the economics, to resist that must have been difficult.

MS. JELLICOE: We were always teetering on the edge.

MR. HALLIFAX: I think *The Country Wife* was done to pick up finances. It was cast with Laurence Harvey, who was a big star and the last person most of us would have thought of casting. And it gave Joan Plowright her chance so it served the company in that way, too. But certainly it was done with an eye to being much safer than what we had been doing.[24]

MR. HOWARTH: Did the play transfer to the West End?

MR. HALLIFAX: Yes, and it was hugely successful.

MR. MURRAY: In terms of money, and of government subsidy, did that have to be fought for?

MR. GASKILL: There was a small Arts Council grant to begin with (of some £7,000) and it stayed small for several years. But most of the plays of John Osborne were successful transfers to the West End, and the film rights were sold. Also, we had a cut of their run on Broadway, and a cut of a Broadway run is a lot of money. That's how for the first three or four years the Court survived.[25] In fact, all the experiments,

23. *Look After Lulu* opened on July 29, 1959, with Vivien Leigh as the star. It ran for forty-five performances to nearly capacity audiences of 97 percent. Production costs were £4,381, and the box office income totaled £12,603 (see Findlater [ed.], *At the Royal Court,* Appendix 2, Financial Tables, 1960).

24. *The Country Wife* opened on December 12, 1956, ran sixty performances, and drew an attendance of 95 percent. Production expenditures were £1,728, and box office income amounted to £13,962 (*ibid.*).

25. At the end of the first season's operation (March 31, 1957), royalties from transfers and rights amounted to £8,505. One year later, that income had risen to £39,631 (see *ibid.,* Appendix 2, Financial Tables, 1958).

all the *Sport of My Mad Mother* types, were financed by John Osborne. Quite definitely. Then gradually the Arts Council subsidy went up.[26] But to begin with, it was touch and go. No one thought the operation would survive more than one or two years. We thought, will we be here next year?

MR. HALLIFAX: The crisis happened in July of 1956. "Will we be here next week?" became the question. But then *Look Back in Anger* opened in New York in October; *The Good Woman of Setzuan* on October 31 was a great failure, but *The Country Wife* in December saved it and was immediately followed by *The Member of the Wedding, Fin de Partie* and *Act Sans Paroles,* and *The Entertainer* in April, 1957. But in July of 1956 I can remember going home and saying, "Well that looks like it." Because it really did look like the finish.

When we opened *Look Back in Anger* on Broadway, Tony Richardson seemed very worldly-wise. We were terribly in awe of him, the few of us who were there, because he knew all about New York, and where to go, and what one said. He became our leader, and at the end of the first night, we couldn't quite tell exactly what was going to happen. Two actresses, Mary Ure and Vivienne Drummond, were with us, and we had been invited to Sardi's by David Merrick. We all thought that was very glamorous. We had no idea where everything was, but Tony, of course, knew. So he said, "Well, while you girls are getting ready, we'll go to the bar next door." And we went into this gloomy cavern, which was absolutely appalling, sort of plastic beige lights and radio on. And this man came on the radio, and he said, "I have just been to the worst play!" Then the girls came in, and we said, "Well, we're just about packing up. But we're hungry. Let's go to Sardi's." So we walked down the road, and Tony was ahead with the two girls, and I was walking with Alan Bates and John Osborne, and I said to John in my usual sort of stage manager–company manager sort of way, "Oh, don't worry about it." And he said, "Well, it was a sellout in Leatherhead last night." We went over to Sardi's. And everybody was applauded, and we thought that was rather good, and we were put at a table right by a corner somewhere. We were rather tired and desperately hungry. The drinks came, and then they stopped coming. And

26. In 1958, 1959, and 1960, the Arts Council grant was only £5,000 annually. By 1974 it had risen to £135,000 and in 1980 to £350,000.

the papers didn't come. And no food arrived. We were actually desperate. At long last, the general manager arrived and said, "The first review by Walter Kerr is good." This began to look a little better, and after that three papers arrived. By that time we were so tired we weren't hungry at all. But one headline said, "*Look Back* lights a Bonfire on Broadway." That was enough to send the menus around.

MR. MURRAY: Did John Osborne exert more influence after that?

MR. HALLIFAX: No, not on the policy making at the Court; he was getting on with his playwriting. But he was around because he was an understudy with us. He understudied in *Look Back in Anger*.

MR. HOWARTH: And the Court had his next three plays on option as well, for £50 per play.

MR. MURRAY: Perhaps we should ask for comments or questions from the observers in the audience at this point.

OBSERVER: May I go back to what Bill Gaskill was talking about—taste. Was it really the taste of one man or of a variety of you who were associated with him? Was taste a matter of championing writers one believed in? I'm thinking about the kind of relationship between David Storey and Lindsay Anderson.[27]

MR. GASKILL: No, I don't think it was the taste of one man. We were all, I think, very close at that time. We did have shared judgments and attitudes among the writers and directors. It was something which didn't last, but certainly for a period of time, we were enormously in sympathy with each other and knew the direction we were going in. I think George was aware of that. But within that general sense, there were individual opinions. For instance, George was not a great lover of Arnold Wesker, and John Dexter was, and to some extent I was, and George would always respond to that kind of pressure among the people he trusted. Tony had a predilection for a particular kind of writing so that was another avenue. We balanced each other. Famously, in the history of the Court, we have rejected plays which have been enormously successful elsewhere, and we've never been worried about it. We did turn down Simon Gray's *Butley,* and I can't remember what else. We probably had Tom Stoppard through our hands at

---

27. Lindsay Anderson directed nearly all of David Storey's plays at the Court: *In Celebration* (1969), *The Contractor* (1969), *Home* (1970), *The Changing Room* (1971), *The Farm* (1973), and *Life Class* (1974).

one time. Someone said to me the other day, "Why is Tom Stoppard not liked at the Royal Court?" and I really couldn't answer that question, but it's true. If you took a straw poll among writers and directors surrounding the Court they would not be Stoppard fans. I think there is a kind of wit tradition of well-written lines which the English critics adore and which I think is really not in the Court tradition. That's the simplest way I can put it.

MR. ESSLIN [speaking from the audience]: I think that Stoppard really represents a kind of English high comedy tradition which goes back to Oscar Wilde, for example. It's the exact opposite of the Court tradition. It is a theatre of wit. Although Stoppard is not as upper class or drawing room as Noel Coward or Wilde were, he continues the same kind of thrust, in a way.

MS. JELLICOE: I think that the objection to Stoppard would be more of a moral objection. The Court, perhaps, suspected that kind of writing was flashy.

OBSERVER: Was political bias at work in the plays selected?

MR. GASKILL: We weren't a largely political group, although the starting of the Court coincided with a political reawakening, I think. It came at the time of the Suez War, and for the first time people who had not been politically involved, like myself, suddenly became aware. This was followed by a nuclear disarmament movement which was very strong in the late fifties, early sixties, which we also became a part of. That's how we first met Arnold Wesker, for instance, who was involved in the movement. So there was a political mood which seemed to throw up certain writers.

MS. JELLICOE: I think our sympathies were left wing, and the plays taken were what we thought were good plays, which happened to be left wing.

MR. GASKILL: We used to say, "Let's see the good right-wing play. Will anyone show us a good right-wing play?" And I can't say we ever saw one.

MR. ESSLIN: Nigel Dennis' *August for the People* is a right-wing play.[28]

MS. JELLICOE: The Court never took to John Whiting, for instance, who was slightly right wing.

28. Dennis' plays produced at the Court include *Cards of Identity* (1956), *The Making of Moo* (1957), and *August for the People* (1961).

MR. GASKILL: John Whiting hated the Court.

MR. ESSLIN: He was never done at the Court.

MR. GASKILL: But he never wanted to be either. He used to write very bitterly about us.

OBSERVER: I was wondering what Ann Jellicoe did before George Devine? And Donald, too?

MR. HOWARTH: Before the Court? I know this is a long story, but I happened to be living in Bradford, which is where Tony Richardson and Bill Gaskill lived, and Tony was a local alderman's son. He started a group called the Shipley Young Theatre, which we joined. And we put on *Comus, Romeo and Juliet,* and *Doctor Faustus,* and then Tony and Bill went to Oxford. I went to a drama school run by a woman called Esmé Church, who had been at the Old Vic with Lilian Baylis and George Devine in the thirties. Esmé Church started the Young Vic School, and George, who was younger than Esmé Church, had been part of the Michel Saint-Denis group running the Vic. Esmé Church moved to Bradford and started her school, which I had joined, and so I knew of George and all that through the Vic, Lilian Baylis, and Esmé Church.

Tony and Bill became involved in professional theatre through the Oxford route. After drama school, I went into repertoire theatre, and six years passed. Meanwhile, George and Tony had met. Bill was working in repertoire companies in various places and for television. By that time, I was in repertoire, stage managing, stage directing, and even acting, for several years. Eventually, I thought, "This is a boring life," and I left the theatre. I worked in a bar in Devon pulling beer. By then the English Stage Company was successful at the Royal Court and everybody wanted to join. I thought, "Hmmmm, all those people are getting their names in the paper now; I'll write a play." So I wrote my first play in two weeks, and I sent it to the Court. Keith Johnstone read it, and Bill, who was at the Court then, said, "I know him—"

MR. GASKILL: "—he can't possibly have written a good play!" And Anthony Page said, "Oh, I think it's wonderful. It is so full of passion. It's like Tennessee Williams." It's not a bit like that, I thought.

MR. HOWARTH: Anyway, I was asked to come in and see Keith Johnstone. We had a cup of coffee, and he said, "You're a very talented writer. Is there any more? It's not long enough to be done as it is." So I went away and in the next four nights wrote another thirty pages. I stuck the glass chandelier sequence on the end and sent it back to him. And they put it on.

MS. JELLICOE: That's absolutely contrary to my experience! I've always wanted to be in the theatre. I knew what I wanted to do when I was four years old, and I never once lost that sense of direction. I was trained as an actress, and, then I started my own theatre club. I went back to my drama school to teach acting, and at this point the English Stage Company was started and I remember going to the first production.

What started me writing was the *Observer* competition. I had always wanted to write a play but had never been able to finish one, and I thought, "Well, if I don't do it now with these judges—and obviously they want something new—if I don't do it now, I never will."

I delivered the play literally on the deadline, ten minutes to midnight on the last day. For me, it was not the "old boy" network at all. I knew nobody at the Court.

MR. HALLIFAX: Perhaps I might say that when we started, we didn't call the plays by their titles. They were known by the author's name because we were a writers' theatre. So we had the Wilson, we had the Miller, we had the Osborne, and there was a slight sort of worry when we had the Osborne Two. We stopped it because nobody could get Sir Laurence to talk about an Osborne Two; so it came to an end with *The Entertainer*.

OBSERVER: We've heard so much this afternoon about the kind of support that Devine gave. Was there practical help given as well? Did he share his experience as a person? Did he work to shape the plays at all? Or was it more a matter of providing the space?

MS. JELLICOE: He had the most fantastic respect for writers; he cherished them. I think it's fair to say that writing is the one thing he couldn't do himself. He could act, he could direct, he had experience with administration. He knew an awful lot about lighting. But I don't think he ever actually wrote. He had extraordinary respect for the creative integrity of the writer. He never meddled with other people's work. It's so easy to say, "I think it would be much better if you rewrote act three." I think one should be very careful before he starts telling a writer what to do, and George certainly instilled that respect into one.

MR. BURGE [speaking from the audience]: George had enough courage to trust the writer. There is no other way to get a fresh approach to playwriting. In the previous ten years the British theatre had a particularly set pattern in playwriting and success in the theatre. But George allowed the writer to lead, because he trusted, and you could trust him. He took the risks.

MS. JELLICOE: It is more than that. The famous phrase "the right to fail" really meant the right to make experiments. George trusted people even when they failed, if he felt real creativity behind that. Failure meant failure at the box office, or failure with the critics, who are always five years behind. It didn't mean failure in George's terms.

MR. HOWARTH: It was Tony Richardson's phrase, "the right to fail."

MR. HAMPTON [speaking from the audience]: Just one exception that proves the rule, as they say. George did cut. He cut Cory out of Miller's *The Crucible* when he did it in 1956. When Arthur Miller found out he sent a cable, saying, "Reinstate, or close." And they had to put Cory back again.

MR. HARE [speaking from the audience]: An attitude very prevalent in America, which is not at the Court at all, is this thing called helping writers with their plays, as if they were cripples and needed help getting across the road. It's a very condescending attitude one finds here. One hears about theatres that aren't prepared to do plays but will "workshop" plays, as a way of not actually taking responsibility. And the good thing about the Court was that there was none of that. There wasn't any of this behavior as if they knew and the writers didn't. On the contrary, the writers seemed to know, and the directors would find out as they were doing the play. I do think this whole attitude of "not to trust" is bad, as if they were doing a big favor to the writer by putting his play on so that he might learn something. They often say, "When the play goes on he will learn more about how to write plays." That is nonsense. He will put his play on, and they will learn something about it by seeing it.

MR. WARDLE: Devine's belief in the writer went back actually to the time of the Old Vic School. He drew up priorities for Vic School students in the early 1950s which said that the origin of all theatrical life was the writer.

OBSERVER: Did Devine choose the writers, or did he listen to good advice?

MR. GASKILL: It is hard to answer that. As for his own choices, I think he was genuinely enthusiastic about John Arden, and he did fight very hard for him. All the Arden plays were financially unsuccessful. He liked N. F. Simpson's work very much. It appealed to that side of George which liked economy and elegance in the writing. He did not really like Arnold Wesker because he was a bit raw for him. But George listened to John Dexter, who did like Wesker. He liked Nigel Dennis, and he committed himself to John Osborne completely and was prepared to see him through. They were very close friends.

MS. JELLICOE: He did surround himself with fine judgments and talents. He listened very often—would take advice sometimes.

MR. GASKILL: One's own judgments are flexible in those situations, particularly in times of change. And there's an exciting climate. You listen and respond to other people and absorb values and give values back and tastes and judgments with which you assess plays. So there's a kind of climate in which that develops.

I remember when I read the first play of Edward Bond, *Klaxon in Atreus Place.* I said, "I cannot understand this play at all. It's rubbish." And Keith Johnstone said, "We must give him a chance. Let's invite him to the Writers' Group. He must write another play." And I trusted Keith at that time so we supported Bond. So it's not a very fixed thing; it's some common awareness among the group.

OBSERVER: Would Devine come to people on the staff to see if they shared his enthusiasm, or did people come to him to advocate new plays and playwrights?

MR. GASKILL: Both, many instances of both. But sometimes he had a strong reaction. I remember that before Pinter had made his name, Harold Hobson said of *The Room* and *The Dumb Waiter,* "These are wonderful masterpieces and must be done at the Royal Court." And George said, "I won't be told how to run my theatre by Harold Hobson." And I said, "Well, I think the plays have something, George." And he said, "No, no, I don't want them." And he was not going to take them. Of course, the outcome is that they were eventually done there.

MR. HOWARTH: Yes, he could have very strong opinions. He was supportive, yes. But I remember when my first play was done on a Sunday night. Miriam Brickman cast the play, and the actress Patricia Jessel (who had won the Clarence Derwent award for her performance in *Witness for the Prosecution*) was to play the main role for two guineas for two weeks' rehearsal. We were delighted that we had this star for it, and we went to George's office and showed him the cast list, rather smug and proud that we had got her, and he looked it over. "Patricia

Jessel?" he said. "Get rid of her." I was already rehearsing the play. We didn't know why he said this. We asked why but didn't get a reply. He just did not want to talk about it. So he could be very firm in his attitude and opinion. I think it was because Jessel wouldn't take over from Diana Churchill in *The Country Wife*. It was for some reason like that. But we didn't fire her. We said, "Let George do it." I didn't want to get rid of her. No, we just let it ride. We rehearsed with her, and he never mentioned it again.

MR. BROCKETT [speaking from the audience]: We get the notion that George Devine was central to this theatre in those years, but I would like to ask, what was your attitude when he announced that he was going to retire? What did you think might happen to the theatre?

MR. GASKILL: George ran the theatre for nine years, the last season of which was largely directed by Anthony Page. The first four years were the most concentrated and fertile, and it became increasingly difficult to maintain the same focus and to keep a group of writers together because the attractions were elsewhere, in commercial managements and the other big subsidies. The whole pattern had been changing, and George had many schemes for rebuilding the theatre, or starting a theatre elsewhere, which came to nothing. So in a sense it had temporarily lost direction, a thing which happens rather regularly at the Court.

It is quite difficult to maintain constantly that level of excitement and concentrated work which is essential. I think George became tired, not so much by the responsibility of it as by the inability to keep the quality as high as he would have liked.

John Dexter and I had gone to the National Theatre. We were very excited about working with Olivier. And George was excited about that, too, because he was very keen on each developing his own career. Jocelyn Herbert had also moved into other theatres. So George was pleased that his work was spreading into classical theatre; many actors, directors, and designers went to the National with us. In fact, we moved a lot of the Court lock, stock, and barrel to the National Theatre, then located at the Old Vic. So we all knew that George's work at the Court was finished, that he had done his task. He was planning to retire, and it seemed to be right that he should, but none of us quite knew what the Court's future should be. In fact, I had been approached to take over. I only made up my mind at the public meeting, when George announced his retirement and Lindsay Anderson made a very emotional speech. Suddenly, I felt that I should take over, if I could, because I felt that there was something still to do.

MS. JELLICOE: In a sense, since one knew Bill so well and had worked with and observed him, one felt there was an absolute continuity going on. It was not George leaving the Court which was shattering; it was George's dying, which was really the terrible thing. He had set to work the most extraordinary influence in the lives of a number of people. I still think of him. I am sure a week never passes without my thinking of George, and I think it is true of almost everybody who knew him. And there was a continuity when Bill took over, with the possibility of a fresh impetus, so that one really felt that it was rather a good thing. It was the dying that was shattering—at a relatively early age. Only a year later.

MR. HOWARTH: When he decided to leave, he formulated what he was going to do with his future, and I have a document in my possession called "The Arts in Society, with a special reference to the University," written by George. It is dated the first of April, 1965; he was dead before the first of April, 1966. That was what he was going to do with his future.

II

Artistic Directors Talk: The Court After George Devine, 1965–1981

MODERATOR: *Brooks Jones, artistic director, Center for the Arts, Purchase, New York*

PARTICIPANTS (PRESENT AND PAST ARTISTIC DIRECTORS OF THE ESC AT THE ROYAL COURT THEATRE):
Max Stafford-Clark, 1979–present
Stuart Burge, 1977–1979
Nicholas Wright, 1975–1977
Oscar Lewenstein (not present), 1972–1975
William Gaskill, 1965–1972

SPEAKING FROM THE AUDIENCE:
Martin Esslin
Amlin Gray
Michael Hallifax
Donald Howarth
Ann Jellicoe
Irving Wardle
and conference observers

MR. JONES: I have the honor of welcoming you, our guests from England, to discuss artistic direction. We are asking you to do a rather difficult task—to dissect matters which don't normally hold up under scrutiny at all.

In America, the artistic director is the person willing to provide some point of view and sense of direction to a company, without any guarantee that that direction will be artistic. We have present here all of the living artistic directors of the Royal Court since George Devine, except for Oscar Lewenstein, who could not attend. Robert Kidd, who was codirector with Nicholas Wright, 1975–1977, is deceased.

I would like to start with one question: How would you characterize the Court as an institution over the long run, and, more specifically, how would you characterize the period of your reign?

Mr. Gaskill, I suppose you have had the longest to think about it since you gave it up in 1972.

MR. GASKILL: It's very difficult to answer the question, in the abstract.

MR. BURGE: I think that the Court's constantly changing. That's one of the exceptional things about it and part of its essential character, because of outside pressures and influences. It started with a splendid idealism. And, fortunately, it was manned by people with fresh ideas and a purpose. As time goes on, that changes, because, in part, of financial pressures. For instance, in the earlier days, one could employ assistant directors for nominal salaries. There were no really stringent union rules about finances for the personnel. Over the years, that has changed considerably so that one is working with an organization now that has many more "hoops of steel" around it. Also, the Court can't now have the same character it had in the beginning because it is now an established theatre. But the value of it is that it IS an established theatre, and yet it is still nurturing new work.

MR. JONES: One of the remarkable things about the Court is the short duration of the artistic directors, and yet the Court has apparently maintained a continuity. What is the soul that keeps going on, even though artistic direction may change every several years?

MR. GASKILL: Well, there are two things. I think I gave this answer once to Irving Wardle when he asked what my policy was. I said, "It's the people I worked with." I still believe that that is an enormous part of it; the people whom you choose to work with and the people who choose to work with you are the key factors. The other thing is the money you get from the Arts Council. When I took over from George Devine in 1965, I was very fortunate because it was at a time when the financial situation of the country as a whole was healthy and became healthier. In fact, during most of the time that I was running the Royal Court the economy was expanding.

Almost immediately after I left in 1972, it receded and has been receding ever since. I think that explains a great deal about why the artistic direction has been so short—because the financial struggles have been great.

But I was fortunate that soon after I assumed the artistic direction in 1965, the Arts Council money literally doubled overnight, and for the first three years that I ran the theatre, I was not dependent upon transfers to the West End or film rights.[1] I actually ran the theatre for its own sake. Eventually, we did transfer a couple of Osborne plays, and their success again financed more experimental work. But I was very fortunate to have a firm financial base for what I was doing.

After four years, I shared the artistic directorship with two directors, Lindsay Anderson and Anthony Page, both of whom had been developed under George Devine and whom I knew. They stayed on when Oscar Lewenstein took over and remained with him during the period 1972 to 1975 so that there was virtually an unbroken succession of people whom George had developed and who went on running the theatre until Nicholas Wright took over in 1975.

What I was trying to do when I took over was to go back to the basis upon which George had started the theatre: to have a permanent company of actors and to play in repertoire. I had just been working with Laurence Olivier and John Dexter at the National Theatre for two years when it was at the Old Vic.[2] Then George asked me to come back, and I did six months before he died on January 20, 1966. I very much wanted to re-create a theatre with a permanent company and with the writers that I had known in the Writers' Group that I had run under George. Those writers were Ann Jellicoe, N. F. Simpson, and Edward Bond; Bond had been developed by the Writers' Group but not performed. Also, John Arden and Arnold Wesker. They were the writers to whom I was closest, and my first season was very much

1. In 1965 the Arts Council grant amounted to £50,555; in the season of 1966–67, £88,650; and in 1967–68, £100,000. In the following three seasons, however, the amount declined: 1969, £94,000; 1970, £94,000; 1971, £89,000. By 1974 it had risen to £135,000, and in 1980 it was £350,000 (see Findlater [ed.], *At the Royal Court,* Appendix 2, Financial Tables).

2. The National Theatre was established at the Old Vic Theatre in 1963 under the direction of Sir Laurence Olivier; it moved to its new theatre plant on the South Bank in 1976. During his directorship of the ESC at the Royal Court, Oscar Lewenstein advocated an expansion of the ESC to include an operation at the Old Vic. In a document dated November 27, 1973, entitled "Suggested Structure for Artistic Direction in the Event of the English Stage Company Taking Over the Old Vic," he argued for a director of the English Stage Company who would govern the operations at both the Royal Court Theatre and the Old Vic. Each company would be run by an artistic director in consultation with the director of the ESC. But a letter from six members of the artistic committee protested the Old Vic scheme. Dated December 19, 1973, the letter voiced "a strong and basic disagreement between the Director of the Royal Court and six out of seven members of the artistic committee." Lindsay Anderson, Jocelyn Herbert, Ann Jellicoe, Anthony Page, David Storey, and Nicholas Wright signed the letter. The Old Vic plan was abandoned.

centered in those particular writers. But what happened was that the controversy over *Saved* and the censorship of it became a great focus for our work, and, in fact, for about three years my life seemed to be a battle against the censor. When the censor finally disappeared in 1968, I did actually feel exhausted; and it was also at that time that I asked Lindsay Anderson and Anthony Page to share the direction of the theatre with me.[3]

So an external force, the Lord Chamberlain, had in fact very much characterized the theatre. We were an embattled theatre. And that united us strongly in a way that the theatre had also been united in the past by its group of writers. All my memories of that period are of fights really, fights with the Lord Chamberlain, with the Arts Council, with the British Council, with members of Parliament. It was draining because it was really external, outside the work itself.

And in the process, a lot of the ideas of developing a company went by the board, and I think that is typical of the Court. In the beginning, one says, we will have a permanent company, we will do plays in a certain style, we will have a permanent surround, we will even have the same costumes. Every artistic director who takes over says at some point, "I'm going to go back to a permanent company." I've heard Stuart Burge say that, and I've heard Max say it, and I laugh. I would never say, "Don't do it."

I remember that I went to George and I said, "I am going to have a company." He didn't say, "It won't work." He said, "Wonderful. Good, I am thrilled. I am excited." He said, "I'll do the budget," and he did do the budget. He asked me lots of questions about how much it would cost, or how many actors I wanted, how many plays, what the changeovers would be; and that became the basis of the work, and for more than six months, nearly nine months, I ran that.

3. The production of *Saved* on November 3, 1965, launched anew an intense controversy over the Theatres Act of 1843, "under which the Lord Chamberlain was given absolute authority" to censor dramatic materials. The controversy was resolved in 1968. Bond's *Early Morning* was the last play banned by the Lord Chamberlain. It had been presented on March 31, 1968, as a Sunday night production; Alfred Esdaile, as licensee of the theatre, canceled the performance for the following Sunday night. Nevertheless, the Court did present what it called a "critics' dress rehearsal" on April 7 for "invited guests," who were admitted through a side entrance. On September 28 the Theatres Act of 1968 became law, ending theatre censorship in Great Britain (see Browne, *Playwrights' Theatre*, 67–70).

But then the politically immediate problem, which was the court case over *Saved,* somehow became much more dominant. I think that also is typical of the Court, that the current political battles become more important than the artistic, than the standards of good work. But if these battles arise, if we have to fight back, we have to do it.

But the idea of a permanent company, with permanent, generalized settings and costumes, never worked. If you have a writer who wants a certain kind of staging, or a certain kind of costuming, you have to go along with that. For instance, if you have a black writer who is writing about Africa, or about the West Indies, you can't say, "Well, I have my company of white actors and they will have to perform it." There comes a point when you say, "No, it's a black play and it has got to be done by black artists." You can't avoid that.

And I think that is right. The moment you say, "Well, I will have my company before everything else," you put an enormous limitation on the plays that you can do. I think that all artistic directors of the Court have to come to that realization. The permanent company idea does not work very well. If you want to do specific casting, either star casting for big parts or casting according to race or with particularly young actors—for example, if you do a play about young boys in London, there is no point in having John Gielgud in the company. It is going to be a waste of time.

MR. BURGE: Unless, of course, you are in a financial situation to be able to project ahead, something like three or four years, so that you can collect a group of, say, half a dozen plays, which you idealistically mean to do. And then form a company to do those half-dozen plays. But that means a projection forward of three or four years, and the Royal Court has never been in that financial position. Certainly, when I went to the Royal Court, I said that's what we have got to do. But we had a deficit of £70,000, or whatever it was.

But one still thinks that ideally one should be able to do this. Somehow, we will get that deficit off and then we will do it. We will find this group of plays, all of which we really want to do, and then find a company to do it. But, of course, in practice, it is impossible because of the finances. That's sad.

MR. JONES: Oscar Lewenstein is not here, but is there anything specific that characterized those years from 1972 to 1975 when Oscar was there? Anything over and above the commitment to running a play-wright's theatre?

MR. GASKILL: The work of the Third World writers; the most impressive thing about Oscar's period was the three South African plays.

MR. JONES: Do you feel that that came out of a point of view of his, or was it chance?

MR. WRIGHT: I can answer that because I was there. I was running the Theatre Upstairs at the time, which had already put on, while I had been working there, *Boesman and Lena* by Athol Fugard.[4] His new play, *Sizwe Bansi Is Dead*, was first mentioned to Oscar by Donald Howarth, I think. At the same time, I had reports of it from another friend in South Africa, and we bought it blind because we had loved the previous show so much.

There wasn't a script, although there was a transcript that was very badly typed and gave little idea of the play. But we brought the company over from South Africa all the same. They did a run-through the morning after they arrived. It was incredibly good. This was for the Theatre Upstairs. Oscar, I think, had considered it for the main bill. I don't know why he didn't put it there. Perhaps he felt he did not yet know it firsthand, which he needed to do.

MR. GRAY [speaking from the audience]: I think Findlater's book mentions that Fugard wanted it to be Upstairs.

MR. WRIGHT: Yes, I think that is true. Because he had done the *Boesman and Lena* Upstairs and he was very happy there. Oscar responded strongly to *Sizwe Bansi* in the Theatre Upstairs.[5] He liked it because it was such a good play, and the actors were excellent. Also, Oscar responded to it politically. He and Athol between them devised the season of three South African plays. It was a great enthusiasm of Oscar's and something he was enormously supportive of.

MR. JONES: Is there anything specifically that characterized your particular artistic direction of the Royal Court?

MR. WRIGHT: There were a few things. It might be worth just going back a little bit. During the late sixties and early seventies there had been a lot of money and activity about in the country as a whole. I don't mean

4. *Boesman and Lena* opened on August 19, 1971.

5. *Sizwe Bansi Is Dead* opened on September 20, 1973. The South African Season, which included *The Island, Sizwe Bansi,* and *Statements After an Arrest Under the Immorality Act,* opened on the main stage in January, 1974.

theatrical activity, I just mean in terms of large social movements. We were able to present an enormous amount of work. The Royal Court's grant increased, and at the same time, and for the same reason, I suppose, certainly during the later years of Gaskill's period as artistic director and throughout the first years of Oscar's period, a lot of money was made on shows that transferred to the West End. As a result, an income from the commercial theatre got, as it were, habitually built into the annual income of the Royal Court.[6]

In the last year or two of Oscar's time there, he wasn't able to find commercial West End sponsors and backers as easily as he had in the previous years, not because they were less enthusiastic but because the national economy was tightening up and the West End was becoming more conservative and less apt to take risks.

When Robert Kidd and I started as artistic directors in 1975, we took over at the end of probably the first year in which the West End income had failed. Not because of the failure on the part of the management of the Royal Court at all, but because the West End itself wasn't in a position to put money into the theatre. The national economy had changed. For the same reason, there was not the prospect of the Arts Council grant going up to make the difference because the Arts Council was feeling the pinch, too. So Robert Kidd and I started as joint artistic directors at the end of a financial year which resulted in a deficit, of I forget what. It seemed a lot of money at the time; probably it was about forty or fifty thousand pounds, or something like that.[7]

It was rather hard to see how that money would be made up. For years before it had been possible to imagine it coming from the West End, but that wasn't true anymore.

So looking at the period ahead was a problem. Robert Kidd, my joint artistic director, was somebody who had worked at the Royal Court for a number of years, and particularly during Christopher

6. During the three years of Oscar Lewenstein's tenure, Arts Council grants rose from £91,250 in 1972 to £170,000 in 1975. Income from transfers, rights, and other sources in his first season was £47,330; in 1973, £55,937; in 1974, £36,913; in 1975, £43,476. But in the year ending April 2, 1977, transfer income plummeted to £16,773 (see Findlater [ed.], *At the Royal Court,* Appendix 2, Financial Tables).

7. Greville Poke, chairman of the council of the ESC, reported on July 22, 1975, that the cash deficit amounted to £47,000 (Minutes of a Meeting of the ESC Council, July 22, 1975).

Hampton's plays and during David Storey's first play there, which were great successes.[8] When I talk of what we did, I am not exactly talking about what either of us would have done individually. It wasn't a good partnership. We both functioned much less well than we would have done in a happier partnership. It is probably not good to have two people running a theatre together, unless they have an unusually good artistic relationship.

A lot of friction developed between us, and, as a result, we looked inwardly and adopted a rather combative stance toward everyone else. The joint creature we had created really lacked the generosity which was necessary. We were both inexperienced in running a large theatre, but, more important, we weren't very good at creating the kind of atmosphere in which it is very easy for people to give advice.

If you look at our record broadly, what happened is that in the first six to nine months there we had some very successful productions. By the time we entered the second year of our tenure we started to lose much more money than we should. Consequently, I think we lost our nerve. I certainly did a show that I shouldn't have done, perhaps because of panic, and partly because of not acting as oneself, really. Also, one of the periodic Arts Council crises started to loom up, and a lot of pressure descended on us and other people. In such situations, one starts to get very paranoid; and then one realizes that he is quite right to be paranoid.

It is a rather complicated story, but, in any event, the financial pressures partly explain why some of the artistic directors didn't last very long. Robert resigned at the end of our second year. Robert's and my contracts were linked. My contract was finished by his resignation, and that is when the council of the English Stage Company of the Royal Court invited Stuart Burge to become the artistic director. Bob left; I stayed on for a little bit, just to help with the transition.

MR. BURGE: Yes, you were very kind to stay. At my request you stayed on to make some kind of link, because, as Bill said, that is the important thing; it is not really the length of tenure of the artistic director, it is the link from one to the other. For example, I had Max Stafford-Clark as an associate director at a very early stage, and he has continued on;

8. Kidd directed Hampton's first play at the Court, *When Did You Last See My Mother?*, in 1966; he directed all of Hampton's plays done later at the Court. Storey's first play, *The Restoration of Arnold Middleton*, was presented July 4, 1967.

that, I think, is a vital ingredient in the decision to appoint the artistic director.

I think the financial crisis that Nicholas was talking about was hugely inflated by the press, perhaps because the various circumstances of the council had changed its usefulness. In the twenty-five years that the Royal Court council has been in existence, its policy has changed considerably. By Nicholas' time, 1975–1976, a large proportion of the council was old and nervous, and also a number of them had been replaced.

In Bill Gaskill's time a number of them were really professional people who were able to lend a certain amount of advice in the early days. Most of those had drifted away by the time this crisis had occurred.

Nicholas Wright and Robert Kidd were pursuing an absolutely admirable Royal Court policy. It is just that the Arts Council, as far as I can see, got nervous because of the deficits, and Nicholas and Robert had an ultimatum, I'm told, by the Arts Council, a letter which I don't think I have ever seen.[9] But anyway, the thing became a huge crisis and appeared in the papers. I suppose they thought that they should get an old hand to steady the nerves, and I was really an old hand. Previously, I hadn't really had anything to do with the Court. I was among the people in the undergrowth prowling around outside, waiting to get in for many years.

I knew George Devine quite well, having at one time worked with him and Michel Saint-Denis before the war and with George after the war in the Young Vic and the Old Vic School. And then I went off and did different things, and it was some time before I joined that group of rather envied people who were working at the Royal Court. In fact, the first time I ever got my foot in the Royal Court was when a

9. In a letter to Greville Poke dated November 26, 1976, Tony Field, finance director of the Arts Council of Great Britain, expresses his extreme "concern at the current financial position of the Company." Later, after "emergency" meetings between representatives of the Arts Council and the ESC on December 4 and 8, the Arts Council notified the ESC "by letter . . . that unless [the ESC] cleared [its] deficit by 30 June 1977 [the ESC] should 'pay off outstanding creditors . . . and then cease operation' in midsummer!" (from Kidd's letter of resignation to the English Stage Company Council, January 10, 1977, in Lewenstein's personal collection, copy in possession of the editors). The previous August, Kidd and Wright had closed the Theatre Upstairs as part of "a radical programme of economies throughout" the ESC.

production of mine was transferred from Nottingham. It was put in for a five- or six-weeks' run, probably because a previously scheduled production had fallen through.[10]

That was my only experience at the Court. In 1976–1977, when I was asked to take it over, this crisis was going on, and I didn't really understand it. There was a feeling that the Royal Court's usefulness had come to an end. I didn't agree with that, and in order to find out a lot more about it, I called meetings of writers, directors, designers, and actors who had worked at the Court; it was illuminating. There were some radical suggestions which, I think, were very well founded, such as, they should pack the whole thing up and start elsewhere in a completely different building and that the ESC should become a kind of cooperative.[11] I found the suggestions valuable, and they were all recorded. Among the suggestions, because there was a great deal of feeling that the council of the ESC was past its usefulness, was the idea that the council should be elected. And then we asked ourselves, by whom?

The difficulty was the constituency. I mean, who would elect the council except the staff working in the Royal Court? The staff amounted to twenty-six people, including the cleaners, and that really wouldn't have been a sensible sort of constituency. Possibly, somebody with a great deal of vision could have found out of that meeting some other way of projecting the Court forward on com-

10. Burge's production from Nottingham, Wedekind's *Lulu*, opened at the Court December 8, 1970.

11. On January 21, 1977, in the midst of the Court's financial crisis, Edward Bond wrote a letter to the ESC Council calling for "a radical change in the membership of the Council." The present council, he said, suffers "from one obvious weakness: few of its members work in the theatre." He urged that a new council be formed made up of "more writers, designers and directors as active, attending members," as well as workers from "backstage and [the] front of [the] house." Oscar Lewenstein found Bond's argument "very impressive"; he wrote to the ESC in support of Bond's "main contention, that the English Stage Company should be run by the Theatre workers through a Council elected by them." Concluded Lewenstein, "I think that the time for paternalistic bodies is over. At the end of *The Caucasian Chalk Circle,* Brecht has these lines: '. . . what there is shall belong to those who are good for it. . . .' So let us with good heart," continues Lewenstein, "turn this present crisis into a triumph, give the theatre . . . to those who have worked in it" (Edward Bond to members of the English Stage Company Council, January 21, 1977; Oscar Lewenstein to Greville Poke, January 24, 1977, in Lewenstein's personal collection, copies in possession of the editors).

pletely different lines. I came to the conclusion that the only urgent thing was to keep it open. But, of course, it's no good just keeping it open and not doing the work it was intended to do.

There's no question that the first six months were difficult and lacked the quality we were searching for. With Max's help and the help of the other people, we decided to take the policy, as far as possible, in the direction of adventurous new work, which we did, I think, on the whole. We had one or two lucky breaks. There was a huge amount of good feeling for the Court among the profession, and financially in the first couple of years we actually did rather well, because a little play called *Once a Catholic,* which had been commissioned by the Court, had its first production at the Court and was well done. It wasn't a play in the true tradition of the Court, but, anyway, it went on and made us a lot of money. And that, together with a huge amount of support from the supporters' group, finally paid off the deficit. [12] Actually, I wanted to close the theatre down, on the advice of some other people, to close for at least six months to get ourselves in order, and then open again. I think Nicholas suggested that, too. It was a very tempting idea, but I discovered that if we had closed it down and saved the subsidy money and then opened again with what we really wanted to do, we would have lost the grant altogether. Those threatening the existence of the Court were like ghouls around the place, or at least that's the way one feels when one's working at the Court. You feel as if you are behind the palisades. Beforehand, I was very envious, jealous of the people working at the Royal Court, but once you are in there, you understand why there is a kind of incestuous continuation of the line, because if you plan to do work in a certain way, the only way to continue is to pass it on. There is a danger in incestuousness, of course, and perhaps it had reached that stage in 1977 when I came in.

MR. GASKILL: We have talked for quite some time, mostly about the difficulties of money and the difficulties of coping with the council. One gets little impression of the plays done. Perhaps we all feel a bit sensitive about our time of running the theatre, but I think it is very

12. Mary O'Malley's *Once a Catholic* opened at the Court on August 10, 1977, and transferred to the West End October 4, 1977. The play had been commissioned by Nicholas Wright and Ann Jellicoe and, says Wright, "programmed for the Court jointly by me and Bob Kidd" (Nicholas Wright to the Editor, *Time Out,* February 7, 1980).

important to know that in the short time that Nicky and Bob ran the theatre they did a program that included David Hare's *Teeth 'n' Smiles,* Edward Bond's *The Fool,* a new play by Christopher Hampton, and a wonderful Beckett season. [13]

It was a good season, which happened to be rather expensive, without, as they say, the money from the West End to help it along. When you are in the job, you tend to see those financial and other problems as dominant, but, in fact, what characterizes the artistic direction of the theatre you run is what you produce, what actually comes out at that time, and if there is nothing that comes out at that time, that is the thing that needs defending, not that you've lost the money. Not that you've quarreled with your acting company, not that you're having trouble with the governing bodies, but whether some of the work was of the standard and the vision that the early works were.

MR. JONES: I would like to ask Max Stafford-Clark a question. By the time you became artistic director of the Court, fifteen years had gone by since George Devine had given up his reign. What do you think characterized the theatre at the time you took over and afterwards? Also, what did you inherit specifically with the Court Theatre? I don't mean the building itself, but is there an aesthetic, is there an ongoing point of view, is there something that has stayed alive through a number of artistic directors that you can identify, so that you each can say, "I am not taking over the National Theatre. I am not taking over the Aldwych, I am taking over something called the Court and here's why."

MR. STAFFORD-CLARK: Yes. It is probably easier to perceive from the outside what the aesthetic of the Court is than once you are inside it. For example, *Tibetan Inroads,* the play by Stephen Lowe that is currently running at the Court, was, he told me, reviewed by the critics as a typical Court play. [14] This is because the first scene contains fully frontal sex followed by dialectic about Marxism and Maoism. So that what is perceived clearly by outsiders as being a Court aesthetic does

13. Hampton's *Treats* was presented February 3, 1976; Beckett's plays were *Waiting for Godot* in German (April 22, 1976), directed by the author; also, *Play, That Time,* and *Footfalls* (all presented May 20, 1976).

14. *Tibetan Inroads,* directed by William Gaskill, opened September 29, 1981; it ran for twenty-one performances and had an average attendance of 34 percent.

not actually seem so when you're inside it. *Tibetan Inroads* is very different from the plays that immediately preceded it at the Court.[15]

A number of factors remain constant and are similar to the initial period under George Devine. For example, it's been said that during George's time there were thirteen plays that made money to seventy-five that lost; I imagine that ratio is still similar. Also, the fact that the Court is a proscenium arch theatre has always had an enormous influence on the work and on the presentation of the plays. It provides a very rigorous examination of new work. I did not work at the Court until I directed David Hare's play *Slag* in 1971. I was brought up in studio theatres and wraparound theatres, where I think the experience is very different. One does realize when he works on the main stage at the Court that, because it is a proscenium, because one is examining the work at a distance, and because it is not warmed by the experience of having the audience around, that the Court stage is a tough test for the writing. That's a crucial factor that has shaped and characterized all regimes.[16]

Perversely enough, I think I absorbed that lesson at the Court not through working there but through working with Bill Gaskill in Joint Stock, which is a kind of tributary to the Court. When Bill left the Court, I had been working in Edinburgh running a company that had a different tradition from the Court. It was more physical work, influenced by some of the American groups like the Open Theatre and La Mama.

A year after I left Edinburgh, and six months or so after Bill left the Court, we worked together on the first Joint Stock play, which was based on Heathcote Williams' book *The Speakers;* he was a writer whom Nicholas Wright had worked with. Nicky directed his play *AC/DC* at the Royal Court. Also, we were interested in experiments

---

15. Edward Bond's *Restoration* (July 21, 1981) and Dusty Hughes's *Heaven and Hell* (September 10, 1981) preceded *Tibetan Inroads*.

16. Elsewhere Max Stafford-Clark has expressed a similar point: "I think . . . attention to detail derives partly from the rigorous demands made by the Royal Court's proscenium and size. The Court is a fine instrument—a microscope that examines and presents the detail of the work placed upon it and exposes the flaws. On the fringe we toured a lot. Each space was different, and usually the proximity of the audience warmed rather than distanced the experience. The exactness of the Court places a particular demand on the work" (Stafford-Clark, "Under the Microscope," in Findlater [ed.], *At the Royal Court,* 198).

in form; for example, in the staging of *The Speakers* the audience moved with the action. There was no formal seating. (The staging is now called promenade.)

Although I think both Joint Stock and the Court had a constant commitment to new writing, the work we did at Joint Stock took as its starting point a subject and a writer and a group of actors, followed by a workshop where one investigated, researched, and improvised on the subject for several weeks. And then we turned the play over to the writer. It was in no sense merely improvised work. An artistic imperative was that the writer be intruded on as little as possible. *Fanshen* that David Hare wrote and *Cloud Nine* by Caryl Churchill both came out of that process.

Going into the Court after working in Joint Stock for five or six years has influenced my work. It is really too close to look back over the last two years and identify the specific characteristics of our running of the Court, but, certainly, we have intruded more in the process of creating new work than what must have characterized George Devine in the early years.

Most plays that we have done over the last two years have had quite extensive reworking from the moment that we received the scripts to the moment they were performed. Paul Kember's *Not Quite Jerusalem,* a new play that has been most financially successful over the last few years, had a rehearsed reading. That is, it was worked on for a week by the director and actors and then given two public readings at the end of that period.[17] Actually, that initiated a redraft of the play which enabled it to be put into a full production some six months later. So that's a specific practice that has changed.

Also, one thing that perhaps remains the same is that although there is a circle of writers whom one looks to and whom one commissions and upon whom one depends to come up with plays to keep the cycle of work going, one needs to look outside of that circle. For example, we have done in the last two years a play called *The Arbor,* which was written by Andrea Dunbar. When she wrote it, she was a sixteen-year-old schoolgirl living on a slum council estate outside Bradford. It is important to look outside our recognized circle of writers.

17. Kember's play, first presented at the Court on December 2, 1980, was revived there on April 15, 1982.

In retrospect, one of the things that I am most pleased about is being able to pioneer new work. The decisions that Stuart took—that there should be a full-time literary manager, Rob Ritchie, has made us more efficient. It's something that I'd like to push further. Other specifics seem not to change, like the failure-success ratio, and as Bill has said, that the battles of the moment tend to become more important than policy. For example, at the moment we have just had a bout with the Arts Council. I think a faction within the Arts Council would like to see the Court's grant cut completely. Certainly, that has been in the air over the last nine months, and, as Bill Gaskill says, once that is happening, that actually absorbs your energy to the extent that it really dictates the policy. The primary energy of the Court over the last six months has gone into fighting that threat.

The country is in a recession. There is going to be less money for the arts next year. New theatres, studio theatres, that have sprung up over the last ten years also give opportunities for new writing (but no proscenium theatres of the same scale as the Court exist). And for that reason there have been suggestions within the Arts Council that the Court is now expendable. But those, I think, have been combated, and I hope successfully.[18]

MS. JELLICOE [speaking from the audience]: Can I ask one question? We have been trying to get to the point of the continuing aesthetics of the Royal Court Theatre, and, of course, all directors have been so intimately involved—but the phrase has come up, at least twice, "we had to put on plays that we should not have put on." Would you define what made them plays that you felt were outside the proper work for the Royal Court to do?

MR. STAFFORD-CLARK: Well, Bill defined that very well in the earlier sessions when he said that *The Country Wife* represented a cynical decision. I think that when you make decisions because you believe that they are going to be financially successful as opposed to believing in the play—that's a cynical decision and a play we ought not to do. It is not difficult as artistic director to decide on plays that you believe in passionately. That is an easy decision. It could be wrong, and it could

18. For the year ending April 4, 1981, the Arts Council grant was £350,000, the same as in the previous year, which, because of inflation, represents a decrease. For the year ending April 3, 1982, however, the council's grant was increased to £424,000 and, for April 2, 1983, £453,000.

lose money, but it's not difficult to feel that you have taken the right decision if you feel passionately about the play.

Whether it is critically dismissed or financially unsuccessful is irrelevant. Those decisions are easy to stand by. I came to the Royal Court from a job as a free-lance director and as a director working for Joint Stock, where I had to commit myself to only three plays a year, but that is not difficult; one can give his total passion and commitment to that. But to give one's total passion and commitment to eight plays downstairs plus another eight upstairs, plus the Young Writers' Festival, plus other aspects of the operation, becomes much more difficult; how can one spread his energy and passion over all that? It's suddenly like having sixteen wives instead of one.

MR. JONES: Ann Jellicoe's point really is, though, what does *The Country Wife* lack? What ingredients are lacking which make it not a Royal Court play?

MS. JELLICOE: That's right.

MR. GASKILL: No, I think Max puts it the right way around, because you see there never is a situation in which you have six plays that you desperately want to do, that you believe are well crafted and mean something. There never are. There never will be either. You are lucky if you have one.

I came to the Court, and I said, "What is there on the shelf?" And they said, "There's a play called *Saved*." And written on the script was "Possible Sunday night but don't recommend." I don't know who had written that, Keith Johnstone, perhaps. And I read it, and I said, "This is a wonderful play. This play I will do whatever! I think it is a masterpiece. I must do it!" There was no doubt in my mind. If you get one such play in your lifetime, you are lucky, you really are.

And even on the secondary level, plays that you like very much are in a small number; then you get to the next stage, where you have a play by a writer whom you know, say John Osborne or Arnold Wesker, which you don't think is very good, but you don't want to break with them.

So you think, "What shall I do?" And then one of your associates says, "I like it very much," and you heave a sigh of relief, and you say, "Thank God, let's go ahead with that."

Or you have two of them at once, and then you are in trouble, and then you have got to say, "I don't know." For instance, a typical situation: John Osborne wrote two plays, neither of which I liked, both of which I thought were West End plays, called *Time Present* and *The Hotel in Amsterdam.* I personally didn't want to do them, but one of my associates, Anthony Page, said, "I want to do them." In fact, Oscar Lewenstein very much wanted to do them, and they both made money. They both had stars in them and went to the West End, and from that money, the rest of the season was done. But if you do it too often, you are in trouble. But that is a typical example of the kind of decisions that you are constantly facing. You never have a lot of wonderful plays you want to do. You may have one. So the decisions relating to the others are very odd and are conditioned by all kinds of factors. So you don't take the whole range of plays; you are conditioned by writers you have worked with before and sometimes by classics that you might want to do which have played an important part in the theatre.

MR. BURGE: Sometimes, even, it could be by way of experiment. At the beginning of my time there, we hadn't the money to fill the theatre completely with productions generated entirely by ourselves so there was a great deal of pressure to bring in other groups. A number of fringe touring groups felt, justifiably, that they never had any kind of showing in London and that they should, at least, have some place that they could come.

And so we did bring fringe groups in, which had not been done before. In 1970 Bill had a "Come Together Festival," which featured a number of fringe groups. But I know that in the first year I was there, we had some companies that did not work out very well. If one saw them in their own space, he'd be very impressed, but on the stage at the Royal Court one finds they don't really work in that theatre and in that context.

MR. STAFFORD-CLARK: The theatre's environment is very important. It is much more difficult to attract stars there now. When I first worked there, there was a differential. The leading pay scale was £50 a week in 1971. The bottom was £25. It varied between those. Now, everybody is paid £100 a week, which is much less in real terms; I imagine that with inflation, £50 then would now be about £150. So that it is much more difficult to attract stars there to play for any length of time because it doesn't actually even begin to pay the mortgage.

In the spring [1981] when I did *The Sea Gull,* with an Irish setting,

71

I offered the part of the doctor to T. P. McKenna, a well-known, excellent actor but by no means a star. His first reaction was, "Well, Max, what's the top whack now at the Court?" And I said, "Well, it is £100 a week," and he said, "Seven centuries of exploitation and you're still doing it to actors!"

MR. BURGE: Also, there is the problem of the big companies now, the National Theatre and the Royal Shakespeare, where the big actors can go. There, in a sense, they have their cake and eat it too, because they are very well paid and act perhaps only once or twice a week. It is a way an actor can fulfill his ambitions to do work that is more interesting than the usual West End fare.

MR. GASKILL: The biggest change, and it happened before George left the theatre, was that because of the other stage openings the writers got more and more opportunities, first with the National and the Royal Shakespeare, and then more particularly with the fringe theatres, whereas before a writer was absolutely tied to the Court because there was nowhere else. Apart from his or her own loyalties and warmth for the people that he was working with, there wasn't anywhere else, but then suddenly there were many, many more places.

No longer could you say to a writer, "Well, look, this play needs more work." Because then the writer says, "Well, I am off to the Warehouse," which was the Royal Shakespeare's small London theatre, or "I can get it set up at such and such a place." So that the actual link between the theatre and the writer diminished, and it has been more difficult to hold a writer to the theatre or to a director in the theatre than it was in the early days. I think the thing which most characterizes the Court's earlier period is that writers and directors were so closely tied to that particular building physically that they had no other life outside.

Now there is endless life outside for writers, and it is very difficult to create the same loyalties toward a theatre, however warmly they feel toward you.

MR. JONES: I have one other question. If all six artistic directors were sitting here at this moment having a beer, and all were alive for the span of time which we are talking about, and they all agreed upon six or eight plays that they thought were just terrific, that the Royal Court really should have done those plays, are there any characteristics you can assign to those plays, politically or aesthetically?

MR. WRIGHT: You could probably get everybody in the British theatre to

72

agree on certain principles. Most people would agree about acting, actually, I think, rather than plays.

MR. JONES: Can you characterize the acting?

MR. WRIGHT: Yes, it is difficult, but it is what I would call classic-realistic English acting, which is very emotional and has temperament but also has the sense of not happening in a social vacuum. It's the way that actors, very fine actors, have of setting what they do in a social context so that it's socially placeable. It's the opposite of a kind of idealistic splurging of emotion—

MR. JONES: Do you maintain, for example, that Laurence Olivier would in his work process work differently at the Court than at the National Theatre?

MR. WRIGHT: No, no, I don't think so. Well, I don't know actually.

MR. BURGE: I think so, yes. Under the influence of the group that worked with George, of which Bill Gaskill is one, there was a fresh concept of acting that emerged. I think it is not too much to say that there was a honing down still further of unnecessary ornamentation in acting. I would acknowledge that that was a tradition set up in the period of the 1950s and later, and it's still continuing.

Also, I wouldn't dismiss the influence of television. I think television screen acting in the last twenty years has been a very good discipline, influencing the kind of acting in the theatre as well.

MR. WRIGHT: Would everyone who has run the Royal Court agree about Edward Bond, in terms of enthusiasm for one of his plays?

MR. GASKILL: No, no. *Saved* would never have been done if, say, Lindsay Anderson had been in charge of the theatre then.

MR. STAFFORD-CLARK: I think that in retrospect there are plays that characterize a particular period, like *Saved* did, and like *Look Back in Anger* did. Those are the two landmarks, aren't they? The decisions were arrived at by people talking. George Devine did not simply make decisions about what plays to put on, nor did he sit back and let other people make decisions about their passions and enthusiasms. So, in fact, the real answer is complex. In any case, there are plays and productions which stand out in the history of the Court.

MR. JONES: You said that you could detect an approach to acting at the Court through the years and that perhaps even Sir Laurence Olivier might have behaved differently at the Court than he would at the National Theatre.

MR. WRIGHT: I was trying to think of things upon which everybody

73

would agree. I find it very hard to think of a play that everybody would be enthusiastic about, but I can think of a number of actors' performances everybody would feel enthusiastic about.

MR. GASKILL: You have to look at it another way. The theatre was started to promote writers. The writers have always been the dominant influence on the directing, the designing, and the acting. Olivier was interested in *The Entertainer* because it was new ground for him; Osborne had created something original which rubbed off on Olivier, and that has been the basis of the work.

To try to define what it is, is something else. Where the Court fails is when it does not have a commitment to writers. It doesn't matter whether the six previous artistic directors would have liked it, or whether there's continuity there. It is whether at any one time the artistic director and his associates feel committed to specific writers and whether they're prepared to put their plays on and develop them. And the history of the Court is the history of those writers. Not really, I am afraid, anything else.

If you look over the years at the Court, what has seemed important as the time fades away, what you are left with are a group of plays by Edward Bond, a group of plays by David Storey, a group of plays by D. H. Lawrence (who became a Royal Court writer!), the plays of Christopher Hampton—these are the plays which actually make up the essence of the Court. It's the continuity of a writer in relation to, perhaps, the same director and, perhaps, a number of actors. That is what's made the work of the Court. It's not a theoretical thing, but the initial commitment to writers; the idea of promoting the writers is an enormous thing. And that was George's original vision. It is very easy to lose this. It is very difficult to maintain it, but, I must say, looking back on my own time, that is what I felt.

People keep trying to define the Royal Court; we used to be defined as a dustbin theatre because there was a dustbin on the stage; and then as a kitchen sink theatre because there was a kitchen sink in a play; and now we are defined because we do plays in which people fuck on the stage and talk about Maoism, which is the last thing that the Court is. The Royal Court never was into sex. That was not at all the Royal Court tradition, absolutely not.

I have heard a group of critics sitting around saying, "This is a typical Royal Court play," but it certainly wasn't. How does it become

74

a typical Royal Court play? Those definitions are in themselves false, but the commitment of a theatre to a writer is not false.

And, of course, if only one person ever believed in Edward Bond, then it would not have been a good or living theatre; if, for example, only I had believed in Edward Bond. There are always other people, actually, directors, designers, who are absorbed in it, and for that period of time their loyalty makes the work "Royal Court." I can't see it any other way.

MR. JONES: Going back to the plays and the playwrights, you gentlemen cover a fifteen-year period of time. Do certain periods of time provide more fertile grounds for playwrights than others?

MR. STAFFORD-CLARK: I think there is a parallel with the economy. It is difficult to run an outstanding theatre, an imaginative theatre, in recessive times. Probably a graph coordinating economic and artistic excellence would have some parallel. *Look Back in Anger,* although it's perceived as a revolutionary play, now seems in form to be rather old-fashioned, whereas the plays that followed, *The Happy Haven, The Sport of My Mad Mother,* and *Inadmissible Evidence,* all seemed to experiment in form. Although the subject matter of the play is what primarily characterizes it, experimenting with form is also important. The Court worked on that in the early days. There was a play with masks.[19] And *The Sport of My Mad Mother* was quite revolutionary and unusual at the time. That's something perhaps that should be remembered, and it is something I've absorbed: that we have to keep thinking of the manner in which the work is presented as well as what is presented.

MR. WRIGHT: Yes. Commitment to a specific writer isn't really just a commitment to do his plays, or even to do them to a particular standard. The peculiar thing about writers, it seems to me, is that they have a particular vision about the world that you actually don't have yourself. I think that commitment to a writer means going all the way with that particular writer, which, in its turn, can influence your attitude to the world and can also rub off onto the political commitment of the theatre producing the work. For example, the fight with the censors over Edward's plays was a commitment to that writer and to the politics of his plays.

19. John Arden's *The Happy Haven,* presented in 1960.

MR. JONES: Since this entire conference is based presumably on the assumption that the Royal Court has affected all of us who are in the theatre, I am curious to know in what ways the American theatre may have affected your work.

MR. STAFFORD-CLARK: It really affected me enormously. I was not working at the Court then. I was running the Traverse Theatre in Edinburgh at the time of that antiestablishment movement in the American theatre, in the late sixties. That led me to believe that I didn't want to run a theatre any longer, as a direct result of seeing those companies. I think I was feeling quite pleased with myself—I was directing plays, and they were being presented in the festival—and suddenly American productions had an impact on us as the Berliner Ensemble must have had upon an earlier generation. A window opened: the physicality and commitment, physically, of those American actors!

I think this experience happened simultaneously to people who saw the Living Theatre and the Open Theatre (which incidentally, were presented at the Court). These weren't really writers' theatres. The writers played quite a small part in that movement. But it was like a new language. Suddenly, music and movement seemed a part of what was important, electric and interesting, and that influenced me enormously. I think that the work I did after that absorbed those influences into the tradition I had already been working in, which had been based on the writer, so that one absorbed that lesson and applied it to the texts he worked with.

MR. ESSLIN [speaking from the audience]: We mustn't forget that Sam Shepard, for example, was at one time nurtured at the Court.

MR. BURGE: Yes, the first play that I wanted to do was *Curse of the Starving Class*.

MR. ESSLIN: *Geography of a Horse Dreamer* also premiered at the Royal Court.

MR. STAFFORD-CLARK: It was commissioned by the Court.

MR. WRIGHT: We've done six of his plays.[20]

MR. ESSLIN: Yes. He was living in London. The Court was his home.

MR. GASKILL: He was the resident dramatist, wasn't he, at the time?

20. Shepard's plays at the Royal Court: *La Turista* (1969), *The Unseen Hand* (1973), *Geography of a Horsedreamer* (1974), *Tooth of Crime* (1974), *Curse of the Starving Class* (1977), *Seduced* (1980).

MR. WRIGHT: He was never officially resident dramatist, but he was close to the Court.

MR. ESSLIN: He was very much connected with the Royal Court. So was Michael Weller.[21]

MR. HOWARTH [speaking from the audience]: Yes, a number of Royal Court writers were Americans.[22]

OBSERVER: What about the Court's production of classics? Max Stafford-Clark just finished working on *The Sea Gull*. And Bill Gaskill did *Macbeth* a few years ago in a controversial way.[23] How do such revivals fit into your artistic direction?

MR. STAFFORD-CLARK: The production of classics is something I didn't appreciate when I first went to the Court. In fact, I have directed only three plays by dead writers! Richard Eyre came to direct *Hamlet* in early 1980. Having been artistic director for a period, Bill Gaskill said, "It's all very well, but if you must do classics, then you must direct them yourself." And I didn't really understand what that meant, but I do now, having done *The Sea Gull*. To see how very important the classics are to the Court, we must measure new writing against the best every so often. It must never be the main drive of the Court's work, but to do a classic occasionally is a wonderful measuring point.

MR. ESSLIN: I remember seeing in 1967 the production of *Three Sisters* at the Court at the same time that Olivier was doing *Three Sisters* at the National Theatre; and the comparison was extremely interesting, and, I think on the whole, in favor of the Court.

MR. GASKILL: Not critically, certainly.

MR. ESSLIN: Not critically, but in my mind the Royal Court won. And, similarly, I thought that one of the finest performances I have ever seen of a Chekhov play was the *Uncle Vanya*.

MR. GASKILL: That was directed by Anthony Page, in 1970.

MR. ESSLIN: It was extremely well done and one of the few performances of Chekhovian comedy which was very funny.

---

21. Weller's *Cancer* (later called *Moonchildren*) appeared in 1970.

22. Other American writers whose plays were produced at the Court include Arthur Miller, Carson McCullers, William Faulkner, Tennessee Williams, Henry Livings, Adrienne Kennedy, Michael McClure, Peter Schumann, Leonard Melfi, Robert Wilson, Thomas Babe, and Wallace Shawn.

23. *Macbeth* opened on October 20, 1966, with Alec Guinness and Simone Signoret. Most critics deplored Gaskill's innovative, "Brechtian" direction of the production.

MR. HALLIFAX [speaking from the audience]: About Olivier's production, at the time he was directing *Three Sisters,* he was going to a London hospital for treatment of cancer. He actually left the production and came back only two or three days out of every two weeks to see what his staff director was doing with the play. When he came back, he was in a wheelchair. He did a fantastic amount of work, but, obviously, he wasn't at his best.

MR. JONES: You characterized the Court as an embattled theatre. I am wondering, what if the Lord Chamberlain had decided to leave you alone, and the Arts Council had decided that everything was just fine so that you were exempt from all that? Would that have denied the Court a certain outside force that helped you rally, or was it simply a sap of energy?

MR. GASKILL: I think it was exhausting, but it did provide a focus, and when it suddenly stopped, I did find it quite difficult to adapt. Also, it was a time of many changes. For example, we had been fighting over whether you could say shit on the stage and suddenly there were people walking around with no clothes on saying whatever language they liked. This was extraordinary when it first appeared, and I thought, God, if we had had to fight over that with the Lord Chamberlain! It was a very strange time. I felt very schizophrenic, and it rather relates to your good question about the American theatre, because I used to go to the Bread and Puppet and think, "Oh, it's wonderful. I wish I could do work like that; it is really great, isn't it?"[24]

I knew in a way that it was a false flirtation because it is inimical to the writers' theatre to enter that world; it makes a statement in which the writer cannot really exist, though they sometimes try. But, basically, it is a nonwriters' theatre. At the same time, I think it made valid criticism of work which was too literary, or too static.

I remember vividly during that period seeing the plays of John Osborne downstairs and thinking, "That's not what theatre should

24. The Bread and Puppet Theatre, founded in 1961 by Peter Schumann, was based in New York until 1968, when Schumann was invited to establish the troupe in residence at Goddard College in Vermont. Schumann seeks to provide theatre experiences as "basic as bread," taking the theatre into the streets and communicating religious and political messages through strong visual imagery (see Peter Schumann, "Bread and Puppets," *The Drama Review,* XIV, No. 3 [1970], 35).

be," and going to see the Living Theatre and really being torn.[25] And I think that dilemma has continued. I think people's attempts to resolve it by making plays more violent or more extravagant in production are false because they only distort the writer's work. I still think that it is something that we haven't sorted out yet.

OBSERVER: I would like to know what Max thinks about that. You were the artistic director during the time of Jonathan Pryce's performance of Hamlet?

MR. STAFFORD-CLARK: Yes. I didn't direct it, but I was artistic director.

OBSERVER: Weren't *Hamlet* and *The Sea Gull* deviations from the playwright's theatre to the director's theatre?

MR. STAFFORD-CLARK: *The Sea Gull* was absolutely dependent upon an adaptation by Thomas Kilroy that I think was excellent. It was very much in the writer's tradition, and, really, the play was his, not the director's. The translation of the action from Russia to Ireland relocated more than the geography; it relocated our whole perception of the play. I found it very difficult to grapple with the classics, to set them in some context which seemed socially and politically real and alive. I found Russia rather hard. I was at university in Ireland, and that parallel between Russia and Ireland struck me about fifteen years ago and made the play vivid and clear to me.

MR. BURGE: I think you have to have a burning reason for reviving a classic at the Court. You can't say, "Oh, well, we've got to make some money; we'll put on *Twelfth Night*." It is important that one have a particular concept.

OBSERVER: What might have been some of the reasons for doing classics? For instance, did you produce *The London Cuckolds* because it was a fine and unknown script?

MR. BURGE: Of course, that play is not a classic. It is a neglected play. Actually, there were reasons that it wasn't performed after a certain period. I think that is another business of the Court, to rediscover the

25. Julian Beck and Judith Malina founded the Living Theatre in 1946; its significance dates especially from its productions of Jack Gelber's *The Connection* in 1959 and Kenneth Brown's *The Brig* in 1963. Thereafter, the Living Theatre toured throughout Europe, becoming more and more devoted to works of anarchy and revolution: *Mysteries and Smaller Pieces* (1964), *Frankenstein* (1966), and *Paradise Now* (1968) (see Pierre Biner, *The Living Theatre: A History Without Myths* [New York, 1972]; and Oscar G. Brockett, *History of the Theatre* [5th ed.; Boston, 1987], 662, 716–17).

past plays that, for some reasons or another, have got buried. Usually, you can find a very good reason. But some plays, because of outside pressures in their day, have got lost, dismissed. I'm not saying *The London Cuckolds* is a great play. But it was interesting because of its context in London at the time. And in its form, it is like an early blueprint for Feydeau. And it contrasted a great deal with the usual repertoire of Restoration plays. It lacked their decorated language; it had clean, clear prose which came easily off the tongue without sounding pretentious to the modern ear.

OBSERVER: Bill Gaskill spoke of the time when he became interested in a nonwriters' theatre but felt that he couldn't do it in the confines of the Royal Court. Did other artistic directors feel at any time an ambivalence between what their own interests were as individual artists and this thing called the Royal Court play?

MR. STAFFORD-CLARK: I don't think one thinks of that as a dominant force. I'm really repeating myself, but you perceive passions for particular plays, and in retrospect, they get turned into Royal Court plays. But, basically, you wouldn't be doing the job if you didn't want to run that particular theatre and inherit that particular tradition. It's really very difficult for us to define exactly what it is politically and socially. But the plays and the work must exist in a particular social context. It's very important, I think.

MR. JONES: If someone brought you a play that you really thought was terrific, but you didn't happen to like the social point of view, would you do it?

MR. STAFFORD-CLARK: I wouldn't think it was terrific, then.

MR. JONES: What if the play played wonderfully and was very exciting in everything but its point of view?

MR. STAFFORD-CLARK: That's like the food is wonderful except for the taste. The color is right and it looks all right on the plate, but it tastes awful. One would not feel passionate about it. I think obviously there are plays one feels passionately about at the time that in retrospect seem silly infatuations. But comparatively few, and one can usually justify those decisions years later with those particular plays. But I think what's most important is finding the passion, finding the one play that you really want to do above all, or finding three plays that you will commit yourself to totally. And, also, the people you work with, their passions are important.

As Bill said, if someone says, "I really want to do that play," that's like a weight off you—the belief that an associate has in a play.

OBSERVER: In each of your tenures as artistic director, did you ever feel a responsibility or a need to do certain American plays? I think American plays have been produced by each of you at some time.

MR. GASKILL: I have never felt that. I always felt that the responsibility was to new British writers first. And if there were other good writers, one would do them. We did present works by Sam Shepard and Michael Weller, but I didn't feel that was laid on us. It enriched the program of the theatre to do it, but it might just as well have been a French play or a German play or a play by any foreign artists who were writing interesting plays at that time.

MR. STAFFORD-CLARK: One of the interesting American writers whose work has been done recently is Wallace Shawn, whose work, I think, is neglected in America. In fact, his plays were first done in Britain by Joint Stock. I directed three one-act plays, which were known as *A Thought in Three Parts*. In fact, a group of writers, David Hare and Howard Brenton, and, I think, Barrie Keeffe, said, "Look, there are these plays we have read which have been turned down by the Court, turned down by Hampstead; they have been turned down by every theatre in London, and, therefore, there is good reason why Joint Stock should deviate from its policy of creating its own plays and perform them, because nobody else will." It was the writers who brought my attention to the fact that Wallace Shawn was an original. I think his work has not really been appreciated yet, nor has been as important as it should be, neither here nor in Britain. I think *My Dinner with Andre,* which was recently performed in the Theatre Upstairs, was a wonderful evening, and, in fact, is much better as a play than as a film. I think he is a major American writer. And because of that we feel a commitment to him. You get over the fact that he's American!

MR. WARDLE [speaking from the audience]: During Devine's time there seemed to be a commitment to the French repertoire at the Royal Court as well as the British. Why was that allowed to lapse so completely after Devine's death?

MR. GASKILL: The French theatre dried up about that time, didn't it, very significantly. There are those so-called international plays which are done, such as Beckett, Ionesco, Genet, which form the repertoire of theatres all over the world, don't they? And a certain number of them found their home at the Royal Court, which has had a very close relationship with Sam Beckett, and, I think, a very successful one. But I don't think there is any responsibility to the French writers, any more than to the Irish writers. The responsibility is to the good writers.

III

Writers and Directors Talk: Finding and Developing New Plays

MODERATORS: *John Dillon, artistic director, Milwaukee Repertory Theater*
Amlin Gray, resident dramatist, Milwaukee Repertory Theater

PARTICIPANTS: *Stuart Burge, artistic director, 1977–1979*
Christopher Hampton, playwright
Donald Howarth, playwright
Ann Jellicoe, playwright
Rob Ritchie, literary manager, 1979–1984
Max Stafford-Clark, artistic director, 1979–Present
Nicholas Wright, artistic director, 1975–1977

SPEAKING FROM THE AUDIENCE:
Martin Esslin
William Gaskill
David Hare
and conference observers

MR. DILLON: Bill Gaskill has said that the history of the Royal Court is the history of its writers; this is the first of two panels to address the question of scripts and writers: how did the Royal Court build such a luminous body of writers? How were the new scripts solicited, developed, and brought to the public?

I would like to begin by introducing the panel members: Christopher Hampton, appointed in 1968 as the first playwright-in-residence at the Court, functioned also as a literary manager; he read many scripts before finally hiring David Hare to help him.[1] Nicholas

1. Christopher Hampton, resident dramatist from 1968 to 1970, had been asked by William Gaskill to become "the first resident dramatist in London." Hampton says: "It was, however, explained to me that I should not be misled by the pomposity of the title, which had enabled the theatre to get an Arts Council grant for me. The Royal Court would make

Wright served as the director of the Theatre Upstairs during Bill Gaskill's reign. I assume you had a voice in the choosing of the scripts that were developed in the Theatre Upstairs?

MR. WRIGHT: Choosing the plays was our job, yes.

MR. DILLON: And Ann Jellicoe served as literary manager while Oscar Lewenstein was artistic director.

MS. JELLICOE: Part of the time, yes.

MR. DILLON: Donald Howarth served as literary manager while Nicholas Wright and Robert Kidd were serving as artistic directors in 1975–1976?

MR. HOWARTH: Yes, for a year, and for six months prior to that during Oscar Lewenstein's time.

MR. DILLON: Following Nicholas Wright's leadership of the theatre, Stuart Burge served as the artistic director. Was there a literary manager during the time that you served?

MR. BURGE: Yes, four. N. F. Simpson had that position when I arrived, and he stayed on in spite of being worn out after three or four years in the job; following were David Mowat, Richard Crane, and Rob Ritchie.

MR. DILLON: Rob came in when you were still there and now serves as literary manager under Max Stafford-Clark, the present artistic director. The final panel member is Amlin Gray, playwright-in-residence at the Milwaukee Repertory Theater Company; he has also functioned as literary manager from time to time.

The Court has used a variety of methods to attract and help writers in the development of their scripts. We would like to look at some of those methods, and then, in the latter part of the session, raise some theoretical questions about the development of writers.

I'll begin by asking Amlin to raise questions about some of the methods that were used.

MR. GRAY: Last week I went through Richard Findlater's book *At the Royal Court,* and I picked out seven different methods that were used to elicit scripts, develop plays, and encourage the writers. I have

---

my salary up to £24 a week . . . and in return I would be expected to supervise the script department." He adds, "There was only one function I could find no time to perform: writing." Gaskill sympathetically permitted Hampton to hire David Hare as an assistant, "for a minuscule amount of money" (Hampton, "Sloane Square Lessons," in Findlater [ed.], *At the Royal Court,* 116–20).

arranged these methods in a rough chronology. How did these methods function, and why were they were abandoned or replaced?

The Writers' Group that began in January, 1958, and lasted about two years has been described in part by Ann Jellicoe in Findlater's book.[2] Edward Bond, Keith Johnstone, and a number of other people belonged to that group. Could you tell us something about that Writers' Group, Ms. Jellicoe?

MS. JELLICOE: Well, it emerged out of George's desire to nurture artists and to give them some reason to come into the theatre. An unknown writer is perhaps not very confident and feels ill at ease in using the theatre building as a familiar base. George wanted the writers to feel that the theatre was their building, and he used several devices. He gave free passes to writers, rarely done in the British theatre, although they weren't used as much as they might have been. Also, a writer could go to any rehearsal. Few went, but when they did, they profited. I remember watching Beckett rehearse *Endgame,* and it was a valuable experience.[3]

Furthermore, George established the Writers' Group, which consisted of a second wave of writers. The first consisted of John Osborne, Nigel Dennis, and Angus Wilson and the second, John Arden, N. F. Simpson, Arnold Wesker, myself, and perhaps Keith Johnstone. In addition, the group included various other people whose work has been produced on Sunday nights.

The Writers' Group started out in a paint shop in Flood Street, Chelsea, in January, 1958. It was a very nice venue, tatty and pleasant, and it felt very romantic. But in the first week, it was rather formal. We sat around on chairs; everybody was there, including George Devine, Michel Saint-Denis, Lindsay Anderson, and Bill Gaskill. Tony Richardson was then in America.[4]

But because our aims were so vague and George's presence a bit awesome, we did not accomplish much at first. After a while we began to meet at a house by the river—a very beautiful house—belonging

2. Jellicoe, "The Writers' Group," *ibid.,* 52–56.

3. *Endgame,* staged by Beckett, was presented in 1976 to honor Beckett's birthday; the Beckett festival also included *Waiting for Godot, Play, That Time,* and *Footfalls.*

4. Elsewhere Ann Jellicoe writes: "There was also John Dexter and Miriam Brickman, the casting director. The writers I remember included John Arden, Arnold Wesker, Keith Johnstone; and about 15 people in all" (Jellicoe, "The Writers' Group," in Findlater [ed.], *At the Royal Court,* 52).

to a fringe member of the group, Anne Piper, who later had a Sunday show produced at the Court; we met once a fortnight.[5]

The interesting thing about the group is that we were absolutely against talking. We never discussed each other's work or the problems of playwriting; we never intellectualized. It was one of the key ideas of the group that we did not talk, but acted. Improvisations became a primary means of exploring our work.

The group included not only playwrights but also certain members of the theatre staff. I have already mentioned Bill Gaskill, who ran the group for quite a long time. Miriam Brickman, who was casting director, also came along because women were very thin on the ground. We needed people like that.

To be a member of the group was terribly important because one could establish and develop friendships. Edward Bond profited in this way.[6] Being a member meant that Edward could begin to feel at home at the Court. He could say to Miriam, "Hello," and Miriam would say, "Oh, come and have a cup of coffee." (They didn't seem ever to have anything to eat on the premises.) George once said to me in a complaining tone, "Do you realize that Miriam Brickman's telephone bill is twice that of the whole of the theatre?" It struck me that everybody used her office as a club, and they all used the telephone. George was nurturing the writer's relationship with the theatre and the workers there. I can't say that you went into the Court to make telephone calls, but one went into the Court because one had made a friend of Miriam Brickman; she was a very warm person. Her office became a sort of center. One could go there and spend ten minutes or two hours.

Certainly, that was one of the prime functions of the Writers' Group, apart from giving writers a direct experience in what it was like to get up on their feet rather than sit down and write. To create those links was a major purpose of the group.

MR. DILLON: Did Devine choose the writers who could participate in the group, or did the group bring in writers?

5. "We began to meet at 7 Lower Mall, in Hammersmith, the home of David and Anne Piper, two doors up from George Devine himself" (*ibid.*, 55).
6. Bond's plays began to come into the Court in 1958, on the basis of which he was invited to join the Writers' Group. His first produced play, *The Pope's Wedding*, appeared as a Sunday night production in 1962.

MS. JELLICOE: I suppose initially it was done on an *ad hoc* basis. For instance, I was asked to the initial meeting because they had just accepted my play, *The Sport of My Mad Mother*. Arnold Wesker's play *Chicken Soup with Barley* had just been accepted so he was asked. John Arden had just had a Sunday night production, *The Waters of Babylon*, and he was asked. Also, we ourselves tended to ask people in. Or, I suppose George would say, "Why not have so and so?" We were very careful about who got in. Donald Howarth has said that it was "exclusive," but that wasn't the point. We didn't want anybody who would rock the boat, who would be disruptive or destructive. There was a very warm atmosphere among the writers at the Royal Court, in my opinion, and we wanted to keep that feeling of mutual support, of mutual sympathy, going. Consequently, it was by invitation. This may well have created an air of exclusivity, but that was not intentional.

MR. DILLON: And the group lasted until 1960?

MS. JELLICOE: Yes, it lasted about two years. I'm not quite sure why it died. I think everybody's plays began to get put on; but it was a very warm and good experience. It was very supportive.

MR. GRAY: Why would getting produced have caused the group to break up?

MS. JELLICOE: One of the reasons those people kept together was that they felt secure with each other. I don't remember actually why it broke up. It could easily be that we simply stopped for summer and didn't start again, not necessarily for psychological reasons. Perhaps Arnold Wesker had a production in Scandinavia or something like that; I don't know.

MR. HOWARTH: That wasn't my reason. I wish I had had a production scheduled in Scandinavia. I stopped going to class. I didn't go to many of them, but I stopped going altogether because I felt a bit of a fool doing the improvisations. I wasn't good at it.

MR. GRAY: Was it conducted like a class?

MR. HOWARTH: It felt like school. One had to get up and become this, that, and the other. And I wasn't good at improvising. I felt very self-conscious. That was the reason that I stopped going.

But I think one of the reasons I *went* to the meetings was that I thought, "If I don't go I'm not going to get my plays on. If I do go, I might." So, I thought, "I'll go and join in." I tried hard, but it wasn't worth it.

MR. WRIGHT: Still, that would explain why once everybody got their plays on, they stopped coming, wouldn't it?

MS. JELLICOE: Oh, no, I honestly don't think that. No, although Bill Gaskill was there, I certainly don't think that one had to go there in order to get his plays on. A lot of people who did not go to it had plays put on at the Court.

MR. GRAY: I got the impression from your essay in Findlater's book that the improvisations in the group made a direct contribution to *The Knack.* Is that true?

MS. JELLICOE: That was true of several writers. I have said we never discussed our plays, and certainly when I am in the middle of writing a play, I don't talk about it because the creativity is dissipated through talk. But I was in the middle of a block in *The Knack.* And, with great caution, I set up an improvisation in which some people came to the junkyard to buy a bed from an old man. I remember the moment clearly; Bill Gaskill and Keith were there, but Bill I recall especially, because he suddenly said to the bloke doing the improvisation, "That's not a bed, it's a piano." And the improvisation took off. And I took that street scene and put it in, working straight into the night.

I recall also that Arnold Wesker participated in an improvisation on the creation of the world. There was a woman (I haven't the faintest idea who she was) who came to only one meeting and disappeared. She got very impatient with the way we were working. We were trying to discover the nature of theatre, what theatre is and why theatre is different from other writing. She got rather snobby, but she set up an improvisation about the creation of the world, in which she sat in the middle and was the Creator.

She named Edward Bond and Arnold Wesker and two others to be the planets revolving around her. And they revolved. We all felt that this was basically a literary idea! And, at this point, Arnold set up an improvisation in which he mimed life with Miriam Brickman. It was very good, actually, and she just stood, imitating what he did— breathing, moving, whatever, and it suddenly seemed to us that those two things set side by side, one intensely theatrical, one intensely literary, was very interesting.

I mean, this idea of the Creator with the planets revolving is an eighteenth-century literary concept about the creation of the world. And that, as I say, was an extraordinarily valuable parallel to have put in front of one. But she buzzed off—she never came back.

MR. GRAY: A prime focus of this workshop was to separate what you all were trying to do from the prevailing literary style of theatre in as clear a way as possible. Is that true? Were you somehow trying to evolve a modern style?

MS. JELLICOE: We were trying to find out what theatre was, as opposed to, say, Shaw, who some of us felt was an extremely literary and intellectual playwright. He, after all, had been a great British genius of the twenties and thirties, and even after the war his influence and that of the poetic writers was terribly strong. We wanted to create something that was different and more theatrical.

MR. GRAY: Speaking generally, do you feel that the writers who did continue to develop their talents as playwrights made germinal discoveries in that workshop?

MS. JELLICOE: Yes, I think that it was very influential. Certainly that is true of Arden, Wesker, Bond, and myself. But, of course, many invited people never came into the group. Wally (N. F.) Simpson never came, probably for the same reason that Donald Howarth didn't like it. Harold Pinter never came, although he was not strictly a Court writer.

MR. DILLON: Did writers feel at home in the Court?

MS. JELLICOE: Oh, yes, they were in and out often because they had friendships. They gravitated to Miriam Brickman's casting office, that curious little coffee room (a slit of a room) where the assistants used to be; people just went in and out. Of course, several of them worked at the Court, keeping alive by playreading, like Arnold Wesker and Keith Johnstone.

MR. HOWARTH: Yes, we were all playreaders. We used to go to the theatre for scripts and return them with our comments written on cards. There was a kind of green room atmosphere. We also were going to collect our ten shillings a week.

MS. JELLICOE: This is really Bill Gaskill's story, but I'll tell it. Before Bill went to the Court he did television. And he wrote to the Court and said, "Have you got any scripts that you're not using? I would love to get new plays going on television." So they looked in all of their old files where they found lots of comments from John Osborne, "suitable for television, suitable for television." So, they sent all of these absolutely awful plays, for whenever John thought a play should be rejected, he just put "suitable for television."

MR. GRAY: In 1963, a program was launched called the Royal Court

Theatre Studio; apparently it was a workshop for actors to undertake research into the nature of improvisation and, especially, public improvisation.

It seems to me that the idea of public improvisation indicates a bit of a departure from what the previous Writers' Group workshop was doing. In the workshop that the writers had started in 1958, was there any idea of taking into public performance the method of improvisation that you all were using to explore the nature of theatre?

MS. JELLICOE: No.

MR. GRAY: The later studio apparently was exploring that possibility, is that right? Was anyone here involved in that? It started in 1963 and lasted about two years.

MR. STAFFORD-CLARK: Bill knows about that.

MR. GASKILL [speaking from the audience]: That studio was, for the record, an actor's studio. And it was for the profession at large. The first session was about comedy and the nature of comic improvisation. It sprang from George's interests in comic techniques.

He used to teach the use of the comic mask, which he had learned from Michel Saint-Denis. And out of that grew Keith Johnstone's work; he eventually ran a group not based at the Court, known as Theatre Machine, which only improvised. Johnstone now works in Canada and has another group called Loose Moose.[7] The studio was not conceived as a writers' group but as an actors' group.

MR. GRAY: But was there from the beginning the idea that some of the improvisations might be developed into public performances?

MR. GASKILL: No.

MR. GRAY: You have said that you never found a way to reconcile texts with the use of masks. When the idea of using masks in performance and using "developed-in-improvisation-pieces" rather than "written-for-performance-pieces" began to emerge, did it then become necessary that that work be continued, not at the Royal Court but in other theatres like the Theatre Machine and the Loose Moose? Is that the

---

7. Keith Johnstone's association with the Royal Court Theatre dates from 1956, when George Devine commissioned him to write a play. *Brixham Regatta,* directed by William Gaskill and Ann Jellicoe, appeared on June 22, 1958. Later he organized an improvisational group, the Theatre Machine, which toured Europe, and then ran the Loose Moose Theatre Company in Calgary, Alberta (see Keith Johnstone, *Impro: Improvisation and the Theatre* [London, 1981], 26–28).

process by which this improvisational workshop became separated from the body of the Royal Court's work?

MR. GASKILL: The studio, with its improvisations, was never designed to produce plays for the Royal Court.[8]

MR. GRAY: It seems to me that some of the work that Max Stafford-Clark and others have been doing in recent years is as close to that improvisational kind of work as any that has been actually generated by the Royal Court.

MR. HOWARTH: I think, in the overview, that George Devine was always trying to make the Court more than just a theatre that rehearsed plays and put them on; he had this thing of being the teacher, of passing on skills to people who didn't really have them yet. The classes that he had formulated and that materialized during his period did so because he saw the Court expanding into an organization with students like the one he had worked with before, the Old Vic School.

It was a characteristic of George to have an organization which had groups working to learn theatre skills, working for an understanding of theatre in a wide sense, not merely in little pockets of writers, actors, and directors. That they all should work and learn together was one of his main objectives during his directorship.

MR. BURGE: Yes, George was always interested in theatre schools. He never lost an opportunity to encourage learning.

MR. GRAY: Another method of play development involved a commission in 1965 for Edward Bond. Was that the first commission, or were plays commissioned at a period earlier than that?

MR. HOWARTH: They were always commissioned, from the beginning. Actually, Nigel Dennis was asked to write a play before the Court was even started. I think the commission fee was £25.

MR. DILLON: What was the agreement with the writer?

MR. HOWARTH: You agreed to write a play, and they had the option to do your next one!

MR. HAMPTON: Actually, later on they improved the deal; it was £100, but they wanted three plays!

8. The Royal Court Theatre Studio opened in 1963 under William Gaskill's direction at the Jeanetta Cochrane Theatre. Findlater notes that the studio sought not only to be a workshop for actors but also to examine the nature of improvisation "and especially public improvisation." Although the studio had not been set up to produce plays for public performance, two works appeared on the Court's main stage: *Clowning* (1965) and *The Performing Giant* (1966).

91

MR. HOWARTH: Osborne is a good example. His contract for *Look Back in Anger* specified that the Court would produce it and that it also had the option on his next three plays, which turned out to be *The Entertainer, Luther,* and *Epitaph for George Dillon*!

MR. GRAY: But there was not necessarily a commitment to produce the plays?

MR. HOWARTH: No. They didn't *have* to produce *The Entertainer*!

MR. GRAY: Arnold Wesker had a commission from the Royal Shakespeare Company, but his play was not produced. Apparently the actors refused to perform in the play after it was cast, and Wesker sued the RSC for not doing the play. So they must have had some kind of agreement in that case, not only to pay him the fee for writing the play but to produce it as well.

MS. JELLICOE: I think we would all like to know a little more about that. I have never in my life heard of a theatre undertaking to commission a play and produce it unseen. It would be insane.

MR. ESSLIN [speaking from the audience]: Well, actually Wesker has written a long article about this case. He sued them for damages because they didn't do it, after they had agreed to do it. He had delivered the script and they said it was all right. They cast it, and then they didn't do it. So he got £4,000 damages from the courts. Of course, this is a unique case.[9]

MR. GRAY: In any case, the commission didn't include a promise to produce the play. The promise to produce it came later.

MR. HAMPTON: It was the exception rather than the rule, I think, that the commissioned plays were performed. Indeed, I think David Hare had a commission from the Court, which was not produced, is that not right?

9. David Jones, at the Royal Shakespeare Company, had commissioned and was to direct Wesker's play *The Journalist,* scheduled for presentation in October, 1972, at the Aldwych, the RSC's London theatre. The play emerged from Wesker's observations at the *Sunday Times,* where he spent two months researching for the projected drama. David Jones apparently lost interest in the play and went off on a holiday. The RSC actors did not like the play and objected to performing in it. Finally, Trevor Nunn asked Wesker to rewrite, offering to produce it in the Other Place, the RSC's studio theatre at Stratford-upon-Avon. Wesker rejected the offer and sued the company for breach of contract. The case was finally settled in November, 1980, when Wesker was paid £4,250, "£2,400 of which went in legal fees" (see Arnold Wesker, "The Strange Affair of the Actors' Revolt," *Sunday Times Weekly Review,* August 30, 1981, and Glenda Leeming, *Wesker the Playwriter* [London, 1983], 92–99).

MR. HARE [speaking from the audience]: That is correct.

MR. HAMPTON: Exactly. This is the point I'm trying to make.

MR. HOWARTH: After my first play was done at the Court, another was commissioned and took me a year to write. I handed it in and was handed it back after six months. They didn't want to do it.

MR. GRAY: Did they still maintain the right to do your next one?

MR. HOWARTH: No. I think what Christopher said is true. Beware of being commissioned. They may not do it.

MR. GRAY: Aside from the financial terms, what other terms are involved in commissions? Is there a stage where the writer has to present a subject or a scenario of some kind and have it approved?

MR. HOWARTH: No.

MR. STAFFORD-CLARK: I think it has become much more formalized now than then—to jump ahead for a moment. Now, a contract with the Theatre Writers' Union is negotiated, which actually formalizes commissions and sets out what should be paid when the play is commissioned, when the play is delivered, and when the rights are taken up on it.

MR. DILLON: For a commissioned play, was a time limit given to the writer?

MR. HOWARTH: No.

MR. HAMPTON: That would have been irresponsibly optimistic.

MR. GRAY: If a playwright wanted to hear a play read aloud, could he go to the Court to have that done?

MR. WRIGHT: During the ten years I was at the Royal Court the workshops and studios and all those activities were peripheral to the main thrust of the work, which was actually the reading, choosing, and producing of scripts. Which plays were chosen, of course, reflected very naturally the taste of the people who were reading them.

MS. JELLICOE: I have never actually seen much value in an unrehearsed reading of a play. Plays are meant to be acted, and this was a great part of our philosophy at the Court. There was little virtue in having a play read for the playwright beyond the sheer ego-building moment of having somebody else actually say your words out loud.

MR. BURGE: I have a different reaction to that; I believe that the full production without decor, with three weeks of rehearsal, and a performance on Sunday night was a valuable thing.

But, unfortunately, since paying a cast for three weeks of rehearsal and for a single performance became impossible, that was replaced by

93

the rehearsed reading, which was second best. Nevertheless, the rehearsed reading had a great value in that we were able to hire actors for a minimum Equity salary for a week, and they could rehearse the play for three or four days with a director and writer and then present a public rehearsed reading on the last two days of the week. And that had a value. I don't know what Max thinks about that.

MR. STAFFORD-CLARK: I think that is a wonderful way of servicing a writer. Of the five rehearsed readings we've done in the past eighteen months, four have gone on to full productions. The faith that you have to present to a writer is that the reading program is not going to be a graveyard for plays that you feel uncertain about. That would be destructive. You have to make it clear by your actions that it is a stage of the process and that the rehearsed reading stands a good chance of leading on to the full production.

MS. JELLICOE: Of the same play, Max, or a different one?

MR. STAFFORD-CLARK: Of the same play. A week's work with actors does stimulate the writer, and a redraft has that body of experience behind it. Certainly, *Not Quite Jerusalem,* perhaps the most successful play which went through that process, was redrafted substantially after the rehearsed reading. The reading was very funny, and Paul Kember, who wrote the play, had some sense of feedback from the audience and some sense of confidence that at least what he had written attracted a response. That became quite a factor when he rewrote.

MR. GRAY: Ann, would you not find a rehearsed reading like that useful?

MS. JELLICOE: Oh, I think a rehearsed reading along those lines is obviously helpful. What I find of dubious value is what happens in many writers' groups—I'm not talking about the Royal Court—where a group of nonprofessionals get together and read each other's plays out loud. Beyond the ego feeling, perhaps, I see very little value in it at all.

MR. GRAY: Was there anything comparable to the rehearsed readings in the earlier years of the Royal Court?

MR. HOWARTH: The Sunday night productions, which Stuart mentioned, had only two weeks' rehearsal, not three. You weren't allowed any scenery budget and perhaps £2 or £4 for props. The actors were paid two guineas for the performance. The writer was paid £5 for the one performance and that was it. But you rehearsed all day for two weeks. I don't know what Equity thought about it; they won't allow it now.

94

MR. BURGE: That's the problem.

MR. HOWARTH: But those productions were completely packed; you couldn't get into them. The Court became the place to go. All the critics went, and the plays were reviewed.

MS. JELLICOE: But they were never very good. They inevitably fell short—sometimes in terms of presentation.

MR. HOWARTH: A few of them were then done in the main bill, but not many of them.

MR. GRAY: This began when?

MR. HOWARTH: My play *Lady on the Barometer* was done as a Sunday night production in September, 1958. Tynan gave us a wonderful review in the *Sunday Observer*. I think the review stated (it's engraved in my mind), "This play must surely have a successful public run."[10] Tynan couldn't be ignored; they were saying, "We'd better put it on if Tynan says so." But the first Sunday night productions were in 1957, such as Lindsay Anderson's first production at the Court, *The Waiting of Lester Abbs,* by Kathleen Sully.

It was a way of using directors. If you weren't sure about a director, you let him do a Sunday night, and so both writer and director were thrown in at the deep end to be judged by the critics in the national press. The presentations were very exciting performances and the audience response was marvelous, because you got five hundred people who wanted to go. They packed into the gallery then.

MR. HAMPTON: My first play, *When Did You Last See My Mother?,* was done on a Sunday night in 1966.

MR. WRIGHT: So was my first play, *Changing Lines,* in 1968.

MR. HAMPTON: The program of Sunday night productions without decor was a very special sort of thing, and it's never quite been replaced. It became redundant, I suppose, with the formation of the Theatre Upstairs in the sense that theoretically the plays that would have gotten Sunday night productions were done in the Theatre Upstairs.

MR. WRIGHT: Sunday nights continued for a while after the Theatre Upstairs was opened, but they never had the kind of prestige you've just been talking about. I think I'm right in saying that after the late sixties there were no more really significant Sunday night produc-

10. The precise wording from Tynan's review is "unless managers are mad [this play] will surely embark before long on a successful public run" (Kenneth Tynan, review of *Lady on the Barometer, Observer,* December 8, 1958).

tions. It was very hard to get them off the ground, largely because new plays at that time were so often written for a small auditorium, like the Theatre Upstairs. This had something to do with the feeling of the times. Also, writers much preferred having plays done in the Theatre Upstairs because the play could be done for a run, not just for one night.

MS. JELLICOE: I first went to the Court as a writer to see John Arden's *The Waters of Babylon* on a Sunday night in October, 1957. That's when I first met all the key people.

MR. HOWARTH: The first Sunday night productions were plays by Charles Robinson and Michael Hastings in May and June, 1957, and plays were still being done on Sunday night in 1976.

MR. WRIGHT: Yes. But I think the function of the Sunday night productions without decor had been taken over by the Theatre Upstairs by then because of its small auditorium and for various other reasons.

MR. BURGE: Also, the cost; it became impossible to open the main theatre on Sunday night except at great expense.

MR. STAFFORD-CLARK: Undoubtedly, the unions were and are a factor in rising costs. I think it should be mentioned that in real terms the salaries and the income of most people working at the Court have been eroded. But not those in the electricians' and technicians' unions, in the sense that their salaries are union-protected and have a cost-of-living increase built into them. This is becoming an issue that we are going to have to face over the next years. The standard of living is dropping for everybody else and being maintained for those few union people. Overtime is becoming like that at Covent Garden: if the opera goes on after midnight, everybody has to be paid automatically overtime, all night. The Court is not as restrictive as the opera, but it is becoming expensive to go into overtime.

MR. GRAY: Are you similarly restricted Upstairs? That must be a union space as well?

MR. STAFFORD-CLARK: We are not similarly restricted. No, it is downstairs that is so expensive.

MR. RITCHIE: There is also a growing trend for workshops and rehearsed readings that needs to be examined. The theatre has had to draw up guidelines for those with the writers' unions. And the agreement does make it very difficult if you want very quickly to organize a workshop of some kind: it now costs quite a lot of money.

So the real choice is whether you do a workshop that may very well be divorced from an actual production structure or use your money simply to produce plays. On balance, I would argue that it is more important to do one play than to workshop six.

OBSERVER: What help did the playwright get when his play was produced on Sunday night?

MR. HAMPTON: In my case it was my first experience with a professional theatre. I had done *When Did You Last See My Mother?* as a student at Oxford, and then it was done by the Royal Court. I didn't really know what this entailed. As a matter of fact, I think that my first visit ever to the Royal Court was on the Sunday night for the production of my play in June, 1966. So I was not in the most expert position possible.

All I can say is that although they were quite cautious about having me in rehearsals (they didn't seem too keen on that), I was not actually stopped from going to rehearsals. But I was told that they could get on perfectly well for a few days now and to come back next week.

Once the play had happened, and it actually was very well received and reviewed, one was made to feel now a member of the Royal Court Theatre. In other words, not necessarily as a result of the success of the play, but after this rather brief apprenticeship, you were welcomed into the building and you started becoming involved in it.

MR. GRAY: And then it was the next year that you were made the first resident dramatist, is that right?

MR. HAMPTON: It was two years later, and although I was called resident dramatist, I was only called that in order to secure a grant from the Arts Council.

In other words, what happened was that Bill Gaskill was concerned about what was going to happen to me when I left the university, and he said simply, "Well, we'll find something for you." And then they got this excellent idea of getting £1,000 from the Arts Council by saying, "We think we might have a resident dramatist." There were no ground rules in being resident dramatist. I just arrived and was put in charge of the literary script department, which had been run by George Devine's daughter for some couple of years before I arrived.

MR. DILLON: That question of scripts brings up another thing; the title of this panel is "Finding and Developing New Plays." I am curious to know about whether the Royal Court found new plays, or whether new plays found the Royal Court. How great was the crush of un-solicited manuscripts coming in?

MR. HAMPTON: It was enormous. My memories of those years have to do with staggering down the street with arms full of scripts. There were never less than twenty a week, usually nearer forty.

Actually, I think the Royal Court's record, certainly at the time that I was there, was rather good with plays, in the sense of processing them and giving them to qualified readers and getting reports and meeting the writers if they showed any promise and returning the manuscripts. The record in that department was much better than at the Royal Shakespeare Company, which was notorious for mislaying scripts.

MR. DILLON: When you contacted playwrights who showed promise, how often would that be?

MR. HAMPTON: We contacted the writers whenever we thought they were any good. But the dispiriting feature of the job was that there were always more good writers than there were spaces to do their plays. The experience that I had a few weeks after arriving turned out to be almost unheard-of: a play came through the post which I and others liked very much called *Life Price* by Jeremy Seabrook and Michael O'Neill, and within two months it went into the main bill.[11]

Having just arrived at the Court, I thought that this was something that probably often happened, but it never happened again. So one would get plays that one thought ought to be done, and they wouldn't be done; but on the other hand, one made contact with the writers when they came there. In my time, I made contact with people like Stephen Poliakoff; I saw his first play when he was a schoolboy. The Royal Court then commissioned a play from him, which they didn't do. But in any case, the contact was set up.[12]

Another was Michael Weller. I saw a play of his at the Student Festival, Exeter, and we commissioned a play, which, as it turned out, we didn't do, but the contact was made. Similarly, with David Hare and with Howard Brenton. And, in fact, during those years we contacted a great many writers.

MR. DILLON: When you say "we contacted," could you take that initiative on your own as the resident dramatist?

MR. HAMPTON: Sure. I was running the script department for only six to nine months, but it became clear to me that it was an entirely full-

11. Presented on January 9, 1969.

12. Poliakoff's first play at the Court, *Pretty Boy,* appeared in 1972, although he had previously coauthored (with six others) *Lay By,* produced by the Court in 1971.

time job, and I couldn't do what I had nominally been hired to do, which was to write a play. And that's when I asked David Hare to join in order to take some of the load off of me.

The routine was depressing, frankly, because there was an enormous number of plays set on park benches, or huge numbers of plays in the style of the current hits of the time; *Rosencrantz and Guildenstern Are Dead* was then a big hit so one would then get "Troilus and Cressida Are Unwell."

In all that time, there would be a huge stack of unworkable stuff which nevertheless had to be gone through, had to be responded to, and all of that was quite conscientiously done.

MR. DILLON: Was and is there much going out to authors who are not submitting to the Court to encourage them to submit to the Court?

MR. HAMPTON: Yes. And it sometimes worked and it sometimes didn't.

I remember Anthony Page being very, very excited about Trevor Griffiths. He tried to whip up enthusiasm in the Royal Court for his work, to get people to go and see his play *Occupations,* to persuade somebody to commission Griffiths, all of which failed.

But there was a good deal of "Oh, I hear so and so is writing." And there were meetings every Monday night when the list of scripts was discussed and gone through; it was all pretty exhaustive and fairly democratic. The meetings were very large, with a lot of people, including the script readers. Actually, any interested party could wander in—anybody who had heard that there was a good play prospect, or a good writer, or something interesting happening. Also, there was a good deal of going out to places around the country to find plays.

MR. GRAY: How were commissions decided upon? What was necessary to generate a commission?

MR. HAMPTON: In the case of Stephen Poliakoff, who was a schoolboy, I went to see his play and thought it was very good. I came back with a copy of the script. We discussed it and commissioned him.

MR. GRAY: David Hare has written of the late 1960s at the Court: "I do remember those years as a time of almost perpetual unease, as I had one fight after another in the place. Every project had to be lobbied for by a medieval series of trials, which became more complex and severe in 1969 when a triumvirate of directors, Lindsay Anderson, William Gaskill, and Anthony Page, took over the theatre and developed an attitude to new work which made the championship of new scripts so arduous and humiliating that it's a wonder people stuck their necks out at all." [13] Was that something that stayed through the history of the Court? Was that a characteristic of the Court?

MR. WRIGHT: There was a strong split at that time; 1969 was the year when a quite coherent generation of playwrights began appearing, including David Hare, Howard Brenton, and Snoo Wilson, and they were being staunchly resisted by the establishment of the Royal Court.

MR. HARE: It was a time when the Court resisted any new ideas. Instinctively, the older generation didn't like the younger generation's style of work. That was basically the true basis of the problem, so that most of the plays that I was suggesting were sneered at.

MS. JELLICOE: By Lindsay? I think we're talking about Lindsay Anderson, not the Court as a whole.

MR. HAMPTON: Anthony Page, for example, was extremely open to new work, rather paradoxically.

MR. HARE: There were differences in temperaments. Everything happened originally at the Court because it was the one theatre with a new play policy. And when many theatres grew up that were doing new works, the Court's position became very confused, and they didn't quite know how to accommodate the fact that there were now so many differences in temperament among new writers.

Certain profound temperamental differences existed between the older people and the younger people of promise. The work not done was overtly political; there was a feeling that that work was not appropriate.

I was all for "helping" writers by putting the plays on. But Bill Gaskill used to ask George Devine's question, which was a good question, "Would you put this play on for four weeks downstairs in a four-hundred-seat theatre?" And if I said, "Well, no," Bill would say, "Then you don't really believe in it, and we shouldn't do it." And he was quite right. But there was a rather closed attitude to new, talented writers. A lot of people were hurt and unhappy about the Court during that time.

MR. DILLON: But apparently throughout the history of the Court there has always been a handful of people in the organization who can go

---

13. Hare, "Time of Unease," in Findlater (ed.), *At the Royal Court*, 141.

out, meet a writer, bring his work in, champion it, and encourage its production until the writer is done at the Court or somewhere else.

MR. HAMPTON: I think you've got to look carefully at what you mean by encouragement, at what that means in practical terms. If you look at just the volume of the material that comes in, some fifteen hundred plays a year, obviously you can't service all of that very effectively; it is encouraging for writers merely to get a reply saying that the play is being read, that it hasn't been lost. And at the end of the day, if the play is rejected (which, if fifteen hundred are considered and fifteen are chosen, the overwhelming odds are that it will be), then you can explain why the play has been rejected.

When I started with the Court, I inherited a system of standard rejection slips, which meant that a play would arrive and be read, and then if none of the readers felt that it was very interesting, the play was returned to the writer with a little photocopy piece of paper saying, "Thank you for sending us your play; I'm afraid it's unsuitable for the Royal Court." This told the writer nothing at all about the quality of the play.

It is important, particularly when production opportunities for writers are contracting rapidly, that one take the time to explain to the writing community exactly what is going on. And if the play is terrible, one should say so and explain why he thinks it's terrible as effectively as he can.

But once you get beyond the correspondence into interviews with writers, which are conducted under the name of encouragement, it does get very difficult. For example, if we get a good play from a writer who lives in Inverness, we don't have the money to invite the writer to come down to the theatre to talk about it. And since the odds against getting the play done are so high, one cannot do much more than say, "Well, you have to keep going and good luck."

MR. GRAY: I want to ask about the practice of collective authorship, which David Hare was involved in. There were, I believe, two projects, *Lay By* and *England's Ireland,* in both of which you were involved.[14]

MR. HARE: We had a conference about writing at the Court to which a lot of writers were invited. It was an attempt to get people who felt out of touch with the Court into the place. We were sitting in the main

14. Hare's coauthors for *Lay By* (1971) were Howard Brenton, Brian Clark, Trevor Griffiths, Stephen Poliakoff, Hugh Stoddart, and Snoo Wilson; for *England's Ireland* (1972),

theatre talking about the theatre's policy and so on, and I put my hand up and said: "Instead of talking, let's write a play. And anyone who wants to help write it, meet in the bar afterward."

Well, there were eleven of us who turned up to start a play. Finally, it was reduced to eight, then seven. And we were promised a production. Whatever we wrote, the Court promised to put it on.

MR. GASKILL: This was *Lay By,* and it was actually put on by the Traverse Theatre Company.

MR. HARE: The Royal Court was very angry about the script; they were terribly hurt by the play—a lot of people were.

MR. HAMPTON: Lindsay Anderson was never pleased by the play. I remember at the reading of the play, he turned to me and said, "I suppose you're responsible for this."

MR. WRIGHT: The play was written by the generation which was a threat. If you cast your eyes down the list of authors, it began with Hare, Brenton, Wilson, and then got worse and worse. I quite welcomed this sort of split in the theatre because it meant that I could do all of those controversial plays in the Theatre Upstairs, which I was then responsible for.

But what was it all about? As an outsider, I did notice that all the people on one side had been to Cambridge, and all the others had been to Oxford.

MR. HARE: I often felt it to be an unfriendly theatre to new writers by this time. As literary manager I felt rather impotent about getting the plays I liked performed.

When the new artistic directors, Lindsay Anderson and Anthony Page, arrived to join Bill Gaskill, there was a meeting at which it was said that there would now be democratic decisions among the staff about which plays to do; and although we didn't agree on what we *should* do, we did all decide under no circumstances to do a rather dreadful play about prisons, which we all hated. Then when the season was announced, the first production was to be this wretched prison play.[15] So whatever the decision-making process was, I knew I wasn't part of it.

---

they were Tony Bicat, Howard Brenton, Brian Clark, David Edgar, Francis Fuchs, and Snoo Wilson.

15. *Inside Out,* by Frank Norman, opened November 24, 1969.

MS. JELLICOE: You've talked about the Court's highly ambivalent attitude to the success of some writers.

MR. HAMPTON: That's a different matter altogether. That has to do with a certain kind of puritanism, that is, not approving of people being successful. For example, reviews could be too good. Young directors were fired for not getting the right kind of vitriolic attack that everybody was used to. You know, "What is wrong with this boy? Why is he getting such good reviews? Get rid of him."

MS. JELLICOE: Can you name names because I've never heard of that case?

MR. HAMPTON: Robert Kidd was fired after the opening of *Marya*.[16]

MS. JELLICOE: Are we quite sure of the reason?

MR. WRIGHT: Yes, I think we are.

MR. HAMPTON: Yes, I'm quite sure of the reason.

MR. ESSLIN: May I say that this is the syndrome of all relentlessly financially weak avant-garde theatres, who are always afraid of losing their best people by success. At the Court, once somebody had a big success, one knew that he was going to be taken up, as indeed David Hare or Howard Brenton was, by the National Theatre.

MR. HAMPTON: *Marya* was considered by the Court to be a very bad production, and it got very good reviews. Therefore, punishment was in order.

MR. WRIGHT: That's right. If it had had very bad reviews, then everybody would have been very loyal about it.

MR. HAMPTON: Yes, if it had gotten the reviews that the theatre felt it deserved, everyone would have rallied around and said, "He'll do better next time."

MR. WRIGHT: But to do a not very good production and to get very good reviews smacked of treachery of some kind.

MR. HAMPTON: Yes. The other unforgivable sin was to write a play which was enormously successful, which some of us inadvertently did.

MR. ESSLIN: Yes, because it meant that the treachery would follow, as it were, because then the big offers would come.

MR. HAMPTON: No, I think not. I think not at all, no. I mean there was no question that my next play after *Total Eclipse* would go to the Royal Court, and I think that was the case for ten years.

16. Written by Russian writer Isaac Babel and adapted by Christopher Hampton; the play opened at the Royal Court on October 19, 1967.

MR. GRAY: Was there an underlying assumption that prevailing critical and popular standards were so corrupt that any shows that succeeded under those terms had to be bad?

MR. HAMPTON: Absolutely, yes.

MR. HARE: We have not spoken about the critics, but a refreshing thing about the Royal Court is that they genuinely took no notice of what was written in the newspapers, except, of course, when it was personally gratifying; they hated the critics. Never for a moment did anybody believe that what critics wrote in a newspaper was the truth. And that is terribly important to the Court's history and very refreshing; it contrasts with the Royal Shakespeare Company. The RSC tends to think there is a kind of rough blind justice, that by and large the truth is told and it all evens out.

Nobody at the Court believed that, but they believed in the work that they were doing. And they believed in each other's estimate of it. And it was not a disgrace to fail. And that, I think, is the most attractive thing about the Court. The criteria were never what critics wrote, and that is very good.

MR. HAMPTON: And rare.

MR. HARE: Rare.

MR. GRAY: This period of bitterness that David is referring to, did that create a break with young writers that then had to be rebuilt for the generation of writers that followed?

MR. HAMPTON: Yes, I think it did.

MR. WRIGHT: I think it did rather. What did happen was that many writers had plays done in the Theatre Upstairs and then passed rather quickly to the main auditorium of the Royal Court, and then perhaps moved on to larger auditoriums, like Nottingham or the National Theatre, for example. That did happen.

A lot of people who, I think, should have settled in the Royal Court, and who would have been very good for it, just didn't.

MR. HAMPTON: That's right. There was a time at the beginning of the seventies when the writers that ought to have been recruited were somehow bungled and not quite recruited, or half recruited, and this formed a sort of opposition within the theatre, which had repercussions for some years.

MR. STAFFORD-CLARK: I think that it is interesting to learn from the lessons of the past.

104

MR. GRAY: May I ask about Nicholas Wright's group of young play-wrights who started in 1979?

MR. WRIGHT: Yes, the Theatre Upstairs was a very important part of the natural development and discovery of writers.

I think that the Royal Court was the first theatre to have a studio in England, that is, to have a small theatre which was a part of that theatre in the same building. It is common now in the regional theatre, but it was started at the Court. The Theatre Upstairs was started in response to the growth of what was later called the fringe theatre. There were a lot of new writers for whom the main auditorium in the Court didn't quite seem right. And people perhaps didn't quite understand this new school but wanted to know more about it.

But the Theatre Upstairs differed from the Sunday night workshop that we were talking about earlier, partly because in the Upstairs space we did full dress productions. Design was important and often elaborate. The theatre was flexible; you could have seats in different places for whichever play you did.

Every time one came to a show at the Theatre Upstairs, the seats and the stage would be in different configurations. We presented many productions for quite short runs of two or three weeks. It's not the kind of program that could be afforded now at the Court because it would be very, very expensive.

But it did mean that we had a lot of shows coming on. There were a lot of hits and quite a lot of misses, but I think it was an exciting time of vitality and life.

MS. JELLICOE: I remember your saying that you never wanted to get the program organized too far ahead because the latest things tended to excite you.

You never really knew beyond two productions, did you?

MR. WRIGHT: No.

MR. STAFFORD-CLARK: What is interesting in hearing about the past is what methods have actually been formalized, like commissions, and have now become accepted as a part of the bloodstream of the theatre, while some like Sunday nights have been superseded.

If I could just say how we work now. The Monday meetings that Christopher talked about began to deal with so much business that it became cumbersome. So I think one of the first decisions I took was to

105

split off the script session from the Monday meetings. It is now a script meeting, which takes place every two weeks or three weeks and to which all the directors in the building come. Sometimes outside directors are invited to it as well, for periods of six months, so that they have an idea of what new plays are going on.

The two resident writers are invited to it, and some other members of the staff, like the electrician, or anyone else in the building who is interested. And at the script meeting, people report back on what scripts they have read. These are rated quite strictly and given either recommendations for production or for rehearsed readings, or for keeping contact with the writer, or for rejection.

As we have heard, the rehearsed reading, the formal rehearsal presentation of a play over a week, has become a key factor in how we encourage writers. Commissions have become formalized. And the Young Writers' Festival that Nicky started has also become an annual event.

It might make sense to talk about that for a second. It is open to any writer under the age of eighteen, and one gets a lot of plays about pixies and elves, and a lot of plays about adolescents, learning about being in love with each other, and a lot of original work, which is quite striking.

I did a play by a sixteen-year-old girl, Andrea Dunbar, called *The Arbor,* which had a wonderful freshness. She had never been in a theatre, she had never seen a play except on television, and she had never been outside Yorkshire, a county in northern England. When she came down to London, when we started rehearsal, it was the first time that she had ever been more than five miles outside her home-town. The originality of her work is quite striking. We came to her work through the Young Writers' Festival.

MR. GRAY: Max, we only have about five minutes left. Could you talk a bit about your continuation of some of the things that began to happen in the Royal Court Theatre Studio in 1963, when what began as a workshop for methods of acting began to generate scripts out of improvisations for public performance.

MR. STAFFORD-CLARK: Through Joint Stock?

MR. DILLON: Yes, I would also like to know a little bit more about Joint Stock and its relationship to the Royal Court.

MR. STAFFORD-CLARK: Right. The danger always in running a theatre committed to experiment and to new work is that you became so formalized that you become fossilized. As I've said, a more efficient way of doing it would be to have regular script meetings but not to let that become so formal that it becomes restrictive.

Ann has talked about the informality of the Writers' Groups in the early days; it was obviously fruitful for that period. But the tendency is that things are fruitful for a couple of years and then lose their purpose and need to be revitalized. That is the lesson from the past one has to learn: you've got constantly to reexamine what methods you are using to promote work; you've got constantly to say, is that working? You must constantly apply that question, Is it going to work in front of four hundred people over six weeks?

The relationship of Joint Stock to the Court is simply that it used some of the same personnel and writers who had been associated with the Court. Because Joint Stock had better working conditions (we were able to work for ten weeks on a play), we were able to take the stage of research and investigation further and feed it back to the writer.

We have always been careful not to see Joint Stock's method as *the* way of doing plays, but simply to present it as an alternative to writers. Writing is a very lonely and arduous job. It is an awful job. I think directing is an awful job, but I think writing is probably worse, and I think that anything that can be done to alleviate the loneliness of the writer is really what we have to keep remembering as our starting point.

Part of the reason for Joint Stock was that it did get the writer out of the garret and get him or her onto the rehearsal floor. And writers saw that as an occasionally refreshing exercise for them.

Some writers, like Trevor Griffiths, have always resisted it. He made it quite clear that he was not keen on doing that kind of work, and he preferred to keep his autonomy, whereas other writers like Caryl Churchill have found it occasionally refreshing to have that instant feedback to their work, in the sense of actually feeding off actors' ideas, and to have that kind of research available.

Maybe this is something we have absorbed from television, the documentary play, but I see that kind of research and that kind of kinship of life with the theatre as being very important. Clearly, what is attractive about a play like *The Arbor* is that it does do just that; it brings life to the stage. Tony Garrett, Les Blair, and Ken Loach's work on television has been influential, and to an extent we have adopted documentary methods; I feel that researched life has accuracy to it.

That work is educative to the people doing it. I'm doing a play at the moment that is set in the Pakistani section of London; it is about immigration and the children of immigrants and how one generation revolts against the strict ideas of the previous generation.[17]

Bringing work that has a political perspective, bringing the street into the theatre, is something that we constantly have to do. The Young Writers' Festival has in the past done that for us. But then, again, it's inclined to become, as I say, formalized and fossilized. It is a matter of constantly reexamining the structure which you are working with and seeing that it lives and is useful.

It's not wrong to throw out Sunday night productions if they have outlived their purposes. It is right to reexamine constantly every facet of the operation and see what works and what doesn't and what serves writers and what no longer has a purpose.

OBSERVER: If the writers could bring back something that the Court did in the past that was helpful, what would it be? The Sunday night productions, or what?

MR. WRIGHT: There isn't enough money to do much work in the Theatre Upstairs. This seems to me to be a terrible loss, because it was simply a way of offering a full dress production to a writer.

The theatre was so small that even if it was a great hit, it wouldn't take in much money anyway so that the financial difference between a flop and a huge hit was limited. It was not worth worrying about; we could afford to take the risk. If very few people came, it wouldn't be an embarrassment. If fifty people came a night, you had a feeling of a full house.

The Theatre Upstairs often provided the excitement of a successful performance, and it was wonderful to be able to offer that, and certainly very attractive for many writers, particularly in the early stages of their careers. It seems to me to be a great loss that the program in the Theatre Upstairs is now so restricted.

OBSERVER: The Court represents an extraordinary period of time, when the development of projects for financial gain was not the goal.

But in America a writer can write one play, which may be done on

17. The play is *Borderline* (1981), by Hanif Kureishi.

Broadway, then promoted, and make an enormous amount of money. That writer will then go away from that institution. Sometimes the institution itself is corrupted by that success. Could you expound on how the commercial theatre has been somehow separated from the Royal Court over this extraordinary period of time?

MR. STAFFORD-CLARK: I think we can summarize what has been said in previous sessions. In the earlier stage of the Court's development, it was very dependent upon income from the transfers to the West End, but transfers began to diminish during Nicholas Wright's directorship, or thereabouts, in 1973–1975.

MR. WRIGHT: Yes, the West End started to dry up.

MR. BURGE: I think that once you start thinking along commercial lines, you are going down a slippery slope. It is okay for the commercial theatre to pick up a play. That's fine. But once you start talking about your repertoire in a commercial sense, you might just as well not have a repertoire.

OBSERVER: Were there any factors in terms of the people or the philosophy of the Royal Court that prevented that kind of thing?

MR. BURGE: Well, one always has to resist it.

MR. HAMPTON: I think that it is differently perceived in America. Success is a much more shiny commodity in America than it is in England. And it is much more greedily desired, and its opposite (noncommercial fare) is energetically shunned. But that's not the case in England, actually.

MR. ESSLIN: Whether one is aware of it or not, the prestige of a theatre like the Court ensures that even plays produced that are completely ignored in England, like Bond's *Lear,* for example, become international successes and the writers concerned become very successful, although the English public doesn't realize that. For example, next season [1982] in Germany, the most produced play will be Nigel Williams' *Class Enemy,* a play that was done Upstairs in 1978. The chap who wrote that will make a hell of a lot of money. This is not perceived in England. But the fact is that once you have become associated with the prestige of the Royal Court, Scandinavia, France, Switzerland, and particularly Germany become outlets so that dramatists like Wesker or Bond who are relatively unsuccessful in England became financially very successful elsewhere.

MR. DILLON: It's appropriate that we're talking about money because this sets the stage for the next session about the business of the Court.

109

THE FAÇADE OF THE ROYAL COURT THEATRE

MAX STAFFORD-CLARK

NICHOLAS WRIGHT

CARYL CHURCHILL AND MARTIN ESSLIN

STUART BURGE

IRVING WARDLE

ANN JELLICOE

MICHAEL HALLIFAX

ROB RITCHIE AND HARRIET CRUICKSHANK

WILLIAM GASKILL

DAVID HARE AND CHRISTOPHER HAMPTON

IV

Managers Talk: The Business of
the Court

MODERATOR: *Alexander Speer, administrative director, Actors Theatre of
Louisville*

PARTICIPANTS: *Stuart Burge, artistic director, 1977–1979
Harriet Cruickshank, head, public relations, 1979–1981
Michael Hallifax, general stage manager, 1956–1959
Rob Ritchie, literary manager, 1979–1984
Nicholas Wright, artistic director, 1975–1977*

SPEAKING FROM THE AUDIENCE:
*Martin Esslin
Gerald Freedman
Christopher Hampton
Donald Howarth
and conference observers*

MR. SPEER: To begin, I'd like to ask some questions regarding the arrangement and structure of the Court. Its council, similar to a board
of directors, has several functions, one of which obviously is to raise
money for the operation and another to choose the artistic director of
the Court. Would you like to expand on that?

MR. WRIGHT: Yes. The arts in Britain are not, as in France, controlled by
a ministry. The body which finances the arts in Britain is the Arts
Council, an independent body, which is itself financed by the government, so it's called a quango or quasi-autonomous nongovernmental
organization. It receives a grant from the government and gives
money to various organizations such as the council of the English
Stage Company. One of the ESC Council's jobs is to receive money
because it's obviously out of the question to give money straight to
those notoriously irresponsible people, the artistic directors. The ESC
Council's other important job is to appoint the artistic director. Once

116

that's done, and once the council has been given the money for the year, the council continues to meet. It reviews the work that's been done at the theatre, and an artistic and economic report is given to it. Of course, the council is bound to comment on what's been happening, but the idea is that it doesn't interfere. After the artistic director has been appointed, it is then his job to make the theatre work as a theatre. That's shown at the Court in that the artistic director is the senior job. The senior administrator, the general manager, is really junior to the artistic director. He runs the kind of theatre that the artistic director wants. And the artistic director makes those decisions himself, in consultation with the people he wants to consult.

MR. SPEER: Would it be fair to say that the council of the English Stage Company exercises artistic control by its choice of artistic director?

MR. WRIGHT: Yes, obviously, the appointment of the artistic director is the crucial decision.

MR. SPEER: What percentage of the total operation does the Arts Council of Great Britain provide the Court?

MR. RITCHIE: For 1981 the grant from the Arts Council was £424,000, which represents 56 percent of the total budget.

MR. SPEER: Where does the balance come from?

MR. RITCHIE: The balance comes from the box office and a small grant from the Greater London Council.[1]

MR. WRIGHT: You referred to one of the functions of the council of the English Stage Company as raising money. In fact, the council is given money by the Arts Council of Great Britain, and it has on occasion raised useful, small amounts of money, but overall, the money it raised was never very significant. There's probably a big difference between the Royal Court Theatre and the way a theatre would conduct itself in the United States.

MR. SPEER: Obviously, they differ in incentives. As you know, in the United States there are tax advantages for both corporations and individuals to make contributions to nonprofit arts organizations, which is not necessarily the case in Great Britain. If you want to be a patron you really have to want to be a patron of the arts directly. Is there much of that?

1. The Greater London Council grant for 1981 was £18,500.

117

MR. WRIGHT: In the time I was there, very little. I don't know what it's like now.

MR. RITCHIE: It's still very little. Under other income, for example, from plays that have transferred to the West End the amount has been nil. That's the climate of the last two or three years; there haven't been any transfers. Also, private sponsorship and commercial sponsorship from indusry is very small. This current year we got £15,000 from Camel cigarettes.

MS. CRUICKSHANK: For Edward Bond's *Restoration,* which opened in July, 1981. They were keen to be associated with a particular production.

MR. SPEER: And did they receive some kind of credit in the playbill?

MS. CRUICKSHANK: Yes. It was carefully explained that we never go into full color at the Royal Court in our playbills because we can't afford it. They had their logo on the posters and on the front of the house outside the theatre and through all the publicity material but not on the front of the playbill. And they got soaked with hospitality at the theatre and some free seats to see the show. One of the conditions of their sponsorship was that we should spend more money on promoting the show. We did some advertising on the backs of buses, which is something I don't think we've ever done before—a revolution it was! So we had the Royal Court Theatre going around on the backs of buses; the rest of the money went to help with the production costs because the show was very expensive. I think that's the first time the Court's actually had commercial sponsorship. When we were trying to raise £42,000 to reseat the theatre, about two years ago, most of it came in small amounts, from actors. Very little of it came from commercial sources.

MR. BURGE: There has been, especially under the present government, a great move to encourage commercial sponsorship of the arts, a kind of pipe dream which it hopes might eventually replace public subsidy. Of course, the record shows that if you're a sufficiently posh theatre company and you're doing the right kind of glamorous productions you can actually raise a great deal of money.

Covent Garden Opera and the Royal Shakespeare Company constantly do productions that are billed as being sponsored by so and so. That's true of festivals, too. Aldeburgh Festival does a lot of that. If what you're doing is a slap-up production of *Cosi fan Tutte,* which appeals to the right kind of audience, then you can get the sponsorship. But obviously, because of its nature, the Royal Court is not a likely candidate.

MS. CRUICKSHANK: Also, Edward Bond was extremely antisponsorship, especially by a cigarette company! I wasn't allowed to show him anything! I had to show him the poster *without* the Camel logo on it because he refused to give his agreement to it.

OBSERVER: Did you say you sought that sponsor or did the sponsor come to you?

MR. RITCHIE: It arose by coincidence. One of the directors at the Court was at a dogtrack one night and was standing next to an executive of Reynolds-Camel cigarettes. The idea came up in a conversation. I think the important point is, as Stuart has said, the nature of the Court's work means that at best we will attract commercial sponsorship from manufacturers of socially unacceptable products. Camel has done disastrously in England in terms of its marketing because it's considered to be a particularly lethal kind of cigarette. They're looking for unusual outlets for promoting their products.

MS. CRUICKSHANK: We did try to raise money for Jonathan Pryce's *Hamlet,* a year earlier. One of the assistant directors at the Court was put on to this job, and he raised absolutely nothing.[2] There was no interest from anybody in supporting even *Hamlet* at the Court.

MR. SPEER: They were all probably sorry, afterward. What was the internal feeling within the Court with this first corporate sponsorship? You said that Edward Bond was not happy about it. What about the other people?

MS. CRUICKSHANK: I think Edward had resigned from something because of cigarette sponsorship; he felt compromised, didn't he?

MR. RITCHIE: That's correct. One of the writers' organizations ran a play competition that was sponsored by a cigarette manufacturer, and Edward had resigned because he wouldn't have any part of an organization that accepted money from a cigarette manufacturer. But for the Court, it was pure pragmatism; in order to get the play on, it was important to get that little bit of extra money. Fifteen thousand pounds made the production possible.

MS. CRUICKSHANK: To be truthful, the feeling within the building was one of cynicism, wasn't it?

MR. RITCHIE: Yes.

2. *Hamlet,* with Jonathan Pryce in the title role, opened April 2, 1980.

MR. SPEER: Was that because you had been compromised?

MS. CRUICKSHANK: Yes.

MR. SPEER: What kinds of strings are attached to the substantial monies that come from the Arts Council of Great Britain?

MR. WRIGHT: You have to charge for the seats is one of them. Also, you have to ask the critics. These are both matters which have been empirically tested. Once when we discussed making the seats free, the Arts Council didn't like the idea at all. Another time when we considered not inviting the press, they didn't like that idea either. I think one discovers most of these strings only by inadvertently pulling on them. There probably are many others.

MR. RITCHIE: The other important one is that part of the subsidy from the Arts Council comes in the form of a guarantee against loss. The Arts Council is human; you are permitted to fail. So a certain portion of your money is kept back and paid at the end of the financial year in the form of a guarantee. And the reverse is also true, that if you make a profit over the course of the financial year, you can't carry that money forward and use it to subsidize work the following year.

MR. SPEER: So in that sense, it is kind of a negative incentive?

MR. BURGE: Yes, that has been a great bone of contention for many, many years, ever since the idea of subsidy came in, because it discouraged companies from getting more than just a break-even figure. And it led to all sorts of devious ways of storing the money away in capital assets and things like that, which was strictly audited by the Arts Council. Fortunately, by a lot of devious work in the last few years, the Royal Court has managed to incorporate some of their profits from transfers and so forth for paying off old deficits, which, strictly speaking, you aren't allowed to use the profit of the current year to do.

MR. SPEER: It sounds like a Catch 22.

MR. BURGE: But by devious accounting, one can actually do quite a lot in that direction in a good year. Officially, the ridiculous thing is that if the theatre has a really good year, one cannot actually exploit that to bolster the theatre in the future.

MR. SPEER: With the £424,000 this year, are specific segments of that money set aside for playwrights' commissions, or is it one lump sum that the artistic director and the management can spend as they need?

MR. BURGE: That's fairly free. That is up to the council of the English Stage Company and the artistic director.

120

MS. CRUICKSHANK: It is done on the basis of a budget presented to the Arts Council.

MR. BURGE: Yes, they do demand a budget.

MS. CRUICKSHANK: Often it is two-tiered; the first budget that we do is what we would ideally like to have, and often we are asking for four or five times the money that we might get. And then they come back to us and say, "Your grant is going to be £424,000; show us that you can work within this." And then everybody modifies the budget to fit that figure.

MR. BURGE: Yes, there is extraordinary fiction in this proposed budget. It's always about twice what we know we're going to get when it comes back. And then you redo all the figures, take 25 percent off, and that's the story of everybody's life in subsidized companies.

MR. SPEER: What is the current situation on the rumor that the Arts Council may cut completely the funding of the Royal Court Theatre?

MR. RITCHIE: Well, what's happened is that in December, 1980, the Arts Council decided to investigate the Court. The specific question was whether its present commitment to new writers justified the level of subsidy that it was getting. There's nothing sinister about that; the Court is the largest producer of new work in London so at a time when the amount of money that the Arts Council receives from the Treasury is declining, it's quite logical that they should review the commission of new drama in London.

However, the drama panel of the Arts Council, which makes the recommendations, made clear to the Court that they were concerned about the relative proportion of the money that was actually used for productions. They wanted to know what percentage was actually going to the physical costs of the plays and paying the writers, and what percentage was used in paying the overhead, central heating bills, the front of the house staff wages, and so on.

The Arts Council's priority at the moment is to ensure that they are as cost-effective as possible. They want to be sure that a reasonable proportion of the money they spend actually goes into producing plays. And, of course, the cost of things like central heating and overhead have been going up astronomically.

MR. SPEER: But that is an interesting example of an artistic decision by the Arts Council. It is a kind of turnaround from perhaps previously, if they're talking about funding much smaller operations, such as loft situations, where one can put on a play very easily and inexpensively. They're making the decision that the production values that are associated with an established institution are not necessary.

MR. WRIGHT: It merely reflects the view of the Treasury and the government, that not just in the theatre but throughout industry in Britain, certain old institutions have become fat and unhealthy, and the Court has at times been perceived by the financial policy arm of the Arts Council as such an institution. For example, it is an old building that has three levels, and so instead of having only two ushers, we need twelve. To a certain kind of bureaucrat it seems obvious that this is a waste of money, and it would be much better if we had a simpler building where one person could stand at the door and we could save costs.

MR. SPEER: No capital funds are available to do that, right?

MR. WRIGHT: No, actually not.

MS. CRUICKSHANK: A very important change in policy was made by the Arts Council a year ago. Previously, when there was no cost-of-living increase in the grant, the policy was to give everybody a little less so that cuts were made across the board. Last year for the first time instead of cutting theatre organizations across the board, certain companies were cut completely, and other companies that the Arts Council thought were particularly effective got more. The latter would actually receive an increase in its grant in contrast to the decrease the Arts Council was getting from the Treasury. And that is the big change. Last year forty-one companies were actually cut, and the Arts Council has not had a history of cutting companies before. And so this year everybody felt very insecure when they realized what the drama panel might do. It has also happened in new music.

MR. WRIGHT: That's right. The Arts Council has guarded its independence over the years by appearing to be a body which doesn't itself make decisions but which gives financial support to the artistic decisions made by the artists of the country. I think the Arts Council has, in fact, made all sorts of decisions in the past. It has always been possible for it to look as if it didn't really make them, or as if it just followed the normal course of events. I think that is one of the ways in which it guards its independence from the government, which it rightfully thinks is very important. But with the country itself in a state of crisis, it is not actually possible to go on doing that. Decisions get forced out into the open.

122

MR. BURGE: Yes, the Arts Council structure works in an expanding situation because on the whole they can do what they set out to do, which is to finance and encourage a seed of enterprise. They can give it a small grant to start it off and then, if it works, expand it. But in a receding situation, where critical decisions have to be made, it is a matter of great question, I think, whether the Arts Council is a suitable body to do that.

MR. SPEER: Whether they're competent to make those decisions?

MR. BURGE: Yes. This particular investigation by the Arts Council last December has partly to do with the expansion of the opportunity for doing good work in other theatres. I think one of the purposes of the inquiry was to assess what proportion of the work of the new writers was done by the Court as opposed to the fringe theatres and the chamber theatres and so forth.

MR. SPEER: But if they were to decide to cut the funding completely, it would mean the death knell of the Court. Am I correct?

MR. RITCHIE: Absolutely, yes. We have had unofficial assurances, that is to say, members of the Arts Council have made statements that the possibility of completely cutting the grant to the Court is not on the agenda. But that's not quite true. It was very much in the air when we met them in May.

So we're going to get some subsidy next year. I expect that we will find out unofficially sometime in November how much will be cut in real terms next year, given the need for inflation and so forth. [3]

MR. HALLIFAX: Yes, because the company could be given some money but not enough to make it worthwhile for that company to go on doing what it wants to do.

MR. WRIGHT: That's right. The terrible thing is that such a huge proportion of the money is spent on usherettes and cleaning the windows. And the amount of money perhaps that you spend on creative work is the cream floating on the top, and it is that which always gets cut first.

MR. SPEER: What is that percentage, the occupancy versus production cost, for the Royal Court Theatre?

MR. RITCHIE: Depending on how good you are at statistics, you can present it in numerous different ways. I suppose the working figure that we use regarding how much money is actually set aside in a year

---

3. For the year ending April 3, 1982, the Arts Council grant was £424,000; for the year ending April 2, 1983, £453,000.

for the production of shows downstairs and in the Upstairs is roughly one hundred thousand for all productions downstairs and forty-five or fifty thousand for the Upstairs.

OBSERVER: I would like to ask if any of you think that the Arts Council can really continue to afford two very highly subsidized companies such as the National Theatre and the Royal Shakespeare Company and other theatres as well if the economy continues as it has been?

MR. ESSLIN [speaking from the audience]: May I say, as a former chairman of the drama panel of the Arts Council and as a member of the Arts Council since 1976, that the assumption that there is any government interference in these decisions is absolute baloney. It is really the drama panel that makes these painful decisions. Of course, the composition of the drama panel is open to a lot of question. I, personally, when chairman, thought that the drama panel was completely wrongly constituted, and now it isn't any better. So if the drama panel comes up with a suggestion, that's the opinion of twenty-five people who have come in from all over the place, and they are as representative as the people in this room.

As a matter of principle, I agree with what Rob Ritchie says. The Arts Council, the drama panel, and the permanent officials, including the secretary general, think that it is bad to cut everybody 10 percent right around. Therefore, one is faced with the frantic situation of whether to cut somebody completely, or by 15 percent or 20 percent, when you may just as well give up anyway, because it will only go on the window treatments.

So the question remains: who to cut altogether. Last year for the first time, they cut a few people at the National Youth Theatre altogether. It becomes a question, really, of asking, "Who is going to be executed?" And that is not a very nice question to have to answer. I think that you have to see that the people involved in making these decisions are in an equally bad position as the people who are receiving them. Probably, if they have said that there is no danger of the Court's being cut, then they certainly will not cut by 15 percent or 20 percent. They may leave it at the same figure of the last cost-of-living increase, which is never representative because the materials that the theatre uses rise in price much more steeply than the general level. Therefore, if the cost-of-living index in the whole country is up at 12 percent, the cost of timber for building scenery might be up by 50 percent. That is really the worst problem at this time.

MR. RITCHIE: I'm not quite as confident. Even having gained the assurance that a complete withdrawal of subsidy is out of the question, I still think that the drama panel has plausible arguments for cuts. Given that the case for continuing the subsidy of the Court is that it's the only proscenium arch theatre in London that regularly presents new work, they could well say, "We will continue to subsidize that side of the operation, but as for the Youth Theatre program and the Theatre Upstairs, they perform functions that are duplicated elsewhere in London and throughout the country, and savings could be made there if those aspects of the theatre's work were closed down." From an accountant's point of view, that is perfectly logical. From an artistic point of view, it would be disastrous to the Court.

MR. ESSLIN: Exactly.

MR. RITCHIE: What is unique about the Court is that it does have that ensemble of resources that enables it to locate work through the Youth Theatre and develop it in the Theatre Upstairs and then transfer it down onto the main stage and address an international audience from that stage.

OBSERVER: Has support from the Arts Council been in doubt in other periods in the history of the Royal Court, or has it always been secure?

MR. BURGE: There have been constant crises. Threats, either veiled or open, have been made that it was no longer logical to continue the subsidy of the Royal Court. After the arrival of the National Theatre and the Royal Shakespeare Company in London, with their chamber or studio theatres, everybody thought that these would replace the function of the Royal Court. In effect, I don't think that's happened at all. But there have been times when they have threatened to cut the grant altogether. When I went there in 1977, there was this belief. An Arts Council letter was sent to the board saying that they weren't going to get the grant next year.

OBSERVER: So it is not just since Mrs. Thatcher's arrival that the grant has been threatened?

MR. BURGE: No. To be fair, I don't think the government comes into it at all, except marginally, perhaps through its hope that some public subsidy can be replaced by commercial sponsorship.

MR. WRIGHT: I wonder if that is as true now as it was years ago. We constantly have to remind ourselves that we're living in quite a new situation in England. When one looks at the massive cuts in health and education, it's natural to expect cuts in the arts as well. But I wonder—do productions like *A Short Sharp Shock,* for example, make any difference to the grant; do they endanger the public financing?[4]

MR. RITCHIE: No. I don't think there is that kind of direct relationship between single plays and the grant.

MR. WRIGHT: It did cause great offense.

MR. RITCHIE: It did. It did produce something unusual in terms of relations between companies and the Arts Council. Generally speaking, the Arts Council operates a kind of arms-length policy—there's no direct interference in the artistic work. On that occasion, because of the nature of the show (which was a political satire about the present government in England), the matter was investigated by the members of the drama panel.

The panel then drew up a highly confidential document, which everyone, of course, saw, itemizing lines and moments in the play which it felt were in such bad taste that it might be better if they were removed.

MR. WRIGHT: They did, in fact, ask for changes in the play, didn't they?

MR. RITCHIE: Yes.

MR. WRIGHT: I think that's an extraordinary thing. I've never heard of the Arts Council doing that before.

MR. RITCHIE: It was very illuminating because one of the things in the play that they queried was a reference to a meeting that took place between Zuckerman and Lord Mountbatten which had been published about three or four weeks previously in a serialization of Cecil King's *Diaries* in the Sunday papers. And yet this was something that was alleged by the drama panel members who came to the production to be total fiction, invented by the writers in order to discredit the people concerned. They recognized afterward that they had overstepped their mark in investigating in that direct way, and I think they would be very reluctant to do it again.

But what's more important is the artistic effect from the contraction of subsidy, which has imposed a limit on the size of casts permitted in studio theatres. A number of theatres in London and throughout the country now won't do plays if they require more than five actors. That is a limitation which permits only certain kinds of

4. *A Short Sharp Shock . . . for the Government,* by Howard Brenton and Tony Howard (a play, said the authors, "that sets out to cheer up all those in opposition to the government"), opened at the Royal Court on July 16, 1981.

plays. Obviously, there are two ways one can respond to that limitation: one either can evolve a style of work that is more epic, where five actors play thirty parts and one does away with the sets and uses a freer form; or, increasingly, what one gets are small-cast plays set in one room, with one set (because that's all one can afford), which look like television dramas.

MR. SPEER: How is the ESC Council membership maintained?

MR. BURGE: It is self-perpetuating. In this great crisis we had when I arrived, we talked endlessly about how that could be changed. Although self-perpetuating, through the years people have been nominated. For instance, when a local authority contributes a percentage of the money, it gets represented on the board. Funnily enough, in that transition during my time, the ESC Council deteriorated because it lost the people who were passionately interested in the theatre itself, and they were replaced by bureaucrats. And although that was absolutely right and fair, it didn't make the artistic director's job any easier because one was faced by people who didn't know what they were talking about.

The first theatre I ran was a truly civic theatre in the sense that it was run by a committee of the council of the local authority, and that was great because we had these monthly meetings on a Friday night, and the last thing we discussed was the repertoire. I must say it was slightly devious, but I used to steer the whole meeting toward the price of light ale in the bar and that sort of thing and leave only five minutes to discuss the plays. I was very independent.

MR. ESSLIN: The Arts Council (I was a member on the drama panel from 1963 until 1977) was extremely anxious to draw a kind of charter for these councils, and especially important was that they should have no influence on artistic policy; in other words, they could only hire and fire the artistic director. Obviously, you had no interference, Stuart, in your operation of the Nottingham Theatre.

MR. BURGE: I think it varies, but I never had any trouble with Nottingham in that way because there was a great deal of independence there, in spite of the local authority representatives. But I know that some councils did and still do exert quite a pressure on the choice of repertoire. At the Court when I arrived in 1977, there was the question of whether the council should be constituted with more professional people on it. There is actually a legal problem there because a theatre's so-called charitable status is governed by the fact that none of

127

the people on the board earn their living at the business in hand. Strictly speaking, people like Jocelyn Herbert, Bill Gaskill, and myself and Harriet shouldn't really be on the council of the Royal Court.

MS. CRUICKSHANK: I remember when I first went to the Court in 1970 the council of the Court was made up of lots of practitioners. On the council were Tony Richardson and Jocelyn Herbert; also Michael Codron and Michael White, two commercial producers.

MR. WRIGHT: The latter two had made enormous amounts of money out of the Royal Court.

MS. CRUICKSHANK: Council meetings were absolutely electric and funny, weren't they? They were very exciting. All these extraordinary people from the past, like John Osborne, Peggy Ashcroft.

MR. WRIGHT: Very, very interested parties.

MS. CRUICKSHANK: Very interested parties who made for these wonderful meetings. For a young person going into management in the theatre, they were the best school one could go to. They were so fascinating.

OBSERVER: I would like to know how the council goes about choosing an artistic director?

MR. WRIGHT: It's gone about it by different ways. It was very much like the leadership of the Conservative party, which, Harold Macmillan used to say, was decided by the usual process of selection, which meant that nobody had the faintest idea how it was actually done, but it was a lot of backstairs work.

MS. CRUICKSHANK: Didn't Greville Poke hold all of these interviews in his house so that nobody at the Court would know who was being interviewed for the position?

MR. WRIGHT: Yes, and everybody knew. Then the post was advertised. You could apply for the job and then you had to go and be interviewed by these people whom most of the candidates had known for years, had worked with quite closely. There was an appearance of method to it, but I don't think that it really had any method at all.

MR. HOWARTH [speaking from the audience]: Each applicant was interviewed by a selection committee of six (Jocelyn Herbert, Lois Sieff, Oscar Lewenstein, Michael White, Greville Poke, Lindsay Anderson). Lindsay had turned down the directorship, but he wanted to continue working at the Court. The Court was "home." Therefore, his influ-

ence on the other five members was crucial in deciding the new
directorship.

MR. WRIGHT: What's happened for many years is that the council formed
a little subcommittee of itself to decide about the artistic directorship
and how they came to their decision is—

MR. SPEER: Known only to them.

MR. WRIGHT: I think so.

MR. BURGE: There is no question that the system is creaky now. Perhaps
we ought to go into the actual structure of the authority of the Court:
there was the council, which usually formed committees, such as a
management committee. This committee at one time was a very
professional group because they usually insisted on having profes-
sionals on the council.

MS. CRUICKSHANK: Fortnightly, they used to meet.

MR. BURGE: And they kept a strict hold over George. I think George was
probably grateful that they were there, because they did actually take
a certain burden of the financial responsibility from him. They were
people who really knew what was going on. The chairman of the
council was the chairman of that management committee. But gradually that professional aspect of the management committee eroded,
and they were replaced by people on the board who really had no
professional knowledge, however enthusiastic they were, and the
management committee became a kind of burden.

MR. WRIGHT: Because the structure insisted that the members of the
management committee were experts. But the real experts were their
predecessors, these pals of theirs who had died years before. And it
became a nightmare by the time I took over. Mind you, if you look
through the minutes of old management committees, during George
Devine's time, they were a nightmare then, too. It is astonishing, the
amount to which George was hemmed in and confined. Neville Blond
had some friend with a flower shop and they decided there ought to be
a permanent display of flowers in the foyer, and George as the artistic
director was told to organize it. Absolute nonsense. It was very difficult when Robert Kidd and I were trying to cope with them. Actually, we had these well-intentioned people with a sporadic interest in
the workings of the theatre, and their unintentional contribution was
to interfere. And you did this wonderful thing, Stuart, of getting rid
of them. I though that was splendid.

MR. BURGE: Well, it was just an evolution.

MR. WRIGHT: You enormously strengthened the position of the artistic director, I believe, by doing that.

MR. BURGE: I attended one or two of these management meetings, and it did seem ridiculous. It was chaired by the chairman of the council, but the members of the committee were able to contribute very little; the meetings took an awfully long time because every item on the agenda had to be explained. It seemed a terrible waste of effort and an inefficient way of going on so that I was able to change that and make the artistic director the chairman of the management committee.

We called it a different name, the executive committee. And members of the staff were the main participants. There was, obviously, the chief person from each department: the general manager, chief of publicity, the head of the technical staff, and the director of the Theatre Upstairs and the accountant, of course, and only two members of the board in attendance. And one was able to choose the two members of the board that actually were competent to make comments. While I was there, that seemed to work much more efficiently. We arranged the meetings to occur two weeks after each production so that the budget for the previous production could be checked and the budget for the next production could be proposed; it was a more streamlined system. The actual way the Court works now is that the council has been reinforced by members of the staff, who are elected by the staff. The management committee, now called executive committee, is manned mostly by those members of the staff, with a copy of those meetings merely circulated to the board. It doesn't seem to risk the board's authority in any way. It seems to work quite well.

MR. SPEER: I would like to move into the area of the financial relationship between the Court and the playwrights. We talked earlier about commissioning playwrights. What kind of contractual arrangements are made with the playwrights regarding transfers and subsequent productions? Does the Court receive monies from a transfer from subsequent royalties or how does that work?

MR. RITCHIE: At present there is a contract that was negotiated between the Royal Court, the National Theatre, and the Royal Shakespeare Company and the Theatre Writers' Union. And that sets standard rates and conditions for any new commissioned play. At the moment, the small print is being finalized. As far as transfers are concerned, the Court's practice is always to negotiate an agreement at the time the plays transfer. It's not written into the contract at the outset. At the moment, there is a dispute about this because some companies wish to specify exactly what will be the split between the writer and the company, and other further exploitation, at the time of signing the original contract. Whereas, the writers want to leave it until the play is actually going to transfer so that, obviously, they can negotiate.

MR. SPEER: With more strength.

MR. RITCHIE: Yes.

MR. SPEER: In this country, there is a great divergence of opinion on the relationship between regional theatres, where a lot of new work is being presented, and what percentage of various subsidiary rights an author might owe the theatre company that originally produced his play. They range tremendously somewhere between 5 percent and up to 20 percent of the author's subsequent earnings from a production for a period of anywhere from five up to twenty years. They also sometimes ask for the film rights, radio and television rights, cable rights, and options to produce the play on Broadway. What are the Court's contractual arrangements to produce a play with an author?

MR. WRIGHT: The original Royal Court contract was, I think, written by Oscar Lewenstein, and it included all sorts of bits and pieces which meant that a percentage of royalties accrued to the theatre in the event of a later production.

MR. HAMPTON [speaking from the audience]: In making a simple comparison between the contract of the Royal Court and the contract which I made in 1980 with the Mark Taper Forum, the American theatres are much more demanding, I would even say grasping.

MR. SPEER: They tend to be at the upper end of what I just described?

MR. HAMPTON: Much higher than the Royal Court ever was. For example, the Royal Court never took any percentage of the foreign language rights, which, I understand, is standard over here or at least it is at the Mark Taper. The Court actually provided a very generous contract.

MR. WRIGHT: The contract, now, I think, is a very good contract for the writer.

MR. HAMPTON: Whereas in America, you get a contract that is approximately the length of the telephone book, which deals with the T-shirt rights and cereal box rights.

MR. FREEDMAN [speaking from the audience]: May I say that in com-

131

parison with European theatres, in America one gets so little subsidy of any sort that unless the theatre can get advantages on the side, such as commercial rights like that, one takes all the risk. There is no other way to run an American theatre.

MR. WRIGHT: Yes, the writer's argument in Britain has always been that a theatre, particularly like the Royal Court, is actually getting its subsidy in order to do new work, largely; and since that's what they are getting their money for, they shouldn't be taking money around the back as well. But that doesn't apply, obviously, to American theatre.

MS. CRUICKSHANK: I think it's become ridiculous in a way; I mean, there's an instance of a play that was done at the Theatre Upstairs earlier this year, an improvised play, *Four in a Million,* evolved by the director, Les Blair. He was invited to choose some actors and go away for quite a long time and work toward developing a piece. Eventually, it was done Upstairs very successfully. It was then bought and filmed by A.T.V., and the Court got not one penny, not even an acknowledgment anywhere that it had anything to do with the show whatsoever. That's a shame.

MR. BURGE: I think the contract recently negotiated doesn't give the Court any subsequent residuals, does it?

MR. WRIGHT: It does actually get some residuals, but the writer gets his first £4,000 per annum from the play before paying any of those residuals, which are not at all onerous to the writer.

MR. BURGE: In a situation where there is very little subsidy, obviously, the subsequent residuals provide an incentive to do new work. That is the situation, I imagine, in the United States. Otherwise, if they didn't have those residual possibilities, there would be no particular incentive to do anything but established work by regional theatres.

MR. SPEER: That's true to a certain extent, I believe. It also depends on what you believe the mission of the theatre is: whether it is to be involved directly in the initial production process or to be involved in subsequent production, which is quite time-consuming and time demanding. Do we spend our time dealing with a revival of a Broadway or an off-Broadway production, as it were, or do we spend time dealing with what we should be about (it's a personal opinion, obviously) of producing a new play in our own theatre.

I think one of the great differences has to do with subsidies; we do not have the huge subsidies in this country, except in a kind of peculiar way. Many of us have huge subscription audiences which provide a financial base, as opposed to huge governmental subsidies.

MR. ESSLIN: You have foundation subsidies and perhaps other subsidies for specific writers which may be divided between the writers and the theatres, when the writer tries to get somebody to produce his play. In fact, I think the subsidy situation in this country is intricately more complicated but I wouldn't say less opulent than England. In fact, in some ways, more.

MR. SPEER: Well, certainly, the private subsidies exist. Foundations are not necessarily where it is happening, I think. The Rockefeller Foundation does provide certain subsidies for the playwright and a smaller amount to a theatre to produce the work of a playwright, should it so desire.

But the corporations in this country have been increasing subsidies for our various regional theatres. And those subsidies sometimes come with strings attached and sometimes they are entirely eleemosynary.

MR. WRIGHT: In the past, the Royal Court always made quite a lot of money by investing the Arts Council grant in West End transfers of its own productions. In these days, this is unthinkable. And I think it's often been said quite confidently, the Arts Council doesn't allow it. But there are a number of occasions (Christopher's *The Philanthropist*, for example) when the Court has profited from the transfers.[5]

MR. HAMPTON: Yes, on *The Philanthropist* it went fifty-fifty.

MR. WRIGHT: Yes, and yet nowadays it seems rather a shocking idea, gambling quite a lot of Arts Council money on the market.

MR. HAMPTON: The sum was small. *The Philanthropist* was cast for four or five thousand pounds, and it made about four transfers, so it wasn't a tremendous risk. The transfer cost was a modest sum, and I think one of the problems today is that transfers cost so much more.

MR. BURGE: Yes, in transferring *Bent* from the Royal Court to another theatre, it cost another £25,000, just for the transfer of the existing production without any rehearsing.[6]

MR. SPEER: What kind of arrangements are made in these instances of the transfer? Does the Court receive a payment for the transfer or participate subsequently in a certain percentage of the box office?

MR. BURGE: It varies. It depends on the kind of bargaining power. Some-

5. *The Philanthropist* opened on August 3, 1970.
6. *Bent* opened on May 3, 1979.

133

times, of course, because of the lack of money, productions are put on at the Court with the participation of commercial management.

A play by Bill Morrison called *Flying Blind,* a very good and funny play about Belfast, was put on with the participation of a commercial company; however, it didn't transfer.[7] But in the case of *Once a Catholic,* by Mary O'Malley, when the financial situation of the Court was dreadfully low, we thought very carefully before putting it on at all.[8] We were racing around to all of the commercial managements, sending the script, seeing if we could get participation, and none of the managers wanted anything to do with it at all.

So when, by some extraordinary chance, it was hugely successful, we were in a very strong bargaining position and were able to auction it so that we could get a very good deal for it. Subsequently, it helped enormously to pay off debts, and it still provides an income. So it depends upon the open market, actually, or the position you are in at the time.

MR. WRIGHT: Sometimes it seems terribly unfair. *The Rocky Horror Show* in the Theatre Upstairs in 1973 (Harriet was the manager then) was a very expensive show for us, £4,000.[9]

MS. CRUICKSHANK: And we had only £3,000.

MR. WRIGHT: We had £3,000 and it was going to cost £4,000 and a very successful impresario called Michael White produced £1,000 so we could put the show on at all, and this involved nicking the carpet from the pub next door to the theatre to cover the stage and getting all of those disgusting knickers from that mail order firm for half price.

MS. CRUICKSHANK: And the seats from the Citizens Theatre in Glasgow.

MR. WRIGHT: Yes, Harriet had the old seats from the Citizens Theatre, which had all been chucked out, brought down on the train so that we could sit on them. They were like very old cinema seats. Do you remember, I said, "Couldn't we keep them in the Theatre Upstairs?" And you said you'd resign if we did because they kept collapsing.

All of that went on, everybody was working around the clock getting this show on, and all Michael White had done was sign a check for a thousand quid. And when the show went on, it made the most enormous amount of money around the world.

7. *Flying Blind* opened June 20, 1978.
8. *Once a Catholic* opened August 10, 1977.
9. *The Rocky Horror Show* opened in the Theatre Upstairs June 19, 1973.

MS. CRUICKSHANK: Yes.

MR. WRIGHT: It has always seemed to me very unfair the theatre got so little out of it.

MR. ESSLIN: What did they get?

MR. HAMPTON: One percent. I looked at the contract, and it was ridiculous.

MR. SPEER: One percent of the profits of the production?

MS. CRUICKSHANK: Yes.

MR. WRIGHT: It wasn't a very good return for an enormous amount of creative work and the nerve to put the show on.

MS. CRUICKSHANK: Yes, and the length of those contracts was five years; it was very funny that when the show actually moved for the third or fourth time to the Comedy Theatre, Jim Sharman had come back to redirect it, and on the first night he got a telegram from Richard O'Brien, the playwright, saying, "Do you know that your rights have expired on this show?" And actually, the five years was up something like two days before it moved into the Comedy and neither the Court nor Michael White had actually the rights to do it at all. They had to renegotiate the contract. It was unusual that the show actually outlived its five years.

MR. SPEER: What percentage of the operating budget is provided by funds from subsequent productions of plays initially produced by the Court?

MR. BURGE: This varies so much from year to year. I know that within a year or eighteen months, *Once a Catholic* produced something like £17,000. And it's made money since. But on the other hand, you can go a whole year without anything at all.

MR. WRIGHT: Stuart, when a commercial management was a partner for a show that you were putting on at the Court, what was your experience of their demeanor? Did they let you just get on with it? How much were they involved?

MR. BURGE: Well, certainly not in my experience has there been any interference. Obviously, there was consultation about casting and possibly consultation about the cost of the set, but funnily enough, it's always difficult to resist commercial management's inclination to feel that if they spend a lot of money they are getting a better show. I had to resist their inclination to spend much too much money on the set, which we didn't want to do.

MR. SPEER: What has been Equity's position in commercial manage-

ment's involvement in productions that subsequently transfer? I mean
by that, perhaps paying lower salaries in a tryout situation?

MR. BURGE: Well, for the last few years, it's been a custom of the Court in
the main theatre to pay the Equity minimum, the West End minimum. The Court is a member of the Society of West End Theatre
Managers. And that leads to all sorts of problems of budgeting, but,
in the end, it doesn't make an awful lot of difference.

Of course, one couldn't pay the actors less than we do. As always,
the actors and the people who have worked at the Court have subsidized it. But they get paid the Equity minimum salary, and it's across
the board, everybody gets the same. And in the Theatre Upstairs,
they get the minimum Equity salary for that particular kind of theatre.

MR. RITCHIE: I think one thing is worth saying about being on the West
End contract. Like everything else at the moment, because the financial situation is acute, one has to look for savings wherever he can
make them, and on the West End contract, for shows downstairs, we
have to have understudies. And at the moment, we are trying to get
off that contract so that we can dispense with understudies and save
on the wages.

MS. CRUICKSHANK: At the Court, there's very little interest in transfers
and in the commercial exploitation of the work.

MR. SPEER: Does the possibility of financial gain at a subsequent time
influence the selection of plays that are produced?

MR. RITCHIE: Not at all, because it would be very bad to try to behave as
impresarios. You would look very foolish if you decided to do a play
for commercial reasons, that is, because you think it will transfer and
make money, and then it fails.

MR. HALLIFAX: The idea of the West End as a gold mine is an illusion.
The transfer costs can be very large, and it takes a long time before you
can pay off those costs. It has to be an absolutely smash hit, doesn't it?

MR. WRIGHT: For the Court, it has never worked unless the theatre was
absolutely packed all of the time.

MR. HALLIFAX: And often West End audiences aren't the same kind of
audiences that have packed the Court. A play that has been a smash
hit at the Court can transfer to the West End and not draw audiences.

MR. BURGE: It would be a recipe for disaster if you started choosing a
repertoire with a view of commercial exploitation. You must keep
that repertoire in terms of your own function.

MS. CRUICKSHANK: There was a time when the main bill of the Court featured, nearly annually, a new David Storey directed by Lindsay Anderson, a new John Osborne directed by Anthony Page, a new Edward Bond directed by Bill Gaskill, and they would all run for six or seven weeks, and it seemed difficult for any other plays to get in.

They were often done as coproductions with a commercial manager as well, and there was a lot of feeling inside the Court at that time that these writers who had established themselves should move on to other auditoriums and that the Court was becoming a way for a commercial manager initially to put on a show quite cheaply. There was a little mini-revolution about it at one stage, wasn't there?

MR. WRIGHT: Yes, from the staff.

MR. BURGE: That was really why we chucked off the commercial managers from the ESC Council, because it looked bad. There was no real corruption, but it looked bad, publicly, to have West End managers on the council.

MR. WRIGHT: On the other hand, I think that with many of those shows the fact that they might transfer was thought of as good and desirable. I don't believe that Oscar Lewenstein was surprised when David Storey's *Home,* with John Gielgud and Ralph Richardson, transferred into the West End. I'm sure that before it opened Oscar thought it might have a further life.

It would be a mistake to suggest that people were always embarrassed by the thought of a West End success. Actually, it could be a very good thing if a production transferred: more people could see this very good play, and it could make money for all concerned, including the Court.

MS. CRUICKSHANK: Oh, yes. I didn't mean to imply to the contrary.

OBSERVER: I suppose that the plays are ultimately selected by the artistic director, but would there be a committee meeting in which some of the business staff and the literary managers would participate? Is there a hierarchy in the play selection?

MR. BURGE: Rob Ritchie, the present literary manager, should enlarge on this because the system of play selection, the search for new work, has developed considerably on the basis of the old system.

MR. RITCHIE: Just after I started at the Court, I talked to one or two people who had done my job before, and I was led to expect that being literary manager of the theatre was a kind of lonely, idealistic crusade and that my ideas for plays would be frustrated or ignored because no director would want to do them.

137

So there was an air of unreality to the whole job, which was mirrored in the office in which I was supposed to work at the Court. When I first started there, I had a tiny office the size of a telephone booth. It was embarrassing because when people came into the office, they assumed they had come in only to hang up their coats. And the actual working conditions of the job were such that I spent all of my time rushing around, up and down stairs trying to find plays, trying to find directors to talk to. What has happened over the years is that the system has been rationalized, in part because the staff is now so much smaller. Now, once the unsolicited manuscripts, agents' submissions, and so on have been read by outside readers, and examined by myself, those that are worth consideration for production are read by all the directors, the resident writers and myself. The plays are discussed in detail at that stage.

Ultimately, the decision of the artistic director is final; on one occasion since I have been there, the staff had fairly good support for a particular script that was not done because Max decided that he did not want to do it.

But generally, I would say that because a smaller unit of people is involved in programming the theatre, there is more of a consensus and not quite the medieval trials that David Hare describes, of wandering around a gloomy building, looking for someone who is going to share your enthusiasm for a particular script.[10]

MR. SPEER: Rob, excuse me for interrupting you, but at the meeting you described, has the business manager projected what the production cost of that particular production might be so that information is also considered at the point of play selection?

MR. RITCHIE: Because of the practical difficulties in running the theatre at the moment, most of the people on the artistic staff have to become financially literate. You have to understand the real basis of the decisions that you can make. It is no use for the artistic staff to sit around saying, yes, we'll do this or these plays, and then go to an accountant who says, "No, you can't afford it." That information is now ingested into the script meeting. So, in a way, the script meeting has become a much more general meeting instead of just a literary meeting; it takes a more thorough view of the whole process.

10. Hare said, "Every project had to be lobbied for by a medieval series of trials" (Hare, "Time of Unease," in Findlater [ed.], *At the Royal Court,* 141).

MR. BURGE: Throughout the period of the Court up until a few years ago, there was an artistic committee and sometimes two. It was a recruited group of people who were connected with the Court but not actually working there on a regular basis, a committee of devoted people, but they didn't actually have the responsibility of staging the plays. I think Christopher was an adviser on it.

MR. HAMPTON: I was on it, yes. Every meeting of the artistic committee began with a discussion as to whether the artistic committee should be dissolved. It didn't dawn on me at the time, but I think it was a kind of a puppet.

MR. BURGE: The fact that those people weren't responsible within the building led to a lot of diversionary discussion which was, in the end, distracting.

MR. WRIGHT: It worked very well when it had very strong directors on it, such as Lindsay Anderson and Anthony Page. It could be an absolute nightmare for the artistic director. But a lot of excellent work came out of it if the artistic committee had a strong director who could say, "I think this play is wonderful. You are all quite wrong, and I think it's very good, and what's more, I'm going to do it." And he would do it, and it would be very good. But it did depend on having people of experience.

MR. SPEER: How many of them actually ended up directing plays in that situation, saying, "Yes, this is a play I like very much and I will direct it." How often did that actually happen?

MR. WRIGHT: Well, it happened to all of David Storey's plays, for example, which Lindsay did, and it must have happened to many of the plays Anthony Page directed.

MR. HALLIFAX: I'm not quite sure how it is possible to produce a budget if you don't actually have your set designed, because surely that's an enormous part of the budget for a production. Did one just guess?

MR. RITCHIE: Well, it's partly guess, but you have in your head a rough working figure. Obviously, if you are doing a play in the Theatre Upstairs and it demands six sets and a cast of eight, you know that it is going to be hard to do it, given the way that you have preset the budget. If you need, then, to investigate the possibilities more thoroughly, you would have to have a more detailed financial discussion outside the script meeting.

MR. WRIGHT: Rob, is it a good thing for the people who are making artistic decisions to be financially literate? Is it an advantage or is it a kind of block you actually don't want in an artistic discussion? I mean, it's sometimes constructive not to be thinking of the size of the cast and all of that.

MR. BURGE: I don't think that Rob means that everybody is versed in accounting, but they are aware of the practical possibilities within the theatre. Obviously, it would be a waste of time to discuss endlessly the possibility of doing a play that you knew from the start was unpractical.

MR. RITCHIE: I have had meetings with writers to discuss a commissioned play for the Theatre Upstairs, where the whole purpose of the meeting has been to work out how to reduce the size of the acting company required.

MR. HAMPTON: I think that is rather disturbing.

MR. BURGE: Surely, no decisions are made on that basis, are there?

MR. HOWARTH: The mere fact that you have the meeting means that a decision is made to ask the writer to reduce the number of the cast needed for that play for the Theatre Upstairs. I find the mere fact of the meeting very disturbing.

MR. HAMPTON: For example, *Total Eclipse* (which I didn't write for the Royal Court but for Michael Codron, who commissioned it) was submitted to Codron, and he very reasonably said, "Well, it's got too many people in it, I can't do it unless you cut out several characters."

And I said, "Well, I can't do that." And I sent it to the Royal Court, and they did it. If the situation now compels people to worry about that sort of thing at the Royal Court, I think it's alarming.

MR. RITCHIE: It's true. In the case of commissioned plays, it is clear that if we are going to put on five or six productions a year Upstairs, we have to have a rough guideline as to the number of actors that each show can have.

Obviously, there is flexibility in the sense that some plays come in with two actors so you have then picked up four credits which you can move forward and then do a larger cast play at the end of the year. But the technical brief inscribed in the commission is much more detailed now, I suspect, than before.

MR. HAMPTON: Well, these considerations absolutely never crossed my mind in the earlier days.

MR. BURGE: I think it is regrettable, certainly.

MR. RITCHIE: The other option is that you just say, "Well, we'll give free range to the commissions and if that means we can only do two shows instead of six, we will do only two."

MR. WRIGHT: But sometimes it's the big shows which are really successful, like *Restoration,* or *The London Cuckolds,* both of which have very large casts. Also, *Hamlet.*

MR. RITCHIE: Well, the first thing that I did with *Hamlet* was to cut it so that we could get it down to a cast of eleven actors.

MR. HAMPTON: This wouldn't be a very good time for Shakespeare to be writing. That's the point I am making. That's what worries me.

MR. RITCHIE: Yes, it worries me; I'm not defending it. But it's increasingly the case that writers, who write on commission for theatres like the Theatre Upstairs, the Bush Theatre, the Traverse, or any of the studio theatres, are told from the outset, "Well, we can only afford four or five actors." And that does produce real constraints on the kind of work that is produced.

MR. ESSLIN: I was talking to Edward Bond about his play *Restoration,* and I said that the only thing that I disliked about it was the terrible microphones that came out for the songs. And he quite agreed with me but had to use them because the Royal Court couldn't afford lapel microphones.

MR. WRIGHT: It's not fair to be shocked by that because once you are doing a play, you have to save money all over the place, and you do end up with things which aren't exactly what you wanted.

MR. ESSLIN: That really spoiled the play to my mind, and Bond agreed with me.

MR. WRIGHT: I don't believe it spoiled the play.

MR. RITCHIE: *Restoration* is an example of a production where we refused to be hemmed in by the financial constraints and said, "This is a good play, for God's sake, we ought to be able to afford it." So we go ahead and commit doing the play because no one else will do it. And it had a big cast, with musicians, which was very expensive for the Court. And then we come up against technical problems like Martin mentions, and we don't have the money to achieve the best solution. But the play was done.

MR. WRIGHT: Yes, that is what is important. Edward Bond might think it a catastrophe that the mikes came up from the floor; actually, it doesn't really matter, compared to whether you actually do the play or not.

141

MR. BURGE: Had that play not been by Edward Bond, if it had been commissioned from an unknown author, and he had come up with that large cast, under the present system one would have had to reject it.

MR. RITCHIE: It's not a system in that sense, but I think the occasions on which you see big casts in new plays in London have been quite rare.

MR. BURGE: But you have to leave a certain margin, I'm afraid, to gamble with. You must occasionally be able to take an enormous risk and do a big cast play. You could name all sorts of occasions at the Royal Court where that has paid off because it's made a great impact.

But to get back to the point of the committee that finally selects plays, it is a very elaborate system of constant reading and passing around and putting on grades. I think all that Rob means, probably, is that those people are more aware of the technical problems than in the old days, the artistic mission notwithstanding.

MR. RITCHIE: I don't know if this is a way of measuring change, but I would say that now commissioned plays are more likely to be done than not done and that the resident dramatist's plays are done.

MR. BURGE: Very often, what happens is that the writer is commissioned for the first time, and his play may not necessarily be done, but it may lead to another play because of his involvement with the Court. I think that has always happened at the Court. It is not gambling just on that one play.

The whole business of commissioning has become more difficult for the Court now because the downstairs commissioning is really quite an investment.

MR. RITCHIE: For the rights now you pay £1,000 on assignment, and when the draft play is delivered, there is a second sum of £750. So before you decide whether you are going to do the play or not, you are committing £1,750.

MR. HALLIFAX: That is, against royalties?

MR. RITCHIE: Yes, but if you didn't do the play, you'd be writing off £1,750. The Theatre Upstairs is more flexible because the up-front money is smaller, £300 on assignment and £200 on delivery. So if you didn't do the play, you would only be writing off £500. For me, it's not the fact that the rates have gone up. After all, they're not all that substantial. If one is getting £2,000 for a play, and he writes two plays a year, you're only talking about £4,000.

MR. BURGE: It's certainly not substantial as far as a writer is concerned, it's just that commissions are tokens of confidence. That's all.

MR. RITCHIE: My view of commissioning is that rather than a random approach where you sow money here and there in the hope that something will sprout, you're a bit more careful in nurturing and in following through on each commission, an intensive rather than extensive approach to developing plays. And crucially, before you commission you see that there is a director committed to the project, who, when the play arrives, will be there to direct it.

Otherwise, it seems to me you get into situations where managers sit and say, "Yes, these ten people are wonderfully talented, and I'll commission them all." And you get ten plays that nobody wants to direct.

MR. WRIGHT: I don't see this at all. It seems to me that if the plays came in and they were good, then they would find directors and slots very fast.

MR. RITCHIE: *Restoration* was commissioned by the Royal Shakespeare Company. But no one in the company wanted to direct it.

V

Playwrights Talk: The Right to Fail

MODERATOR: *Joel Schechter, associate literary manager, Yale Repertory Theatre, and editor of* Theater

PARTICIPANTS (PLAYWRIGHTS WHOSE WORK HAS BEEN PRODUCED AT THE ROYAL COURT THEATRE):
Caryl Churchill
Christopher Hampton
David Hare
Donald Howarth
Ann Jellicoe
Stephen Lowe
Snoo Wilson

SPEAKING FROM THE AUDIENCE:
Stuart Burge
John Dillon
Martin Esslin
William Gaskill
Max Stafford-Clark
and conference observers

MR. SCHECHTER: The Royal Court has a long and varied history, much of it dependent on and changing according to the writers. It might be useful to begin by briefly surveying the connections each writer has had to the Royal Court.

MS. CHURCHILL: I first knew about the Royal Court in 1956, when I had just come back from Canada, where I had been living for quite a long time. I went to the first production of *Look Back in Anger* when I was about seventeen, and I remember liking that and having no idea that it was anything new. I mean, I didn't know what plays were like.

When I was at Oxford, I started writing plays there, and John

144

McGrath and Anthony Page saw one of my plays, and I knew that they were connected to the Royal Court, and I talked to them. And they sent my play to an agent.

I certainly thought of the Court as the only theatre there was to work for. It was very different then from what the situation would be were I just starting now, because writers have a lot of places to go. I did some student productions, and then I wrote quite a lot of short plays, which were done on radio. In 1972, I wrote a full-length play, *Owners,* which was done at the Theatre Upstairs in November of that year.

MR. SCHECHTER: Did you submit it to the theatre?

MS. CHURCHILL: No, Michael Codron, who produces plays in the West End, commissioned me to write the play, which I did. And when I had written it, my agent sent it to the Royal Court.

MR. SCHECHTER: So, in a sense your agent introduced you officially to the Royal Court.

MS. CHURCHILL: Yes. There had been one other contact with the Court. I had sent them one other full-length play before that, and I got one of those encouraging, friendly letters.

MR. SCHECHTER: From anybody we know?

MS. CHURCHILL: I can't remember. I think it was Keith Johnstone. That was my only other connection before 1972.

MR. WILSON: I was commissioned by the Royal Court in 1971–1972 to write a play, and that was my first connection. And before that, six other dramatists and myself had written *Lay By,* so I knew a little about the writers. I believed that it was another facility for showing work at that time.

I had been working with the Portable Theatre, which David Hare started, and I didn't really have any idea of how plays got on professionally.[1]

I was keen on the proscenium stage so my first play was written

---

1. The Portable Theatre, founded by David Hare and Tony Bicat in 1968, "had no permanent base," taking its new plays "on the road round the university circuit." The Portable produced plays by, among others, Howard Brenton (*Christy in Love*) and Hare (*How Brophy Made Good, What Happened to Blake*). See Naseem Khan, "The Fringe," *Drama,* CXLIX (Autumn, 1983), 9; and Jonathan Myerson, "David Hare: Fringe Graduate," *ibid.,* 26.

deliberately for that kind of space. And Oscar Lewenstein said, "Well, this is a very smart play; we will put it on in the Theatre Upstairs."[2] I was delighted to see it put on anywhere. That was my first encounter with the Royal Court. I had been reading plays occasionally for them.

MR. SCHECHTER: Probably many of you began working at the Royal Court, even before you were produced there, by reading plays.

MR. HAMPTON: It was not true of me. My first play was done by students at Oxford in 1966; the play attracted some attention. I think my tutor bribed a man who used to write for the *Guardian,* and he wrote, at any rate, a favorable review, and a certain amount of interest was generated. I then got an agent, Peggy Ramsay.

At that time, the Royal Court was more or less the only outlet for new plays. So without any further ado, she sent it to the Royal Court, who accepted it for a Sunday night production.[3] So the play was on in Oxford in February, and the Sunday night performance was in June of 1966, and that was a very fortunate start for me. But I had no connection whatsoever with the theatre and, in fact, had never seen a play there.

MS. CHURCHILL: It might be worth saying that my agent is the same agent.

MS. JELLICOE: And mine.

MS. CHURCHILL: Peggy Ramsay has played a very large part in all our lives.[4]

MR. SCHECHTER: When the scripts are received by the Court, do they pay special attention to certain agents? Is preference shown to particular writers because of their affiliations?

MR. HAMPTON: Peggy Ramsay's submissions were taken quite seriously.

MS. JELLICOE: Christopher Hampton and I have both been literary manager for the Court, David Hare, too; if Peggy sent a play, you knew she wasn't messing about, and it would be read straight away. It might

2. Snoo Wilson's *The Pleasure Principle* opened in the Theatre Upstairs on November 22, 1973.

3. Hampton's *When Did You Last See My Mother?* appeared as a Sunday night production, June 5, 1966.

4. Margaret Ramsay became the agent for many Royal Court writers, including Edward Bond, David Storey, Arnold Wesker, David Hare, and Howard Brenton. For a profile on Ramsay's career, see Mel Gussow, "Profiles (Peggy Ramsay)," *New Yorker,* May 23, 1988, 35–60.

even bypass the literary manager, but this didn't mean that the other plays weren't very carefully looked at.

A play went through a sifting process, of going out to first readers, who sent a report back to the literary manager. Speaking personally, I would read all of the reports, and I would look at a few pages of every play. And any play that the reader had any doubts on, he would send for a second opinion so you would either read it yourself, or you would send it to a second, even more experienced reader, probably within the theatre. And if it's fine with him, then you would definitely read it. But with the number of scripts coming in, you had to have that process. I was reading three scripts a day. I couldn't manage any more than that and absorb them.

If a play came in from an established writer, naturally it would go straight to myself or Oscar Lewenstein or Nicholas Wright or somebody like that.

MR. SCHECHTER: There is a famous story that John Osborne, having submitted *Look Back in Anger,* had his play selected from something like 675 scripts. No one else wanted to produce it. That must be the exception rather than the rule.

MS. JELLICOE: Well, that was terribly early on before anything was organized. I don't know that story at all.

MR. SCHECHTER: How did your original affiliation with the Royal Court begin?

MS. JELLICOE: I had won the prize in the *Observer* playwriting competition. When they told me that I had won, they said, "Would you like us to submit this to the Royal Court for you?" And I say, "Oh, yes." And within twenty-four hours I was having lunch with George Devine and Tony Richardson. It was a very weird experience.

MR. SCHECHTER: David, how did your connection begin?

MR. HARE: Well, I was literary manager first because I was an old friend of Christopher's, and I was willing to do the work load, which was very heavy for not much money. That is how I started at the Royal Court. I wasn't a writer, and when I did write a play, I didn't consider submitting it to the Royal Court.[5] It never occurred to me because, partly, I sensed that they had standards which I didn't understand and which I knew my play would not meet. I knew they wouldn't like it,

5. Hare began his career as a director for the Portable Theatre in 1968.

and I therefore didn't dream of submitting it to them. And so it was done at the Hampstead Theatre Club; it was called *Slag,* and then a year later, Bill Gaskill revived it at the Court.[6]

So I became a Court writer by a very curious process and, as I've said before, never really felt that I was something called a Royal Court writer.

MR. SCHECHTER: Did you submit other plays later on?

MR. HARE: Well, what then happened was that I became resident dramatist, whereupon they wouldn't do any of my plays. And it did, indeed, confirm the feeling that somehow I didn't fit in as a writer. In fact, it was only through working with Joint Stock with Bill Gaskill and Max Stafford-Clark that we, the three of us, so to speak, became—I like the phrase that Bond used—the Royal Court in exile. There is a sense in which Joint Stock did have that feeling. And then I did feel at home, but I never felt at home in the early days because the writers that I tried to champion were not really wanted. But, again, I didn't fight as artfully as I should have for their production.

MS. JELLICOE: Please don't imply that any of us fought artfully.

MR. SCHECHTER: But you did have to fight?

MS. JELLICOE: No. I had no art for it; I'm incapable of artful fighting.

MR. SCHECHTER: Donald, you were at the Royal Court rather early, I believe.

MR. HOWARTH: Yes, I wanted to direct, actually, so I wrote my first play, *Lady on the Barometer,* full of stage directions to show anybody who read it that I was really a director.[7] I sent it in, and they sent for me. I was immediately shown into an office to talk about the play, and I kept wanting to say, "Yes, but when can I get into production?" But somebody else directed it so I was still not a director. Instead, I was commissioned to write another one. So I had to become a writer. If anybody's got a job, I'm a very good director!

MS. JELLICOE: That was precisely why I wrote my first play, Donald. It was in order to break into directing.

MR. HOWARTH: Yes, directing is exciting. Writing's boring.

MR. SCHECHTER: Well, the Court has allowed some of you to direct.

6. *Slag* opened at the Royal Court Theatre on May 24, 1971.

7. *Lady on the Barometer* was a Sunday night production, September 14, 1958. In the following year, the play appeared on the main stage for a regular run under the title *Sugar in the Morning.*

Maybe that was one benefit of writing. Stephen, how did you go to the Royal Court?

MR. LOWE: I had a number of false starts with the Court. I sent my first play there; I had no other place to produce. Ann Jellicoe and some other people at the Court read it, and it was considered for a rehearsed reading but wasn't given one. That was about 1975. I was working as a clerk in the civil service at the time and did some script reading for the Court for about three months or so.

MS. JELLICOE: Then you went up north, didn't you?

MR. LOWE: Yes. And I think during that time at the Court, the only person I met was Ann. It was probably my fault. But I had no real sense of contact with the Court. Then I changed my name and became an actor and wrote a play, *Touched,* for the Nottingham Playhouse, which at the last minute I submitted for the George Devine Award, an award of money given by the Court.[8]

MS. JELLICOE: The money for the award was raised by the presentation of a memorial performance, given in June, 1967. They raised £20,000; the interest pays for the George Devine Award annually.

MR. LOWE: In 1976 my award amounted to £750. Later, Max Stafford-Clark commissioned me to write a play, which took a long time for me to do. And then, to my amazement, *Touched,* the play that I had done for Nottingham in 1977, was revived by Max at the Court in 1981. At Joint Stock I had done a play called *The Ragged Trousered Philanthropist* that Bill directed in 1978. But I came back to the Court when Bill directed *Touched* for the Court's main stage. *Glasshouses,* the play that I was commissioned to do, we did Upstairs at Easter, 1981. We've just done another play at the Court that I had, in fact, written for the Royal Shakespeare Company, *Tibetan Inroads,* which Bill also directed.[9] Suddenly, after a long period of time, I found the press saying that I am a Royal Court writer, whatever that means.

MR. SCHECHTER: Is there such a person as a Royal Court writer? The Royal Court has provided a number of you with not only productions but good employment at times, and I wonder if there was an effort on

---

8. Shortly after Devine's death in January, 1967, the George Devine Award was established. Jocelyn Herbert and John Osborne, among others, promoted the idea for "an annual award open to promising writers, designers or directors." They sought £20,000 to establish it (see Wardle, *The Theatres of George Devine,* 280–82).

9. *Tibetan Inroads* opened at the Royal Court September 29, 1981.

the part of the Court to provide a home for writers, a place where they could not only see productions but earn a living.

MR. HARE: It was a very fruitful experience for me in the sense that the things that the Royal Court represented, the values that they represented, I learned a great deal from. I'm talking primarily aesthetically. I learned a lot about good acting, good stage design, good lighting, the look of things, the appeal of an event that has to appeal to a bigger number of people than I'd met at the Portable Theatre. Everything that had to do with the aesthetic side of the theatre I admired very much. But the actual plays that I thought they should be putting on and the plays that they thought they should be putting on were different.

It therefore became a little hard. And because I couldn't get any of the plays on I liked or felt passionate about, it became increasingly difficult.

MS. CHURCHILL: Did those plays then get done elsewhere? Who did the plays that you felt passionate about?

MR. HARE: They were mostly done in the fringe theatres.

MS. JELLICOE: What sort of plays were they, David?

MR. HARE: I tried to get Howard Brenton's work done at the Court for a long time.

MR. SCHECHTER: He did have productions done at the Royal Court, didn't he?

MR. HAMPTON: They were always sort of grudging about it.

MS. JELLICOE: It doesn't matter whether it's grudging, as long as it gets put on.

MS. CHURCHILL: I think he was a resident writer there, wasn't he?

MR. HARE: But that was during a period of time when it was somehow incorporated into the unwritten constitution that whatever else you might do with your resident dramatist, doing his plays was not one of them.[10]

MR. SCHECHTER: And how did it evolve that the resident dramatist would not be produced?

MS. JELLICOE: Many resident dramatists' plays were knocked down. But surely your plays were done.

10. The plays of several resident dramatists were, in fact, produced by the Royal Court, including Hampton's *Total Eclipse* (1968), Whitehead's *Alpha Beta* (1972), and Brenton's *Magnificence* (1973).

MR. HAMPTON: The one that I wrote was done. It had a certain amount of difficulty getting on, and it went through a good many directors before it was finally staged, but they did do it.

MR. HARE: To get back to your question, is there such a thing as a Royal Court writer? If you look back at the people who were produced at the beginning, like Ann, John Osborne, Arnold Wesker, John Arden, they are very different sorts of writers. You can see that the Court has always been kind of pluralist as far as writers are concerned. It has done N. F. Simpson, and it has done Samuel Beckett.

MR. SCHECHTER: But certain writers returned, yourself included.

MR. HARE: Well, the only reason that writers return to a theatre is that they feel comfortable there, and the reason that they feel comfortable at the Royal Court is because it pays attention to their requirements. You get the feeling that the play is being put on in the way you want it done, and for you, and not, as often tends to happen in the theatre, for what the management can get out of it.

MR. SCHECHTER: To be more specific in terms of production, what would the Royal Court do that would encourage you as a writer, once the play had been selected for production?

MS. CHURCHILL: It would involve you. You were always involved in the casting, in rehearsal, in working intensely with the director; it is increasingly so elsewhere, but it wasn't and still isn't a totally accepted thing by all other theatres. Also, the text was taken very seriously; you didn't feel it was just an excuse for a director to do something.

MR. SCHECHTER: Did you choose your own director; how did that evolve?

MS. JELLICOE: That depended on status. Christopher has always chosen his own director.

MR. HAMPTON: I always worked with the same director, Robert Kidd.

MS. JELLICOE: Yes, but that was your choice.

MR. HAMPTON: Well, it was his choice in the sense that he chose my first play. When the script came in, he passionately wanted to do it, and it was actually his very first production ever. So we had a very close relationship, and he did all of my plays at the Court.

MS. JELLICOE: It's a mechanical thing. The directors are often meeting with the artistic director, and in the corridors directors are seeing each other every day, and seeing the artistic director every day. Obviously, if a director likes a play, he's going to push that play. Do you see what I mean?

151

MR. SCHECHTER: Would the resident dramatist or the literary manager also be involved in "pushing"?

MS. JELLICOE: Yes, absolutely, but directors tend to fall in love with plays, and if they do, they'll fight for that play because they want to do it.

MR. SCHECHTER: To what extent would it be a director's theatre, and what if a director refuses to do the play?

MS. JELLICOE: There were other directors who would do it.

MR. HAMPTON: Not necessarily. No, I think that's where the problem began to arise.

MS. JELLICOE: Can you think of an example?

MR. HARE: Yes, I think it became a director's theatre in the sense that if you have four artistic directors, the likelihood is that they are going to have four favorite writers. And, indeed, it was a happy system whereby Lindsay Anderson did Storey's plays, and Bill Gaskill did Bond's plays, and Anthony Page did John Osborne's plays, and Peter Gill did the Lawrence plays. That was terrific. Any theatre would be pleased to have those writers as regular blocks, and they were regular blocks for some years. There was a quite long period in which those people were writing a play every year or every eighteen months. But it did mean that it wasn't a writer's theatre; they were the writers whom certain directors wanted to do.

MS. JELLICOE: I remember that I didn't normally attend meetings of the council, but for some reason I was there, and Lindsay was saying something to the effect that plays should be chosen not because they were necessarily good nor because of objective standards but because Lindsay wanted to do them. And I remember feeling rather strongly that this was the wrong thing to do.

MS. CHURCHILL: But you can't choose a play on some cold objective criteria and say this is a good play.

MS. JELLICOE: True, but there should be room for that play within the repertoire so that somebody else can do it.

MR. HAMPTON: I think the point is that Lindsay is not famous for his catholic taste; therefore, the number of plays that Lindsay might want to do would not be very large.

MS. JELLICOE: True.

MR. HAMPTON: And the number of plays that he would possibly not want done—

MS. JELLICOE: Would be enormous!

152

MR. HAMPTON: Would be enormous.

MR. HOWARTH: And a director saying that he doesn't want to do a play can sink its chances, because if that director doesn't want to do it, then the management begins to have doubts about the play.

That happened with me outside the Court. Michael Codron was very keen on a play that I had written. And within two days, he had read it and was warmly ringing me up about it. What about so and so to direct it? Yes, okay. And the director read it and bowed away from it, and Michael sent the play back because he then agreed with the director. To management it is the director who has successes or is known to take plays into orbit. This was in the commercial theatre, but I think it works that way at the Court, too. If a director has reservations about a play, his disenchantment is contagious and can affect its chances of being done. More options lapse than are realized.

MR. SCHECHTER: Once the play was chosen for production, would you feel that the theatre and the director were fully behind you? There have been references to half-empty houses for certain productions, and I assume this is a sign of integrity, if nothing else; they will stand behind the work.

MS. JELLICOE: Don't say integrity with such reservations. It was very important.

MR. SCHECHTER: Would the theatre stand behind you, in the sense that they weren't concerned about whether the audience would like the play?

MS. JELLICOE: Yes, absolutely.

MS. CHURCHILL: We all felt a half-empty house was a shame because you would like more people to be there, but you didnt' feel that it had all gone wrong and that you were a failure. Nor that you were no longer a writer that they wanted to work with. You did feel supported.

MS. JELLICOE: Yes, that was one of the great strengths of working at the Court. *The Knack* was a success. But you could have a failure there, and they still wanted to see you the next day. My play *Shelley* opened Bill Gaskill's season in 1965, with disastrous notices.[11] I went in the next day, and Bill was as comforting and friendly as ever, in fact, rather more so.

MR. SCHECHTER: A few of you mentioned a policy of revivals, of bring-ing in a play from other institutions or from the fringe. This suggests

11. *The Knack* opened on March 27 1962; *Shelley* on October 18, 1965.

perhaps a different function at the Court, as a second stage in production, or a chance for a play to be seen by a larger or different audience than it might have had in the fringe.

MR. LOWE: My play *Touched* was not done on the fringe. It was done by a main house. But, in fact, when it did reach London on part of a tour, it folded on the second night. I went in on the second night, and we were closing. As it was my first play seen in London, it was a very brief stopover for me. But the Court revived *Touched*. I never felt that they had any thought about it closing, except that it should be seen, and they mounted it. One of the great things about the Court, from my point of view as a writer, is that you can create a whole team for each show. You can draw from a group of very good designers, actors, and directors. The Court is good with the kind of play that has particular types of casting problems. Mine was a regional play, and the age groups were difficult to cast. It is very difficult to do a play like that at the RSC or the National and cast it successfully. But at the Court you can do all of that with enormous care, and the prework on the play is especially good, in my experience. I have worked twice with Bill Gaskill.

MR. SCHECHTER: Is Joint Stock another variation on that? Does it have a team of sorts?

MR. LOWE: Yes, I think of Joint Stock when there is a type of subject matter that would need a workshop situation, and when you don't know that you can do it in a proscenium arch or whatever; you may want to experiment in the full, which we did do with *The Ragged Trousered Philanthropist*. I don't think that the Court can do that very successfully. I had a play at the Court which had a week's workshop and a reading at the end of the week.[12] I personally hated the reading, but I understood why we had it. And I found the week's workshop good in opening up a few things, but not in any sense in the way that Joint Stock works; it's very different, basically.

MR. SCHECHTER: Is that in part because you have more time to work at Joint Stock?

MR. LOWE: Well, at Joint Stock we took the entire company, including the designer, outside London for a month and divided half of the time in painting, decorating, and physical work. And that's very difficult

12. Lowe's *Glasshouses* was given as a rehearsed reading on September 6, 1980, and a full production in the Theatre Upstairs the following April.

154

to do; you need a structure that is not weighed down with having a theatre that has got to be open every day, and so on.

MR. SCHECHTER: Caryl, you worked with Joint Stock?

MS. CHURCHILL: Yes, in 1976 I started writing for fringe companies, which I suddenly found a lot more attractive. I wanted to work with touring companies, and with people who had more political interests, and in workshops. I wrote *Vinegar Tom* for the Monstrous Regiment that year and *Light Shining in Buckinghamshire* for Joint Stock. The latter production came back to the Court. Another play, *Traps,* which I had written earlier, was done at the Court in early 1977. The next one I wrote was again a Joint Stock play, *Cloud Nine.*[13]

MR. SCHECHTER: David and you have mentioned that the political aspect of your writing may not have been suitable for the Royal Court.

MS. CHURCHILL: No, I don't think that it is a matter of suitability. It's a matter of having a director and actors with whom you can share certain assumptions and not have to feel that you are constantly the one to be trying to push things in the direction you want them to go.

MR. LOWE: And, of course, the Royal Court is a London theatre.

MS. CHURCHILL: Yes, and London theatres have certain types of audiences.

MR. LOWE: And with Joint Stock you can tour where you want and you can pick spaces that are not theatre spaces, and so on. The Court simply can't do that. There it is in Sloane Square, with a certain type of informed audience.

MR. SCHECHTER: When the Court began, it seemed to be serving a function unusual at the time, which was to produce new plays by relatively unknown writers, who had not had any commercial success or any productions. As the fringe developed in later years, this function of the Court became less unique. Other theatres emerged to offer playwrights a chance for a first production or a London production.

MS. JELLICOE: Yes. That's because the Royal Court had led the way. That was a result of the Royal Court.

MR. SCHECHTER: This was its legacy, perhaps.

MR. HOWARTH: I think that the fragmenting occurred because of that, actually. Suddenly, the Royal Court was not the only place you could go; now there were many other places. That was a healthy develop-

13. *Light Shining in Buckinghamshire* opened in the Theatre Upstairs on September 27, 1976; *Traps,* Upstairs on January 27, 1977; and *Cloud Nine,* in the main theatre, March 29, 1979. The latter was presented again at the Court in a revised version on August 30, 1980.

ment in the theatre, but it didn't help the Court. In fact, it knocked it sideways somewhat for a year or two. From its position as a monopoly, it suddenly became just one of many theatres. There was a fundamental realignment at the beginning of the seventies.

MR. SCHECHTER: I think that this has happened within the past ten years in the United States, too, with the resident theatre movement. Theatres now actually compete for plays, usually for first productions that will create a lot of publicity or funding for the theatres.

I don't know if it is always healthy that playwrights may be treated more as property or commodities in the theatres which are seeking to buy this property. It verges on commercialism, although this sort of competition is not quite as fierce or as financially profitable in England.

MS. CHURCHILL: I didn't get the feeling that the Royal Court was competing for plays, but more of their rejecting plays they don't want, which are then sent elsewhere. It's good that there should be other places and good that the Royal Court shouldn't do plays which it feels aren't right for it.

MS. JELLICOE: What is not a Royal Court play? When I was literary manager, a play came from a woman whom I had met; she said, "Oh, I've written a play." And I thought, "Oh, my God." And I read it, and it was very good, in fact, but it was not a Royal Court play. It was a commercial play. This happened twice, and in each case one put them in touch with commercial management. They were very good commercial plays, but they were not Royal Court plays.

I tell you this to my own disadvantage, but I disliked Robert Patrick's *Kennedy's Children* so much that I turned it down; it was later a great success elsewhere. But I have no regrets about that. I don't like the play.

MR. SCHECHTER: Since you have mentioned that a few of you have served as literary managers or play readers, was that of any benefit to your own work?

MR. HAMPTON: No, I think that what would make fascinating reading is for some scholar to have the readers' reports of the Royal Court Theatre. I think people often sneaked back when, say, *Rosencrantz and Guildenstern Are Dead* was running into its third year at the National and quietly destroyed their reports. A great many very successful plays were turned down by the Court for one reason or another.

I remember finding a report on my first play which said, "I see no reason why we should do this play." And Robert Kidd, who then directed it, had written on the bottom, "Why not? I like it." But it had been filed, and it was there. Those reports are all on file at the Court.

MS. CHURCHILL: I have never looked up mine. What a wasted opportunity. Heavens!

MR. HOWARTH: John Osborne was the reader who sank my second play; he gave a negative report on it. It is not only directors who can sink your plays, colleagues can do it, too. The Court did two other plays of mine, after the first one, years later. I went away and had plays done in other theatres. I was rather like David Hare, you go and find another home. One was done in 1967 at the Court, and I was back there again in 1970.[14] But you just get your plays done where you can.

MR. HARE: I think the exhilarating thing which gets forgotten about the Court is simply that they do the hardest job in the English theatre. Any other job in the English theatre, like running the National or running the Royal Shakespeare, is a cinch compared with the job of trying to be the front-line new play theatre. That's the hardest job imaginable, because every play is a stomach-turning crisis. When Max first took over as artistic director, I met him when *Hamlet* had just opened, and he said, "Oh, I'm rather enjoying this job, you know, it's really not as bad as I thought it was going to be." And then six weeks later, he had something which was doing rather less well than *Hamlet,* and he was looking ill and down.

It is the worst possible job. And what's wonderful about the Court when you first go is that you meet people who are used to trouble; they are used to trouble with the public, they are used to seats flipping up, they are used to critical trouble, they are used to fighting the Arts Council, they are used to fighting the government, they are used to fighting the Lord Chamberlain. And so there is this minority spirit of knowing that you are doing something very, very difficult and that you are practiced in the art of doing something very difficult.

And that, to walk into the Court as I did, is very exhilarating. Particularly, if the official culture, that is, what is generally regarded

14. OGODIVELEFTTHEGASON opened on July 24, 1967; *Three Months Gone* on January 28, 1970.

as good in English culture, seems to you not terribly good. It was exhilarating to come into an organization which took minority taste seriously and never doubted its taste, although it was not the fashionable taste (and we do not stress how unfashionable the Royal Court has often been as a theatre; it is out of favor more years than it is in favor, critically and in general with theatregoing audiences)—the ease with which it accepts that role is very cheering.

MR. HOWARTH: And once a writer has had his play accepted for production, the commitment is total from all departments in the theatre. Everybody is totally behind the decision to do it.

MR. SCHECHTER: We have only a small number of the writers who have been produced at the Royal Court here, but if I'm not mistaken, there has been proportionately a smaller number of women produced in the Royal Court than in other theatres.

MS. CHURCHILL: I don't think that's true. Recently, they have been doing a lot of plays by women, though in the Theatre Upstairs, mainly. I think the majority of the new writers being encouraged by the Court at the moment are women.

MS. JELLICOE: Caryl, did you think it was a disadvantage to being a woman at the Court when you first arrived in 1972?

MS. CHURCHILL: I don't think so. No.

MS. JELLICOE: In retrospect, I feel very bitter that it was an immense disadvantage. It is very difficult territory, because it is so easy for one to say, "Oh, yes, but she wasn't very good." You know what I mean. "She wasn't such a good director or she wasn't such a good writer." I say this in light of hindsight and in light of education by the women's movement, which I think has been incredibly valuable to women. I feel that I operated, always, under a tremendous disadvantage as a woman.

I'm now going to tell a story which illustrates that bitterness I still feel, and I have never told the story in public. I apologize to Irving Wardle now, because I didn't tell it when he asked me during the writing of his book on George Devine. But I feel it is worth saying, because I want to redeem some of the sweetness and light that I spread over George Devine in our earlier sessions here. And I also want to say that I nevertheless still love him and love his memory; when you have friends, you make space for the wicked things they do.

It must have been around 1959. Keith Johnstone and I had been lovers for nearly two years. No one at the Court knew. But George found out. There was a meeting—I must have been doing something at the time—which took place without me there. And somebody complained to George that I was being a bit troublesome. Like, for instance, I wanted a pink wall instead of a green one, and George said, "Oh, just say to her, 'Shut up, you silly woman. Keith will screw you later.'" George said that an hour after he'd found out about our relationship. And that seemed to sum up for me—it wasn't the bitterness of the betrayal, it was that (even now, I feel intense resentment for that attitude) my value and work could be dismissed at that level.

And, as I say, you make room in your friendships for these things, but it seems to me of vast significance. I think I was up against that attitude all the time. And I am really quite glad to tell the story after all of these years.

MR. HAMPTON: Do you think it's changed now? Do you think that attitude still persists?

MS. JELLICOE: I think some germ of it still persists, yes, I do. I don't know how much, because now I take my life into my own hands and run my own company.[15] But it had something to do with George's nature. I was told the remark twenty minutes after he had made it. Another interesting thing about that was that Arnold Wesker knew of this affair; I mean, it was quite a relief that the news of the affair was out because it had been going on for two years. But Arnold Wesker knew almost from the beginning and never said a word to anybody. And I remember that loyalty.

MR. ESSLIN [speaking from the audience]: Wasn't there a period when Jane Howell was assistant director at the Court?

MS. JELLICOE: Jane should have taken over the theatre, but she was passed over and thus left the Court.

MR. ESSLIN: She was a sort of heir apparent, wasn't she?

MS. JELLICOE: Yes, she was a very good director.[16] She was also the

15. Ann Jellicoe founded the Colway Theatre Trust in Lyme Regis, Dorset, and served as director from 1979 to 1986. The Trust presented plays written for and put on by an entire community, using a professional core of author, director, designer, and stage manager.

16. Jane Howell directed several significant productions at the Royal Court between 1965 and 1971, including Arden's *Sergeant Musgrave's Dance* (1965), Wesker's *Roots* (1967), and Bond's *Lear* (1971).

obligatory woman. I've been sitting here feeling very paranoid about this woman's thing, because it seems to me there are so many men here at the conference and so few women.

MR. HAMPTON: Yes, but I think that there are, in fact, more women now writing.

MS. JELLICOE: Yes, but it is thanks to the women's movement, not thanks to the Court.

MR. HAMPTON: I'm not saying that it is thanks to the Court, but what I'm saying is that when I was literary manager, I remember being aware of the fact that an extremely large percentage of the plays sent were by men. And I don't actually think that's the case nowadays, is it?

MS. CHURCHILL: I don't know, but there certainly are more plays being done by women now than there were.

MR. HARE: Yes.

MS. CHURCHILL: Going back to your point, Ann, I must say that I didn't feel that. I do think there is probably a difference for women who are working within a structure for a long time, as you did; probably you do begin to realize the disadvantage you have as a woman. Whereas, if you are just working as a writer, and come along and work on a play, then it is easier not to notice.

MS. JELLICOE: Yes, but there is another thing that operates against women in the theatre, and that is that most critics are men. Irving, I hope you don't take offense. Irving Wardle is a good friend and has always, even when he's felt he had to be negative, tried to be kind, shall we say. But theatre is based upon identification. And if you are a woman writing plays, you are only too conscious that the critics are men and are, naturally, not going to identify, in a way, with women.

When I was literary manager of the Court, quite unconsciously I discovered at least three women playwrights, not because I was looking, or was positively biased, or anything like that, but simply because I was interested.

MR. SCHECHTER: Since you bring up critics, let me ask, would the impact of critics have affected your own attitudes toward production at the Court? For a time, I worked at the American Place Theatre, where we gave the playwrights the option of not having the critics review a play. Would this have been preferable at times, not to have had the Court production reviewed?

MR. HAMPTON: When we tried that the critics had a strike against the

160

Royal Court because one of the critics was excluded. Not excluded but, in fact, not invited.

MS. CHURCHILL: Not given his free seats?

MR. HAMPTON: *Her* free seats.

MS. CHURCHILL: Who was it?

MR. ESSLIN: It was Hilary Spurling.[17]

MS. JELLICOE: Don't joke. I'm in no mood for joking.

MR. ESSLIN: I'm not making this into a joke. It just happens to be a woman.

MR. HAMPTON: It so happened that Hilary Spurling left a production in the Theatre Upstairs and was therefore no longer invited to the new productions. And then all critics stopped coming for awhile; is that not right?

MR. HOWARTH: It's true, yes. There was a sort of boycott.

MR. HARE: Yes, a boycott by the critics. This mysteriously annoyed everyone at the Court. I would have thought it was what they had been wanting for years.

MS. JELLICOE: Critics are free publicity. There is no getting away from it.

MR. HAMPTON: I suppose so.

MS. JELLICOE: An avant-garde magazine called *Time Out,* which the Court has discovered that it relies on, has been on strike for several months; correct me if I'm wrong, Max, but the notices not appearing in *Time Out* have had a tremendous effect on the box office. Am I right?

MR. STAFFORD-CLARK [speaking from the audience]: It did. It did not have much effect on the play running downstairs because we had reviews on that play when we opened it. But upon the new play opening Upstairs, it had a certain effect.

Let me take up your point about women writers. It's certainly true that the best plays about personal discovery have been written by women over the last five years. It certainly is true that a great deal of the best unsolicited work is by women, such as a play I did by Andrea Dunbar, *The Arbor,* and one by Sarah Daniels, *Ripen Our Darkness.* It is also true that the plays that experiment in form have tended to be by women.

17. On October 2, 1969, the Court announced in a press release that it would no longer provide free tickets to Hilary Spurling, theatre critic for the weekly *Spectator.* When the Arts Council threatened to withhold the Court's grant unless tickets were restored to the *Spectator,* the Court acceded (Browne, *Playwrights' Theatre,* 88–89).

MS. CHURCHILL: *Cloud Nine* had some good notices on tour, but in London the first-time notices were quite mixed. And I did feel very conscious that the critics were men. But the second time around, having been successful and having had full houses, we got notices saying, "I like this even more than the first time. We're glad to welcome back this wonderful play." But the first time, they were disconcerted, I did get the feeling.

MS. JELLICOE: I remember now that the Hilary Spurling in question was the only female critic who reviewed one of my plays, and she was the only person who gave that particular play a good notice. I'm not saying that women critics should write good notices of women's plays, but I say that they are more likely to empathize with them.

MR. SCHECHTER: I have one other question. Since I have asked you about your entrances at the Royal Court, I would like to ask about the exits. Most of you have already worked with other theatres or did so prior to the Royal Court productions that you had. As a result of having had a production at the Royal Court, have you found that you have benefited in other productions? Christopher, you have said that, now, for the first time, you are writing for theatres other than the Royal Court. Is this a different experience?

MR. HAMPTON: I have written a play now for the Mark Taper Theatre in Los Angeles, and it's my first play which will not open at the Royal Court.[18] And so far, we are in an initial stage. It's very hard to say what the differences are. Immediately, the difference seems to have to do with the difference between the American theatre and the English theatre. In America the play is regarded as a sort of mass of raw material to be somehow improved and knocked into shape, whereas that would not be the case at the Royal Court. They took one's play, warts and all, and did it.

Now, I don't know that at this stage I'm an authority to argue one case against the other. All I know is that it is something that one has to deal with; one has to decide, am I going to go with all this business of improving the play before it opens, or am I going to resist it. I can't tell you what the result will be.

18. Hampton's *Tales from Hollywood* was produced at the Mark Taper Forum Theatre in March, 1982, and appeared at the National Theatre in London the following year.

MR. SCHECHTER: Well, at the Court, I would think that there were times when you were asked to rewrite or suggestions were made?

MR. HAMPTON: Hardly ever. There was a problem with my play *The Philanthropist,* which seemed (to everyone) headed for disaster, and I did try to rewrite it during rehearsals, without any success at all. I don't know whether this is a good thing or not.

It's not that I didn't want to rewrite plays, it's that (a) no pressure was put on me to rewrite, and (b) I felt disinclined to rewrite, and therefore the scripts were considered "done." What would be for an American theatre a first draft, was, at the Court, "done."

MR. SCHECHTER: I find this very unusual.

MS. CHURCHILL: At Joint Stock you're under the pressure of time and people are seeing the script the minute you've written it so you rewrite during rehearsal. Whereas, my plays for the Court were put on virtually without any rewriting.

MR. SCHECHTER: Was this always the case at the Court, that the play was more or less finished?

MR. LOWE: I really didn't rewrite until we worked with Joint Stock and then there's so little time, you tend never to stop writing. *Touched* was done fairly intact. The latest play at the Court, *Tibetan Inroads,* I was still rewriting two days before we opened. I will rewrite as long as the actors are willing to learn the lines and remember the cuts, and then I tend to stop.

And I don't mind that at all because often, particularly if you do very exotic work, decisions about the staging will begin to affect the way that it is done; they're normally technical considerations.

OBSERVER: Bill Gaskill has said that now with the increased opportunities for playwrights at other theatres, at the Court you can no longer say to them, "If you rewrite the play, we'll do it." Because then they would just say, "Right," and take the play elsewhere. What was the Royal Court's policy on rewriting? Were productions offered contingent on rewriting?

MR. GASKILL [speaking from the audience]: We might say, "Look, it needs work and let's not schedule it until it is reworked."

But I would think that that is rare in the Court. We tend to say, "Look, I think it needs work, but I am prepared to do it as it stands if you can't make it any better." You know, there is that initial commitment to a writer. "Well I might do it if you make it better" is a very poor commitment to a writer. That puts him in a terrible situation, and then he goes away. But at the Court, most of the time we say, "Well, if you can make it better, rewrite." I think that all of the plays at the Court are really done on that assumption.

OBSERVER: Christopher, did you do any rewriting on *Total Eclipse* when you worked with David Hare? [19]

MR. HAMPTON: Yes, to a certain extent. When there is a thirteen-year gap since the original production, there are clearly defects in the play, which over the years sink in, although during the time of the initial production, I was still very pleased with the play. I think that's often the case; I think it does take a few years. Because the emotional intensity of having the play done is so great, it is very hard to find one's way to what is wrong with the play. So thirteen years passed, and David was extremely clear on what he thought needed attention. Since in most cases it coincided with what I thought needed attention, it was not a difficult job. It was very easy to do, and I think the play is much better as a result of that.

OBSERVER: Did you rewrite before you went into rehearsal?

MR. HAMPTON: Yes.

MR. HARE: It is true that there was a certain point at which there were things upon which we agreed. I thought, "Oh, this is rather youthful overwriting here." But then I suddenly thought, "Fuck that, youthful overwriting is what this play is. Part of the joy of this play is its youth, and if we start taking that out, then we are actually destroying what the play is." And most important, we have no duty to incorporate the arguments against this play. It's not our job to put in what the likely objections to this play are going to be. The play, by being something, by definition will not be something else, you see. And I think Bill is right that a lot of unscrupulous rewriting is done which results in making plays more like each other and less like themselves. There is a certain point at which the writer has to say, "No, that's what I think. That's what I believe, and if you don't like it, don't do it."

I think this sort of endless tizzing about is a neurosis that comes out of commercial pressure or the director wanting to bump himself up beyond the job of director, which is a humiliating job for a fully grown man or woman to do for a living.

---

19. *Total Eclipse* first appeared at the Royal Court in 1968, directed by Robert Kidd; it was revived in 1981 at the Lyric, Hammersmith, with David Hare directing.

MR. SCHECHTER: Perhaps we should open the floor to questions.

OBSERVER: I am curious about the creative process. Do most of you work from a scenario at all?

MS. CHURCHILL: None of us know how we work!

MR. WILSON: Usually, the idea of writing a synopsis in advance is quite a misleading one for a writer. A synopsis generally, for writers, comes at the end of a piece of work.

MR. HAMPTON: Exactly. That's true.

MR. BURGE [speaking from the audience]: I think sometimes there are justifications for asking an inexperienced writer who obviously has a blazing talent to do some rewriting. I can give you an example of that. I'm not sure who was at the Court at that time, but *The Ruling Class* by Peter Barnes was controversial; it had been rejected by the RSC and nobody really had any interest. I just happened to be in a good mood when I read it and seriously thought it should be done, but it was a practical problem of sheer size and length. I helped Peter Barnes edit it, and we put it on at the Nottingham Playhouse. And to a certain extent that was true of *The Glad Hand* by Snoo Wilson at the Court.[20]

MR. WILSON: Oh, yes. Very much so. *The Glad Hand* was a play that was definitely reassembled with the director, because the author was incompetent to do so. And another play before that, *The Pleasure Principle,* which David Hare directed, had a really depressing third act with two prematurely aged people sitting in a garden talking—I can't remember about what—but they were sitting there, and it was all very gray and David said, "Well, this is a bit bleak, you know."[21] It was in three acts, and even if the audience had to sit through only two acts, they'd get totally depressed. So I thought that was a reasonable point of view from the perspective of the director. I took it away and relocated it and rewrote it and gave it an ironic happy ending. And I think that improved the play enormously.

The problem with *The Glad Hand* was that it had kind of fallen apart in my head, and only the smaller pieces could get out. The author had lost control. At the time I wrote it, I was dramaturg for the RSC, and I had written one play for them which did not do terribly well. Then I wrote another one, and I couldn't interest any of the directors in it, and they just let it go, and I had to put it in workshops

20. *The Glad Hand* opened on the Court's main stage on May 11, 1978.
21. *The Pleasure Principle* opened in the Theatre Upstairs on November 23, 1973.

to demonstrate it to them. And I got very depressed, and because I got depressed I lost control of the structure of the play. And I think the idea of warmth and welcome, however grudging it is, the idea of contact with a theatre is terribly important to writers. Writing is such a boring job. No one in his right mind would do it.

MS. JELLICOE: On the contrary, I think it's a privileged job. I know it's hard. It's terribly hard. But it's a privilege to anybody who can have this extraordinary alternative—between working intensely hard on one's own, and then working intensely hard with people who are incredibly dedicated to what you are doing.

I would like to take up this business of scenarios. I think every writer works his own way. Some people work it out in their heads entirely, like Edward Bond. I doubt that he would submit a scenario.

I think scenarios are beloved of people who want to chop plays or films about. In my opinion plays are not written, certainly not by me, stage by stage, in scenarios. They are written as a sort of three-dimensional thing in one's mind; one senses along. Frankly, I think a scenario is a hostage of the devil, because the reader starts saying, "Well, don't you think that if you did this, it would be better?" It is a means whereby essentially untalented parasites can keep their tabs on the artist while they put in their three pence worth.

OBSERVER: Is there an imbalance between the new writers coming up and the older writers of the Royal Court?

MR. HAMPTON: Yes.

OBSERVER: Could you give a clear reason why?

MR. HAMPTON: I think the most obvious reason to me is the availability of alternative theatres.

MR. GASKILL: During my operation of the Court, I think we had become conservative, I mean, myself, Lindsay Anderson, and Anthony Page, who were running the theatre. Perhaps we weren't altogether in sympathy with the new movement. I was very ambivalent.

The Court went through a rather schizophrenic stage when the Theatre Upstairs was formed in 1969; but when you have a studio theatre, you immediately have a division. You say, "Right, we'll put the experimental writers upstairs, and we will do the safe plays downstairs." A division in the theatre emerges.

At the Court that division lasted for quite a long time. In a way, it is still there. I don't think the Court's ever recovered from it: "This is an exciting play and we should do it in the Upstairs."

166

Certainly, Edward Bond's plays were developed in the main house from the very beginning. He was a big stage writer and his epic plays, like *Lear,* were staged on all the vast stages of Europe; he was never a fringe writer. Most new plays now go on in fringe theatres, and they are never exposed to a larger stage, a more severe critical apprehension. The critical scrutiny of a proscenium stage production is tougher than that of an experimental theatre.

MR. SCHECHTER: There is a parallel in the American theatre at present; a number of resident regional theatres have developed what they call their second or smaller stage, and they attempt to relegate experimental writing to this other smaller space as if it's a second-class form of drama that has to be tried out and proven extensively before it can move to the larger space and larger audience. So it may be an international phenomenon in some ways.

MR. DILLON [speaking from the audience]: I think at the Milwaukee Rep we actually have the opposite problem. The second stage becomes the playground and the main stage starts to get very startling shows.

MR. ESSLIN: This is the case with the National Theatre, where the Cottesloe is by far the more popular theatre with directors, and certainly, also with the theatregoers. So that's where the best work is being done.

MR. SCHECHTER: So we need more smaller theatres?

MR. ESSLIN: No, I think that the point that Bill makes is absolutely true. Playwrights tend to write for the venues which are available, and if suddenly a venue is not available, then they will tend to go somewhere else.

MR. HOWARTH: The danger in the bureaucracy of institutional theatre (which the Court is) lies in deciding what sort of plays should be done. It has to be left to the writer, not to the theatre, to decide how many characters there are going to be, whether twenty or seven, and the theatre has to cope with that and not prescribe when they commission a play what they want to fit in their building.

If the writer is writing a play which he hopes will be performed, he must be trusted to have enough sense to know whether ten or eight people or twenty are right for the piece of work he's creating. If that is not going to be within the theatre's capacity, and they are going to withhold the thousand pounds, then that theatre shouldn't interest that writer. I think there's a danger when the commissioning of work involves certain things a writer should be expected to come up with.

167

MR. STAFFORD-CLARK: I think that the times have changed a great deal, and it seems quite clear that we would be unable now, however enthusiastic we felt about Wesker's *The Kitchen,* to mount a production of it.[22] It is quite inconceivable for us to do a production of a new play with more than ten or eleven characters downstairs because that would take a whole year's budget.

MR. SCHECHTER: Is this primarily an economic problem? You can't afford to do it?

MR. STAFFORD-CLARK: Yes, certainly. If you look at the history of the Court, the average size of the casts for new plays done has shrunk year by year. We can no longer afford to take a chance on plays like *A Patriot for Me* or *The Kitchen* because, regardless of the play's success, there would be no money left to do any other plays that year.[23]

MR. SCHECHTER: Does this mean that by default the National and, perhaps, the RSC would be the only theatres left that can do these large-scaled plays?

MR. STAFFORD-CLARK: I would say so, yes, the large-cast plays.

OBSERVER: But even they don't do the large-cast new plays, do they?

MR. HAMPTON: They do, yes. Such as Howard Brenton's *The Romans in Britain.*

MR. HOWARTH: Is Edward Bond's *Restoration* a big cast?[24]

MR. STAFFORD-CLARK: *Restoration* has ten actors in it and six musicians as well. So that's the absolute limit.[25]

MR. HARE: Another advantage of the National Theatre, which is worth saying, is that because it is a repertoire system and presents a new play only twice a week, one is not so dependent on the critical reaction. My play *Plenty* was rather glumly reviewed, which did hurt the box office at the National for about two or three weeks, and then the audience transformed the play into a hit. It then ran a very long time to full houses, but it went through a period which the Royal Court could not have sustained. That's to say that it went through four weeks of playing to low houses and only twice or three times a week. Then the

22. The original shortened version of *The Kitchen* was given a Sunday night production on September 6, 1959; the full-length version opened for a regular run on June 27, 1961, with a cast of twenty-seven.

23. Osborne's *A Patriot for Me* opened on June 30, 1965, with a cast of thirty-seven.

24. Bond's play opened at the Royal Court on July 21, 1981.

25. Actually, there were thirteen actors.

number of performances can be increased once the audience creates the word-of-mouth.

And, for that, I was immensely grateful because otherwise the play would have gone down the funnel. The repertoire system is very good for large-scaled new plays.

MR. STAFFORD-CLARK: That's quite true. Even though a play is a hit at the Court, it takes about two or three weeks to take off.

MR. BURGE: The Court really has no means of selling a play except by transferring it to the West End.

MR. SCHECHTER: What is the length of a play's run at the Royal Court now?

MR. STAFFORD-CLARK: The runs do vary. For example, Bond's *Restoration* ran for eight weeks, *The Sea Gull* ran for two weeks, while Andrea Dunbar's *The Arbor* ran for four weeks in order to recoup the production costs.[26] As a matter of policy, I would run the play that is successful and make room in the program for the plays I'm taking a chance on.

The average run is four weeks with an option for another two, whether it is taken up or not. If we think the houses will be good, we run for ten weeks. But we have to run that long to recoup production costs.

MR. HAMPTON: That's a real change, isn't it?

MR. STAFFORD-CLARK: Not really. It's actually a policy that dates to a very early stage. *Look Back in Anger* had over 250 performances at the Court. And it was revived twice or three times.[27]

MR. GASKILL: In the first two years at the Court, and briefly later, we could not entirely do new plays; we had to have a new play bolstered by a revival.

MR. STAFFORD-CLARK: Ionesco's *Exit the King,* with Alec Guinness, played sixty performances in 1963.[28] A look at the calendar of per-

26. Of the three productions, only *The Arbor* did not recoup production costs, which amounted to £9,452, while box office receipts were £6,897. For *The Seagull,* costs were £37,370 and receipts, £41,687; for *Restoration,* costs were £39,368 and receipts, £39,899 (see Findlater [ed.], *At the Royal Court,* Appendix 2, Financial Tables, for the years ending April 4, 1981, and April 3, 1982).

27. *Look Back in Anger* initially opened on May 8, 1956, and ran 151 performances; it was revived March 11, 1957, for 104 performances and had a second revival on October 29, 1968, for 52 performances.

28. *Exit the King* opened on September 12, 1963.

formances over the years reveals very clearly that the long run is not unusual.

OBSERVER: Did you run *Hamlet* long?

MR. STAFFORD-CLARK: Yes, and we could have run *Hamlet* longer, but a shorter run was necessary because of the economic conditions the actors were working under. In order to run it longer, one would have had to up the actors' wages or move into a larger theatre where the production could have a bigger return. Besides, Jonathan Pryce's commitment to the play was for ten weeks, and he would have been reluctant to remain any longer.

The West End is no longer the enticement for actors that it used to be. Certainly, *Cloud Nine* had the possibility of transferring, but four out of the six or seven actors in the cast didn't want to commit themselves for as long as six months or whatever.

MR. BURGE: A huge advantage to the Court would result if one could schedule runs for at least ten weeks and then make decisions about whether to continue it or not once the play recovers its costs. Under our present restraints, one can't schedule, certainly a new play, for more than, say, six weeks, because you must be prepared for the next production before that play opens. Otherwise, in the event of inadequate box office the theatre will be dark during the preparation and rehearsals of the next play.

MR. STAFFORD-CLARK: I think that we are now considering quite seriously the option of fewer productions for longer runs because it is quite clear that the grant, as we said earlier, might be withdrawn completely. That's not likely, but it is possible. I think it's very, very likely that we'll have a standstill, and that amounts to a cut in real terms.[29] I think we will have to consider our options very carefully and that may well be to go dark for periods, to shut the Theatre Upstairs, or to go cooperative.

MR. ESSLIN: At one time, the Court ran a play without charging admission. That was a very important experiment, too.

MR. HAMPTON: That was *Life Price,* which came through the post by two unknown writers, and it was directed by Peter Gill without any well-

---

29. As it turned out, in 1982 the Arts Council raised the grant to £453,000. The previous year, the grant had been £424,000. The increased grant still did not match inflationary costs.

known actors.[30] And after two or three days, the audiences were very, very small and the management decided to make the tickets free, which caused an absolute outrage and furor in the Arts Council, together with a very strongly expressed theory that nobody would come. The thing was announced on the weekend, and by Tuesday at lunchtime, all seats for the entire run were gone. The audience enjoyed the play enormously. It transformed what seemed like a deathly failure into a real success. It would be a wonderful policy, actually. In an ideal world enough subsidy would be forthcoming that people would not have to pay for their tickets.

MR. SCHECHTER: This might diminish royalties somewhat.

MR. STAFFORD-CLARK: Let me mention a theatre ticket dilemma for Edward Bond's *Restoration*. On Monday nights, tickets are £2, the rest of the week they're graduated from £5.30 to £2, or with bad sight lines, £1.50.[31] In fact, although the house averaged 40 percent attendance throughout the run, the only nights the house was full, absolutely full, were on four Monday nights out of the eight Monday nights the play was done. So Monday night changed from being invariably the worst night of the week to the best in terms of attendance.

MS. CHURCHILL: For some productions, all the seats were under £2.

MR. SCHECTER: Maybe you should lower all the seats to £2.

MR. STAFFORD-CLARK: If we did, we wouldn't even make enough money to pay the cast. We take £650 net on Monday night if the theatre is full, £1,350 on Saturday if it's full.

MR. HOWARTH: In conclusion, I would like to make a personal statement regarding the sensitivity that Ann was expressing about what female writers felt.

Imagine that you were a black female writer or a black male writer at the Court, which is run by a completely white artistic committee (most institutions are run by white artistic committees). If you were to try to get your play on, you would have a much tougher time than if you were just a white woman.

---

30. *Life Price* opened on January 9, 1969, and for the first ten days played to virtually empty houses; for the last two weeks of its run, seats were offered free, which the public quickly grabbed up, filling the theatre to capacity every night.

31. In 1985, ticket prices at the Royal Court Theatre still ranged from a low of £2 (or £1.50 to members of the Royal Court Theatre Society) to a high of £6, or about $3 to $9.

MS. JELLICOE: I don't agree. I think the black writers were treated very well at the Court, and there were quite a lot of them. And actually, maybe Americans will put me right on this, but American black women have said that it is a far more difficult situation being a woman than being black.

MS. CHURCHILL: I would agree with Donald about the present situation. At the moment, women can feel reasonably welcome at the Court, and there is quite a good feeling among women for what the Court has been doing. But some black writers feel very bad about the Court at the moment. They don't feel that their plays are as welcome as before.

There was a time when black writers were being done, but the new generation of black writers that are coming up are choosing to go elsewhere; some do feel unwelcome at the Court.

VI

Designers Talk: Objects in Open Space

MODERATOR: *Karl Eigsti, designer, New York*

PARTICIPANTS: *Deirdre Clancy, designer, 1967–1973*
William Gaskill, artistic director, 1965–1972
Michael Hallifax, general stage manager, 1956–
1969
Donald Howarth, playwright

SPEAKING FROM THE AUDIENCE:
Stuart Burge
Caryl Churchill
Martin Esslin
Christopher Hampton
Stephen Lowe
Irving Wardle
Snoo Wilson
and conference observers

MR. EIGSTI: Our participants in this session on design at the Court have worked at the Royal Court Theatre over a number of years. I would like to ask each of you to give his or her own view of design at the Court. Perhaps you could focus on the visual aspect with regard to a writers' theatre. It seems to me that one of the important aspects of designing plays, new plays in particular, is to arrive at the successful visual imagery that those plays suggest.

In addition to questions about the historical and pragmatic aspects of design at the Court, I would like to ask, how do you achieve a visual style out of plays which have never seen the light of day?

MR. HALLIFAX: I think very interesting is the original conception that Margaret "Percy" Harris, of the Motley design firm, had for what was really meant to be a permanent surround for the Royal Court. Although Richard Findlater's book *At the Royal Court* notes that the

173

white canvas surround with black netting was the original design, it wasn't. Initially it was to be white canvas. As soon as we got on the stage (after Sam Wanamaker's production of *The Threepenny Opera* left toward the end of February, 1956), we had about a month to get ready for the first season of the English Stage Company. We put up the white canvas so that Percy Harris at last was able to see it. The actual design very simply was a canvas cloth against the back wall. In front of that, there was an opening of ten or twelve feet, and then on either side was a curve, a complementary curve, and joining the gap, at about three feet downstage of the gap, was a panel, again of canvas, which could close the gap or, obviously, when it was flown, you could see right through to the back wall. And then downstage, left and right—down the right-hand side and left-hand side of the stage— were some slow S's that were battened out on metal tubing. These made the sides look slightly more interesting.[1]

The stage therefore had not only the assembly entrances (which were through the stage boxes, left and right) but also had downstage entrances, *i.e.*, downstage of these slow S's, one side of which went, practically, into the stage manager's lap. And on the other side, one was practically against the side wall of the building. Then there were two entrances upstage of the slow S's and also one had the two entrances either side of the center panel upstage.

But, of course, the effect when we saw it in Berlin during *Mother Courage* was, as far as I can remember, just clear canvas.[2] At the Court it was too bright and sharp; it looked too hard. So Percy Harris said, "Oh, I know a little man in Northumberland who makes fish netting. We must get some of that." We got in touch with the little man, and

1. Wardle has written, "In his brief to Harris, Devine had asked for the stage masking to be shaped so as to suggest that it led on to further space beyond; and executed in some non-associative material through which light and air could pass. 'We want something which will seem as impermanent and of the moment as the life that takes place on the stage.' Harris [solved] this problem by making a divided surround, consisting of two S-shaped side pieces and a panel that dropped in connecting with the two upstage ends of the S. Viewed from in front, the effect was that of a wrap-round cyclorama equipped with six invisible exits. The panel, when not required, could be flown, opening up the full stage area to the back wall" (Wardle, *The Theatres of George Devine*, 172).

2. Hallifax was stage manager for Devine's production of *King Lear*, which played in Berlin in the fall of 1955. At that time, Devine met Brecht and Helene Weigel, and many of the company went to East Berlin to see the Berliner Ensemble perform.

he sent down this enormous amount of netting, and it worked fine. You weren't conscious of it, but it did break the solidity of that wall.

So we were ready for our first production, Angus Wilson's *The Mulberry Bush,* which opened on April 2, 1956. The set had a door, and I think, a French window; in one act we were on the inside looking out of it, and in another act, we were on the outside looking in. And we had a huge mulberry tree which had no leaves; all of the branches were very spiky. I can remember the absolute horror of it because all those little branches caught in the netting when we were trying to do the change. But it all worked for the first play. For the second, *The Crucible,* Stephen Doncaster designed an excellent, very simple setting. He had just a ceiling, open beams that were put in various angles to indicate the size of the house and the shape of roof, so that when one got into the house and the girl sees the bird under the beam, that actually worked very well.

We then did *Look Back in Anger.* That was the first clash I had with a designer, Alan Tagg, who went on to do an enormous number of productions at the Court. Poor chap, he said, "Well, here's my set." And I said, "Well, we're not allowed to use sets." Needless to say, I lost. He said, "There has got to be an attic. You have to contain these people." You had to have the window so that when the "bloody bells" were ringing, the window could be slammed down to reduce the noise of the bells. You had to have a place where Jimmy Porter was going to play his trumpet, and so on. So, very unwillingly, we had this set. There was very little space offstage, if any, and the only storage space was up left where there was a dock down a couple of steps, where we had to put everything. And so Alan Tagg's actual flats for *Look Back in Anger* were irritating to say the least.

MR. EIGSTI: With *Look Back in Anger,* what did you do with the basic surround?

MR. HALLIFAX: That stayed. It was visible.

MR. EIGSTI: So that the set for *Look Back in Anger* was basically a room surrounded by—

MR. HALLIFAX: It was a room with a view at the top. But, of course, the surround was a bit dark, and you weren't conscious of it.

MR. EIGSTI: Was it a conscious decision to incorporate the surround or to try to ignore it?

MR. HALLIFAX: I think if you put it that way, to ignore it, yes.

175

MR. EIGSTI: But later on, in 1959, in Arnold Wesker's *Roots*, Jocelyn Herbert used it.[3] In actual fact that is a typical thing from the Berliner Ensemble, the room cut off at eight feet, or something like that, and then seeing over it into the theatre void.

MR. HALLIFAX: Yes.

MR. EIGSTI: I was wondering whether, as a compromise, it became a design decision or if it was just, "Well, this is all we can do."

MR. HALLIFAX: It was a design decision because there it was, really, from the early days. And that was where it was going to stay; therefore, the designers had to adapt into the surround. But it worked very well for *Look Back*. It was just a part of the scenery, that's all. The surround wasn't lit, but, of course, it got reflections of light.

MR. EIGSTI: Were the lights exposed for that production, too?

MR. HALLIFAX: I can't quite remember. What I do remember is taking the borders out. We obviously had them for *The Entertainer* because I can remember taking them out.[4] I won't go through the whole lot, but really that initial concept of the surround stayed for a long time. The first production that really broke away from it was *Member of the Wedding*, at the beginning of 1957. It had a house, trees, and Spanish moss. There was massive scenery in that one.

MR. EIGSTI: That was the first production without the surround? The surround was gone by that time?

MR. HALLIFAX: Apparently it hadn't gone completely because I can remember it coming back in other things. We used it in *Purgatory*, for instance. And Jocelyn Herbert used it in *The Chairs*.[5] In some way,

3. Before World War II, Jocelyn Herbert was a student at Michel Saint-Denis' London Theatre Studio, managed by George Devine. In 1956 he engaged her as a scene painter for the Royal Court, where she designed her first production, Ionesco's *The Chairs*, and thereafter became recognized as one of the leading designers in contemporary English theatre. Her designs for the ESC include Ionesco's *The Lesson, The Chairs*, and *Exit the King;* Beckett's *Krapp's Last Tape* and *Endgame;* Wesker's *Roots, The Kitchen, Chips with Everything, Chicken Soup with Barley*, and *I'm Talking About Jerusalem;* John Arden's *Sergeant Musgrave's Dance;* Osborne's *Luther* and *A Patriot for Me;* Chekhov's *The Seagull;* Christopher Hampton's *Savages;* David Storey's *Home, The Changing Room, Cromwell, Life Class*, and *In Celebration;* Joe Orton's *What the Butler Saw;* and David Hare's *Teeth 'n' Smiles* (see Jarka M. Burian, "Contemporary British Scenography, Part I," *Theatre Design and Technology*, XIX [Spring, 1983], 7–9).

4. John Osborne's *The Entertainer* opened April 10, 1957.

5. Carson McCuller's *The Member of the Wedding* opened on February 5, 1957; Ionesco's *The Chairs* on May 14; and Yeats's *Purgatory* on July 22.

there was some gauze involved in *The Chairs* because I remember that she suddenly found that if you get lights on the gauze at a certain angle, it makes an extraordinary sort of watered silk effect. And I can remember her discovering that, simply because of the effect of the light as we caught it there.

Because of working in repertoire, the business of taking scenery in and out of the dock in these small theatres always is a matter of having to take about four lots of sets out, in order to get the one you want, or when you are packing them away at night, making sure that the next one you want is brought to the front.

We had no permanent stage staff as such, except for one stage manager. The boys who used to come in had a variety of jobs, such as working on the tube (London underground transport system), and two of them were meter readers for the London Electricity Board. But they would come in whenever they were free. They used to go out to read meters at a terribly early hour in order to be able to work in the theatre. And they used to come with these horrific stories about how they had to waken people at an early hour in order to get their meters read so they could come along and work at the Court. They were incredibly loyal and a very, very good bunch of people. In fact, it's often those sort of people that kept the Court going.

MR. EIGSTI: This was preunion days?

MR. HALLIFAX: Oh, yes, yes. I ignored the union then, I'm afraid. We had nothing to do with it.

MR. EIGSTI: Were the plays in repertoire?

MR. HALLIFAX: In the beginning, yes.

MR. EIGSTI: When did that system change—going from repertoire to a single run?

MR. HALLIFAX: I think it changed with *Good Woman of Setzuan* in October, 1956. And then *The Country Wife,* which opened in December, had a solid run. I'm sure that wasn't in rep.

MR. EIGSTI: So did the visual look change with that shift from plays rotating in repertoire?

MR. HALLIFAX: Oh, yes.

MR. EIGSTI: That surround probably disappeared shortly after the rotating rep closed out. Yet it didn't quite disappear because one had to have some sort of a backing and obviously it saved money. It served as an eye, of a kind?

177

MR. HALLIFAX: Yes, that's right. And *The Country Wife* was very interesting. The design was, again, by Motley. It was a black and white
production, and she wanted it so that one could practically see
through everything, so we made the furniture quite thick. I think it
must have been in perspex, or what was called perspex in those days,
and then she painted the shape of the Chippendale chairs, or whatever
the period was, on to this quite thick perspex, which had the effect of
being able to see through. In Richard Findlater's book a steep ramp is
mentioned. The stage at the Court was slightly raked, with a steep
ramp; the actors wore high scarlet heels in *The Country Wife,* and it
was very difficult. They were playing in a period piece, which, for
many, wasn't their forte. But we had a repertoire company, and they
had to join in.

   When we did *The Entertainer* we used the traps which were there.
They were the original traps in the theatre, the kind in which the
panel dropped and then it slid down on these very beautifully made
runners. I suppose they were the original 1880s traps.

   The floors were beautiful wood. Once we started using the trap in
The Entertainer, Tony Richardson became besotted by it. When we
took *Look Back in Anger* to America, we went into the Lyceum, which
was enormous, and our tiny set appeared as if in a great ocean. But we
had some gauzes there and an enormous surround. Also we did have a
trap so that we could see when Cliff went down to get the soap.

   I remember, also, that Faulkner's *Requiem for a Nun* in November,
1957, was beautifully designed by Margaret Harris, and I think we
must have used again the permanent surround simply as a cyclorama
for that. We dropped the repertoire idea because it was too costly.

MS. CLANCY: I think Michael touched on some of the essentials of design
at the Court. The two magic words were *size* and *Berlin*. The Royal
Court stage was small; the proscenium opening was about twenty-two
or twenty-three feet wide. One man in a chair can easily dominate
that space. And there was an area, as I remember, about twelve feet
square set on a point starting about two feet back from the front of the
stage that was visible from every seat in the house. Every other place
on that stage was not seen by a portion of the house. And those two
facts actually completely dominated all our discussions; they were
always in one's mind. The style, as I understand it, had to evolve from
that because clutter was unseemly and unnecessary. It didn't work.

178

There was a visit from the Berliner Ensemble—in 1966, I think, which had an immense influence.[6] The visual images of the Berliner Ensemble were of startling austerity, and at the same time, they had the most beautifully worked hand props, which, of course, were perfect for the Royal Court because of the small space.

Because of the closeness of the actors to the rest of the house, what they held in their hands and what they sat on had to be perfect. Otherwise, it would be very tatty and theatrical in the wrong kind of way. And this vision of a way of presenting design in the theatre kind of sanctified the style that was most appropriate to the physical aspects of the Royal Court. I think it went on from there, and the reason for that permanent surround was not only money. It was also because it was, in fact, the only feasible method of making a tidy, reasonably spacious-looking background against which to present the actors and their immediate trappings. And even though the particular surround that Percy Harris designed ceased to be used in its entirety, the one thing that remains constant in my mind about designs at the Court is—until such a time as the back wall started to be used—that nearly always there was a surround of some sort, because it was almost the only way. There wasn't room for wings. There wasn't room for complicated periaktoi. It simply had to go straight up and down. It was tied to the galleries at the side in front of the counterweight. And that's all.

MR. EIGSTI: At the beginning was any consideration given to a more conventional masking which has legs running up and downstage, so that you could get side lighting coming in?

MR. HALLIFAX: Yes, oh yes, there was side lighting.

MS. CLANCY: There were a couple of curtains behind the proscenium.

MR. EIGSTI: Yes, but then when you have the S curve coming downstage, that sort of eliminates anything from that downstage tormentor position?

MR. HALLIFAX: No, the perch lighting came through there. And in the next opening halfway up the stage, one had huge thousand-watt

6. The Berliner Ensemble performed in London at the Palace Theatre in 1956 and at the National Theatre in 1966. During the latter visit Helene Weigel and the ensemble visited Devine and attended a performance of Osborne's *A Patriot for Me* at the Royal Court (Wardle, *The Theatres of George Devine,* 277).

lamps; there were no ladders invented in those days, which gets everything up off the floor. People had to make entrances around the lamps.

MR. EIGSTI: You described what you called a slow S. Was that broken in the middle so that there could be lighting through there?

MR. HALLIFAX: No, no, that was a solid S.

MR. GASKILL: You could light from above it.

MS. CLANCY: The proscenium was eighteen feet high, which brought the gallery up to about twenty-five.

MR. GASKILL: I think there were borders in the whole of the first period of the Court. In fact, you sometimes see them in photographs.

MR. HALLIFAX: Yes, yes. It was only later that we got rid of the borders altogether, I think.

MS. CLANCY: Andrew Phillips started designing light grids to suit the design of the setting.[7]

MR. GASKILL: I think that was a significant development. Although George's idea was to open up the proscenium and take away the house border, initially the lighting was still masked. I can't remember when the lighting was deliberately exposed, but certainly it was during most of the time I ran the theatre. That convention of the lighting being seen was, I think, Jocelyn Herbert's original idea. The lighting was seen by those people who sat in the front of the stalls, but then gradually we lowered the lights on frames which could be seen by the whole audience.

MR. EIGSTI: Yes, I have seen pictures with the frames having some kind of a design to them.

MR. GASKILL: That became standard after that. We used it a great deal. And we used it in realistic-naturalistic plays.

MS. CLANCY: Certainly the D. H. Lawrence plays used them.[8]

MR. GASKILL: I remember when we went to Europe with the Lawrence plays, people were most astonished that we should do a play which demanded detailed realism and yet exposed the lights. They thought

---

7. Andrew Phillips, resident lighting designer at the Royal Court from 1965 to 1972, started there as chief electrician and subsequently designed more than eighty consecutive shows for the ESC. He has designed for the National Theatre and frequently works abroad in opera and drama.

8. Three Lawrence plays, directed by Peter Gill, opened at the Royal Court in 1968: *A Collier's Friday Night,* February 29; *The Daughter-in-Law,* March 7; and *The Widowing of Mrs. Holroyd,* March 14.

that was a very individual convention. They were used to having the lights rather exposed, but in stylized productions. And the combination of realism, plus a kind of external statement, I thought, was very particularly Royal Court, and they seemed to acknowledge it.

MR. EIGSTI: Do you think that that was an innovation that came out of the work itself rather than any debt to Berlin? I don't think the Berliner Ensemble particularly makes a fetish out of exposing the lights.

MR. ESSLIN [speaking from the audience]: They do.

MR. GASKILL: But not to the extent that we did. We should explain that the lighting design rig often follows the actual ground plan of the set so if it were on a triangular basis, then you would have a triangular lighting rig. It became more and more complicated so that the rig hanging up there became a very strong design feature mainly due to the work of the lighting designer, Andy Phillips, who was there nearly the whole of the time that I ran the theatre. He devised a very particular style.

But I would say, its ancestor is Berlin. I mean the design theory, certainly, initially stems from Berlin. Also, one has to say, from much earlier, because the Motley sisters, Margaret Harris and Sophie Devine, were strongly influenced initially by the Compagnie des Quinze, which first came to London in 1931, and which, also, if you remember, used large expanses of white cloth in *Le Viol de Lucrèce* and *Noé*. But that style was already part of the thinking of the designers, and the Berliner Ensemble, in a funny way, reinforced that concept.

MR. EIGSTI: I think, to put it all in perspective, there is quite a natural evolution in the theatrical tradition in Europe. In the twenties was the Dadaist theatre in Paris, and then the poor theatre in Germany. I mean *The Threepenny Opera* kind of poor theatre, and the two evolved a sort of design style out of austerity, which then became formalized in the Berliner Ensemble after World War II. Now that they had the money, they wanted to do what they had done with the cabaret out of economic necessity. They used some of the same devices, such as the half curtain; these things are part of a tradition that is twenty or thirty years old. Is that more or less what you are saying or implying?

MR. GASKILL: Yes, but I think it also corresponded to a certain kind of puritanism in the English aesthetic, as shown by people like Jocelyn Herbert, who resisted decoration for its own sake and did not want more than you need on the stage. So it is rather like Shaker furniture, which was designed as maximum austerity. In fact, it's the height of aesthetics in England because it is so pure. I think something in that side of the English temperament responded to that so it became a preference rather than a political weapon, which was the original case.

MS. CLANCY: But it was also the most suitable for the physical space.

MR. GASKILL: Yes, but Michael described so clearly what happened in the first season: the plays that were done didn't conform to the epic pattern. Only *The Crucible,* which did look beautiful, was an epic play, that is, a play which has different scenes in different places, some of them inside and some of them outside, and which tries to present a cross section of social happenings.

Look Back in Anger is a play of three acts and one set, set in an attic. It could be quite conventionally done, and has been, in any proscenium theatre. It has no epic form to it at all.

MR. EIGSTI: So, in a sense, Alan Tagg was right when he was saying that you needed to have all that.

MR. GASKILL: Absolutely. The struggle between the Brechtian theory and the plays that were being written, I think, finally produced that compromise of style. Many of the plays were not epic, although we often tried to reimpose that style. When I took over in 1965, I again went into repertoire, and again we had a regular designer, John Gunter, and again we had a permanent surround, and again we tried to re-create something of the epic style.[9] And, perhaps, some of the plays, like Ann Jellicoe's *Shelley,* were more epic in feeling.

I think the most interesting of the works of Edward Bond are his first performed plays, *The Pope's Wedding* and *Saved.*[10] Although apparently extremely naturalistic in dialogue, they are very carefully controlled, and underneath them is an epic statement. That is, the plays seek to make a statement about society outside what is seen.

Now, *Look Back in Anger* doesn't actually do that. *Look Back in*

9. John Gunter designed for the Royal Court from 1965 to 1970. His designs there include the D. H. Lawrence trilogy, David Storey's *The Contractor,* Christopher Hampton's *The Philanthropist,* John Osborne's *West of Suez,* and Joe Orton's *Entertaining Mr. Sloane.* He now designs for the National and the Royal Shakespeare Company with occasional projects in Europe and the United States (see Burian, "Contemporary British Scenography, Part I," 9–10).

10. *The Pope's Wedding* was a Sunday night production without decor, December 9, 1962; *Saved* opened in the main theatre on November 3, 1965.

Anger says these things happen in this room. It's claustrophobic and intense and has a great deal of passion. The characters talk about life outside, but we only experience life inside.

Now, I think Edward's plays are essentially concerned with the larger scale of life, even though he concentrates sometimes on quite small areas. His visual sense of how that should be presented was already clearly defined in his first plays; he knew what he wanted. They are very simple things like the scene in *Saved* where they are in a boat, and we literally put a rowing boat in the middle of the stage against a background. It's a very peculiar epic statement. I can't quite describe why that's so. The scene is very warm and pastoral, and yet there is something very hard about putting the object, in itself, in the middle of the stage. And a lot of Bond's early work was very concerned with that. For example, he first said to me, "Well, I want this room to be like a bowling alley." And I said, "What do you mean?" He said, "Well, there's a door in the back." And I said, "Oh, you mean a door in a floating piece," like we used to have when we were flying a door with a particular flat around it just to say, "This is the door of a room." It became almost standard practice for indicating living rooms during that time. He said, "No, no. It should be angled. There should be a door and there should be two side walls." And I said, "Oh, I see. And you put the furniture inside." And he said, "No, no, you put that at the back and you put the furniture downstage of it, so that it doesn't relate. You just put the chair and the sofa and the table in front of it, and you just use that as the entrance at the back, and you can also use it as the door for the bedroom." This was from someone who was not brought up in the theatre, no theatrical background.

MR. EIGSTI: Where do you suppose these ideas came from?

MR. GASKILL: I don't know except he has a wonderful eye.

MS. CLANCY: He has the most extraordinary eye.

MR. GASKILL: And he says, "Yes, that would be right." And then that set a whole peculiar style. It wasn't Brechtian, and yet there was something about the detachment of the objects. It was very hard and quite different. And he always insisted that everything be modeled, like the pram in *Saved*. John Gunter made it the wrong color, and Bond was appalled. He hadn't said what color, but he had in his mind what color it should be.

And the scene was made up of these beautiful objects. It's a pity

183

John Gunter isn't here because he made such beautiful models. The actors were all very careful of them, and I remember the whole of that production being a series of objects in space: a pram, a table, a chair, and that set the whole style. I think it was not very surprising that, eventually, Bond started to write plays which were not about the twentieth century, but which were epic plays on a really big scale, like *Early Morning,* a fantasy about Queen Victoria, which Deirdre designed, and *Lear,* his own version of the Shakespeare theme. The scale of the design became much nearer to what one thinks of as the Berliner Ensemble designing, but something about his own philosophy was in his eye and fed into a lot of work that followed, I think.

MR. EIGSTI: It seems to me that there is a very distinct break in the stylistic trend that Jocelyn Herbert represented up to 1965. Do you think that that kind of stylistic period ended and then something else began?

MR. GASKILL: I didn't feel so at the time.

MR. EIGSTI: In retrospect, do you feel that?

MR. GASKILL: I think there is a Court tradition which is expressed by the Arnold Wesker plays that were so beautifully designed, and the David Storey plays, most of which were also designed by Jocelyn Herbert. They are plays about the texture of living and are strongly atmospheric, and she used detailed realism, but also a quality one can only call poetic. She did use projections, and she has what I call the pastoral side of the English temperament. I wouldn't say those plays are very hard or violent. But Edward's plays are strongly *about* violence, and there is an element which enters. I think you can see that difference in the design.

Of course, after the sixties people take their clothes off and start hitting each other. That is very clearly demonstrated in the plays of that period. Suddenly, you see real violence and passion.

MR. EIGSTI: I believe Berlin and Warsaw had a definite influence in New York. When Grotowski came to New York, La Mama and Tom O'Horgan were influenced by that style of theatre. Also, Eastern European theatre is much more visually oriented in many respects, because it's easier to get something past the censors when it's merely on the page and they can't see what it's really going to be; it comes out more as a form of a political cartoon. Is there any of that from Eastern Europe, do you suppose, that affected the Court in the late sixties and seventies?

184

MR. GASKILL: I wouldn't really say so, no.

MR. EIGSTI: There were no visits to Grotowski, for example?

MR. GASKILL: I think we were, and to some extent still are, rather puritanical. We thought a lot of Svoboda was excessive, you know.[11] We were constantly fixed on the idea of the play and that nothing should interfere with the play, nothing should make a statement beyond the play, and the design was always at the service of the play, so the tradition wasn't broken in that way.

MR. HALLIFAX: We had a lot of foreign companies coming to the World Theatre seasons at the Aldwych in the middle of the sixties, and we used to say, "That's a good design," but I can't remember them ever affecting anyone.

MR. EIGSTI: You don't feel there was a sort of cross fertilization there as Eastern Europe opened up?

MR. HALLIFAX: No.

MR. GASKILL: In fact, it became more austere. I did a production of *Macbeth* in 1966 in which one solution to the stage masking was eventually to make a kind of box rather than having wings or a soft S. We ended up having a rigid frame box with entrances either side upstage of the assemblies downstage and two flat walls which varied. That became standard and then got taken up by the Royal Shakespeare Company because Christopher Morley, who designed *Macbeth*, went to the RSC, and they took up the austerity element, I think, as a direct result of the Court's style.[12] And for quite a long time, and perhaps still, they worked in that kind of surround.

MR. EIGSTI: Wasn't Peter Brook's *King Lear* somewhat before that, though? About 1963. The set had two white walls. I'm thinking of when Alan Webb came on, for example, in the last scene and sat down in the middle of the stage and it was just a big empty stage.[13]

11. Jerzy Grotowski, director of the Polish Laboratory Theatre, called for a theatre stripped of its trappings, with the primary focus on the actor. Josef Svoboda, designer for the Prague National Theatre and other Czechoslovakian experimental companies, became especially influential after 1959 because of his integration of multimedia techniques into stage design.

12. Christopher Morley designed a number of productions for the RSC, serving as head of design from 1969 to 1974. He continues to design for the RSC as well as theatres in Coventry, Leicester, Los Angeles, and New York and for opera in England and Denmark.

13. Peter Brook directed *King Lear*, with Paul Scofield in the title role, at the Memorial Theatre, Stratford-upon-Avon, in 1962. It later played at the Aldwych, the RSC's London house.

185

MS. CLANCY: By that time, a break between the Court and the RSC was pretty thorough, wasn't it?

MR. GASKILL: No, no. I would say not. I would say that we were very close at that time. Jocelyn and I went to work in Stratford, as I remember. In fact, I did about three or four shows for the RSC at that time, and there was a quite definite move for Peter Hall to bring in directors and designers from the Royal Court.[14]

MR. EIGSTI: In actual fact, John Bury's design philosophies, which at that time were coming from Joan Littlewood, were similar to what we have been talking about here as well. He was a great exponent of a no-nonsense, no-decor, no-frills design. That grew out of the play and out of some kind of sensibility toward a certain spareness—[15]

MR. HOWARTH: Economics.

MR. EIGSTI: Economics. *Oh, What a Lovely War!*, of course, was a similar style to this—[16]

MR. GASKILL: In that period the feeling through the theatre, through the emerging National and the RSC and the Court, was very close.

MR. EIGSTI: This was the time that I spent in England, and I felt there was a current of electricity going through the whole English theatre; a seminal feeling toward the change in design was taking place.

I think the design you're talking about in *Macbeth* is very interesting because it did take it into another step. It does seem, when you look at pictures of your *Macbeth,* that the production went a little further than Brook's *Lear* did.[17]

MR. GASKILL: Yes, and because its statement was very hard and bright,

14. Gaskill directed *Richard III* for the Royal Shakespeare Company at Stratford-upon-Avon in 1961. It was designed by Jocelyn Herbert. Other productions directed for the RSC by Gaskill include *The Caucasian Chalk Circle, Cymbeline,* and *Infanticide in the House of Fred Ginger.* Herbert designed *Ghosts* and *Saratoga* for the RSC.

15. John Bury joined Joan Littlewood's Theatre Workshop in East London as an actor soon after World War II. In 1962 he joined the RSC, and in 1973 he moved to the National Theatre. In time, he turned his energies to lighting and then to stage design. He has described his work as "essentially realistic, even when abstract. . . . It's all very real, but selective realism, not naturalism. There's no distinction. The human action is always the measure and the center of my stage" (Jarka M. Burian, "Contemporary British Scenography, Part II," *Theatre Design and Technology,* XIX [Fall, 1983], 7).

16. Joan Littlewood directed *Oh, What a Lovely War!* at the Theatre Workshop in Stratford East in 1962.

17. An expert in lighting, Devine stated as early as 1955 that plays should "be per-

which some believed to be against the feeling of the play, the production was considered very shocking.

MR. EIGSTI: I would like to go to the period when Jocelyn Herbert was at the Court. She is obviously quite a dominant force, and no discussion of design at the Royal Court could be complete without an extensive illumination of her works. Could you express some of your views on that in particular?

MR. HOWARTH: Jocelyn's influence is strong. She's marvelous; she always designs from the text. The visual is secondary to Jocelyn. She reads the play over and over and over. She gets the demands of the scene and what the actor has to do and what the scene is trying to say, and then the design comes from that. She starts from the text, and the design follows. That's why the lack of clutter.

MR. EIGSTI: When you discussed design with her, what do you remember talking about?

MR. HOWARTH: The demands of the scene. For instance, in *Three Months Gone* in 1970, which she designed, I wrote an almost impossible task. It was a bungalow, with about eight doors in it—the bathroom, the kitchen, two bedrooms, the front door, the door into the garden, and a door into the living room from the hall. They were all essential, as it were. But if you'd done everything that I had written you'd have had structures holding doors up all the way, and it would have been awful. So we had to resolve that, and by a process of elimination, I said, "Well, it's all right to let go of that door." And finally she got me down to where there had to be five doors, and then the design sort of grew up from that. And when you looked at it, it was like a doll's house actually. She made the front cloth come in, which limited the set to a roof and the shape of a house; it looked rather like a toy and layers of things dropped in behind that. In fact, that design was unusual for Jocelyn because she had to have flats. She doesn't like flats, really, unless they are absolutely essential. In summary, Jocelyn works from the text, designs from the text, and the visual follows that.

MR. EIGSTI: Does any particular production stand out in your memory in those first years?

---

formed in full light with actors *acting* darkness where necessary," an idea Wardle says Gaskill used in his production of *Macbeth* in 1968 (Wardle, *The Theatres of George Devine*, 165).

187

MR. HOWARTH: Yes, *The Chairs* in 1957, which was for me a watershed.[18]
I couldn't believe what I saw: two actors in the dark, George Devine
and Joan Plowright, on this black, empty, seemingly empty stage,
coming in and mumbling the text. Gradually, as the play went on,
they bring the chairs on and the lighting comes in, and it was a
miraculous transformation of the space. It seemed to get longer and
taller and taller. I don't know how she did it; I suppose the lighting
grew, and it seemed to be about the height of a church steeple by the
end of the play, with these tiny people at the bottom of it. The sound
was also part of the design, as well as the lighting, and the whole was a
coherent thing that sort of grew as you watched the performance. And
the visual element was part of the fabric of what the actors had to do in
the play, which was to escalate toward the moment when the man
comes on to make the speech, but he doesn't talk. Jocelyn's design was
a revelation to me. The set reached a climax with the actors, which
was extraordinary. And the transparencies that Michael spoke of, this
gauze effect, actually seemed twenty-five feet high; these hangings
became transparent higher and higher up. You could see through a bit
more very gradually. And at the end, it was like cascading water. It
was amazing but very simple.

MR. EIGSTI: Any other ones?

MR. GASKILL: Well, *Chips with Everything* in 1962 was wonderful. That
had a really difficult problem. It had to have a hut with twelve beds in
it, and at the same time, the actors had to go in and out of the hut into
the parade ground, so the whole stage had to be clear for all of the boys
to drill in, which isn't all that big a space, so the entire space had to be
cleared.

And Jocelyn actually had made beds that were less than full size,
though one couldn't perceive it because no one ever laid down flat on
them. They were all about eighteen inches shorter than the human
body. They were swung out to the sides, to clear the whole space. It
was the most difficult show, but the actual technical solution of it was
brilliant. The design never obtruded. Her actual control of the poetry
was such that what we remember are the images of the play and not
the mechanics, which must have been fiendish for her. The beds
"concertinered," so that after they swung out to the sides, they went

18. *The Chairs* opened on May 14, with Giraudoux's *The Apollo de Bellac;* it was revived
on August 5 with Oliver Wilkinson's *How Can We Save Father?* In June of the following year
(1958), *The Chairs* was paired with *The Lesson,* and this double bill returned on August 4.

in on themselves. And I think they then made a wall out to the side so it made a surround when they were out. It was very clever. But it's so long ago that I just remember the skill involved.

MR. EIGSTI: Are there further visual images that come to the mind of anybody here?

MR. HALLIFAX: Can I just say a little more about *The Chairs?* We obviously looked at this as very hard work, and it was another one of those production weekends where we seemed to spend the whole day up in the grid, crawling along and lighting down through all these gauzes. But what Donald hasn't mentioned, actually, was the number of doors. I can't remember how many there were. There were at least four on either side, and they had to be doublehinged, and we had only an interval in which to set this up, because preceding *The Chairs* was a production of Giraudoux's *The Apollo de Bellac,* which had a full set of a salon or an entrance hall with an enormous staircase going up to a first level.

And having got all that and dressed it with these beautiful Oliver Messel–type curtains and swags, we then had a chandelier about the size of this room. And I said, "We can't have this fantastic crystal chandelier." We had not sufficient room to fly it so we had to drag this awful thing out of the way and then set up all these doors and make them work. If you remember, in Ionesco's play, they fill the stage with chairs, and they come pouring on through door after door so that offstage, where we had eighteen inches of room, chairs were stacked up. We were having to prepare them for Joan Plowright. It was the most amazing evening, but the design was absolutely incredible. It worked so well.

MR. EIGSTI: That is an interesting image of the thin line between magic and reality. Magic is on the one side, and then backstage, the reality of all of this, with the chairs.

MR. GASKILL: Well, one of the good things about the Court is that although it has no wing space, the flying space is very good. We used flying a great deal; we still use flying quite a lot.

MR. EIGSTI: Deirdre, what is a memorable performance image that pops to mind?

MS. CLANCY: I don't know. I think I spent my first couple of years there in a state of complete confusion.

MR. EIGSTI: What do you think of when you think of the Court? As a designer or as a spectator?

189

MS. CLANCY: Well, I had only been working professionally for hardly a year when I went to the Court. I was dead green. I had never done anything. Jocelyn decided that I was to have the job of wardrobe supervisor at the Court; I had gone to work as her assistant.

And then suddenly I went to her wonderful apartment in a place called Flood Street, in Chelsea near the river. She was actually playing Gluck at the time on the radio. She was driving an ancient Alvis, which had belonged to George.

MR. EIGSTI: She plays a harpsichord, too, doesn't she?

MS. CLANCY: No, I don't think so. Stylish she is, twee she isn't. And I thought this was wonderful. This was design; this was the theatre. Jocelyn got me the job at the Court, where Bill employed me as wardrobe supervisor, at which, I have to say, I was very, very bad. And then I did the costumes for the D. H. Lawrence trilogy, which Peter Gill directed. Images do stick with me partly because of the torture of getting it on. If you are a designer, you like to have somebody who is a wardrobe supervisor or production manager to whom you give notes. I was my own wardrobe supervisor so any notes that were given would have to go to me. I cut all the costumes as well for that particular show. Luckily, it was very small, but it was quite a baptism in fire. When the costumes turned out on John Gunter's set, beyond his wildest expectations, it was an extraordinary experience because the mind had become so cluttered with these terrible horrors and rows and my sheer terror. I was very frightened of Peter Gill at first. He was a very cross little man when he got going.

MR. GASKILL: He still is.

MS. CLANCY: And it took years, in a sense, before the agonized terror subsided in me.

MR. EIGSTI: Can you expand on the whole aspect of costume design? Just talk to us about the overall approach to costuming at the Royal Court: where does it come from, where has it gone, where is it going?

MS. CLANCY: It was exactly the same as the approach to all of the other aspects of design. If it didn't grow out of the needs of the text or what the actor could do in it, if it wasn't beautiful because it was suitable, then it was wrong.

MR. EIGSTI: So it's basically a shared sensibility, which is just what we've been talking about.

MS. CLANCY: Yes, yes. And the best part of it was—conceptual theatre was rather a dirty word—it did allow the designer to kind of grow up.

The designs were a genuine and, as you've heard from the description of Jocelyn, a most appropriately crucial part of the whole presentation, and the costumes were the same.

MR. GASKILL: The function, yes, the function is the thing.

MS. CLANCY: The design did, occasionally, where it was applicable, become very beautiful and effective, but because of the rigorous examination of what was required, I hope.

MR. EIGSTI: *Ubu Roi* was designed by David Hockney. The sketches by Hockney—remarkable as they are—seem to be a bit out of the mainstream of what we've been talking about.

MR. GASKILL: Hockney was brought in while I was running the theatre; it was my idea. I think I had kind of Diaghilev ambitions at that time. One also has to say that it was the time of swinging London, and Chelsea was rather at the center of that. I had employed, to everyone's chagrin, Marianne Faithfull, the girl friend of Mick Jagger, for the production of *Three Sisters,* in which she was quite remarkable, wonderful. And it was also the time of the fight with the censor. It was a time of trend, one has to say, a very trendy time. And so lots of ideas were buzzing around when Iain Cuthbertson said, "I am going to do *Ubu Roi,*" and I said, "Well, why don't we get David Hockney? And we'll have Max Wall play Ubu." [19] It was those kinds of ideas, and Hockney's design was wonderfully beautiful and, of course, the colors—his color sense is so extraordinary. All of the ideas about the production were really his ideas. They weren't the director's ideas. He would say [imitating Hockney's Bradford accent], "We'll have this thing—that says, 'Royal Palace,' and p'haps the 'ace' can fall off after the battle and it will say, 'Royal Pal.'" He was kind of naïve, and when he first saw the scene, he said, "Oh, they have reproduced my brush strokes exactly, only it's much bigger, isn't it? I didn't mean it to be like that a'tall. I just meant it to be kind of white, you know."

MS. CLANCY: Isn't there a story that the painter got extremely cross when being told to do it exactly like the drawings, and he actually did reproduce the thumb prints?

MR. GASKILL: I don't remember that the Hockney work fed much into the tradition. But I think it was well worth it. I don't, in any way, feel ashamed of it.

MS. CLANCY: Yes, but it opened it out, didn't it? I mean, I do remember

19. *Ubu Roi* opened on July 21, 1966; *Three Sisters* on April 18, 1967.

very vividly there were about two or three productions that were outside the Court. Do you remember that one that came from Bristol?

MR. GASKILL: Oh, *Dingo,* yes, wonderful.[20]

MS. CLANCY: But I remember that it was not very good. We all went in to scoff, actually. It was considered to be rather vulgar, tasteless, and not the thing at all, but there was something about the vigor and the untasteful and austere images that could get a little precious, if not watched. In fact, it did have a very invigorating effect, and I think that it achieved something like *Ubu Roi* must have done, exactly the same thing in a different way. It reopened rethinking. It was really a part of that movement of swinging London. We weren't really influenced by Europe at all.

MR. HOWARTH: It was the Americans.

MR. GASKILL: I was most excited by the Bread and Puppet Theatre, which we brought to the Court; also, the Open Theatre.[21]

MR. ESSLIN: And you had Andrei Serban doing a Café La Mama season.[22]

MR. GASKILL: Yes, that's right. And we were very excited about *that* visual input, which was brighter, more color. I think we never really got into all of that Polish gloom at all, you know.

MR. EIGSTI: What are some of the other productions that you had at the theatre? Deirdre, you mentioned that there were two American productions.

MS. CLANCY: Yes, van Itallie's *America Hurrah* and Michael McClure's *The Beard,* on a Sunday night.[23] Those American plays were a revelation.[24]

MR. EIGSTI: What was the difference in terms of what was happening at the Court at that time? Why did those stand out in contrast?

20. Charles Wood's *Dingo* opened on November 15, 1967, at the Royal Court. The play was first performed at the Bristol Arts Centre, April 28, 1967. Wood later adapted it for the film *How I Won the War,* which featured John Lennon.

21. Joseph Chaiken brought his Open Theatre to the Royal Court on August 2, 1967, in Jean-Claude van Itallie's *America Hurrah: Interview, TV, Motel.* Peter Schumann's Bread and Puppet Theatre performed *The Cry of the People for Meat* on June 23, 1969.

22. The La Mama season opened on May 19, 1970; Jarry's *Ubu Roi* and *Arden of Faversham* (anon.) were directed by Andrei Serban; Leonard Melfi's *Cinque* and Adrienne Kennedy's *Rats Mass* were directed by Ching Yeh.

23. *The Beard* by Michael McClure was produced by the Court on November 11, 1968, as a late night show.

24. Ellen Stewart's Café La Mama first visited London in 1967, "bringing not only Sam Shepard's surreally sparse plays but also a style of acting different from anything [in Great

MR. GASKILL: Well, they were sexier, I think. They were very sexy.

MR. HOWARTH: The energy. The American energy.

MS. CLANCY: Yes. And we were so puritan and chaste at the Court at that time.

MR. GASKILL: You know that scene in *America Hurrah* when he writes obscenities on the wall with lipstick and tears the woman's clothes off and all that. We'd never done anything like that at the Court.

MS. CLANCY: It was so wonderfully uninhibited. That was the thing.

MR. HOWARTH: As for the influence of the Americans, they showed us in England that you could have trash and vulgarity and still have marvelous taste. You could be tasteful with graffiti and vulgarity and coarseness. You didn't have to be superior to it; you could actually join in and do it elegantly. That was quite a cultural shock.

OBSERVER: So everything kind of exploded with sexuality?

MR. HOWARTH: It also gave license for one's own behavior, you know. You thought, the things that one does in secret, one need not be ashamed of if done with grace.

MR. GASKILL: Can I tell a story about *The Beard?*

MR. EIGSTI: Go ahead. Sure.

MR. GASKILL: Those of you who know the play know that it ends with the man going down on the woman—"The Hallelujah Chorus." And sometimes we would hear out of the darkness the American actress Billie Dixon, who played Jean Harlow, saying, [Gaskill speaks in an American accent] "I told you not to do that." But one night she was receiving in her dressing room, and the stage manager came and said, "I have washed your knickers, Ms. Dixon." And she said [Gaskill uses whispering voice], "You are not supposed to say that. I'm not supposed to have any on." And the stage manager said, "This is the Royal Court Theatre. We don't believe in illusions."

MS. CLANCY: Oh, that's lovely.

MR. EIGSTI: I do want to talk about the early seventies. Do you think that the Royal Court has led or followed? Deirdre, you've been working a lot in the theatre in the last ten years. What do you think of it, or is it too close for you to tell?

Britain]. Tom O'Horgan's actors . . . were performers, musicians, dancers; they combined all those skills and more in a theatre bounding with physical energy and a quality of raw shock" (Khan, "The Fringe," 8).

MS. CLANCY: I'm not sure that I can say. It doesn't actually seem to have improved quite as much as you'd have imagined in the last few years.

MR. EIGSTI: One of the things that happened in reaction to the sixties, especially in this country, was a whole renewed interest in naturalism and realism. What is happening in this country with the playwrights' theatres like Circle in the Square, the Public Theatre, and the Manhattan Theatre Club is the reversion, or the progression, toward realism, toward naturalism, toward real spaces as opposed to the Bread and Puppet Theatre and that kind of abstract illusion. Is this a part of the Court tradition?

MS. CLANCY: Well, it was always doing that. That's what it was.

MR. GASKILL: In the sixties, we imagined that some of that influence would feed itself into the kind of plays that were being written. I don't think that really happened very much at the Court. It happened on the fringe itself. But then, the fringe became politicized and not concerned with aesthetics. I think one of the tragedies of a lot of fringe theatre in England is that it is so ugly. You have never seen anything so ugly as some of the productions of 7:84.[25] They are so appallingly designed. They think that if they say the right thing, that it will be all right, but it's not all right. You have to have an aesthetic as well. The great thing about Brecht, really, was that his work was not only political but it was also beautiful, and I think the two things together are essential.

The fringe became politicized and turned its back on what it saw as the American influence, which I take to be largely an aesthetic influence. The fringe became concerned once again with social problems, not in the realistic way, but the economics have become very dominant.

MR. EIGSTI: Which brings us to a very important point of the seventies. In a strange way, maybe we are still feeling the influence of the seventies, a decade of reduction and contraction, because of the oil crises and the various scaling down of one's expectations, which in the sixties, perhaps, were limitless. I think the set designer, who spends the most money in the theatre and gets the most grief for it, does have that problem of reduction of budget. The theatre is going that way. And there is a problem of trying to make an aesthetic out of austerity,

25. 7:84 is a strongly political theatre, aiming its messages at "trades' union halls, working men's clubs, political conferences and community centres" (*ibid.,* 9).

as opposed to an aesthetic out of what it is that you are actually doing. And whether or not poverty alone is something that you can actually make beautiful is one of the problems these theatres face, isn't it?

MS. CLANCY: We all got used to that at the Court.

MR. EIGSTI: Making poverty beautiful?

MS. CLANCY: Yes.

MR. GASKILL: I don't think so. There was more money, and the poverty was always expensive. But today, you could not afford to do Osborne's *A Patriot for Me* or Wesker's *Chips with Everything*. You couldn't afford the size of the casts, nor that amount of scenery.

When Max asks me to do a show at the Court now, he says, "Well, you can have nine actors if one of the boys doubles as one of the girls." You say, "Okay, right." That would have been unthinkable at one time. Then he says, "This is all you are going to have." In fact, *Tibetan Inroads,* a new play of Stephen Lowe's that we have just done, looks rather splendid, but it cost a great deal more than anything has for some time.

MR. EIGSTI: Was there ever any consideration at any time of leaving the Royal Court in Sloane Square and building a space that would be able to fulfill all of your dreams in terms of production, in terms of going out and raising the money and building the theatre? In this country most of the theatres that started out in the sixties now have permanent homes and spaces that were designed by their founders. Was there ever any consideration of that?

MR. GASKILL: Occasionally. George had a big plan to reconstruct the Court itself inside its own shell. It was the last thing that he tried to do, and he was very disappointed when it didn't happen.[26] And there have been times when we have been invited to set up in other theatres like the Old Vic, or an old music hall in the Edgeware Road, the Metropolitan, neither of which happened.

And we all had a dream at one time of moving into the annex that the Old Vic used for the workshops and making that into a studio

26. Irving Wardle provides a detailed account of Devine's "last big dream for the Court." His "architectural ideal" called for "a covered multipurpose performance and community centre." It involved a complete rebuilding of the Royal Court's interior, as well as extensions to the building. Devine wanted a new auditorium with a "single sweep of seats and its stage shorn of the proscenium," demolishing "the hierarchy of stalls and circle." But ultimately he had to settle for merely cosmetic improvements (Wardle, *The Theatres of George Devine,* 243–56).

195

space. Over the last few years we have all felt that it would be wonderful to have flexible space, but larger than the Theatre Upstairs, in which you could seat perhaps 250 to 300 people and which you could convert to the round.

The proscenium theatre does demand a certain kind of excellence and a certain kind of visual satisfaction, and if you can't afford to give it to the audience they do feel that there is something lacking. Some of the excitement one feels about some of those earlier productions was that they were beautifully designed and staged, and they cost quite a bit of money. And, honestly, we can't do that now, and I don't know whether Max is thinking of a move. I certainly think if he were, it would not be toward building a theatre, which I think is a terrible, awful thing to do, but to finding a space that one could use, a large, open space.

MR. EIGSTI: So there is thought of that?

MR. GASKILL: Well, there is always thought of that.

MR. EIGSTI: Is the Royal Court a kind of captive siren of Sloane Square: you don't want to get out of it, but you don't want to stay in it?

MR. BURGE [speaking from the audience]: There is a very simple reason that everybody comes back to: if you move out of that theatre, you would have to call it something else.

MR. EIGSTI: Royal Court II.

MR. BURGE: I don't think anybody underestimates the real value of that theatre as a proscenium theatre of its time. If it were closed, it would be very hard to replace. But what we're hearing constant talk about, I think, is an alternative space to the theatre, a more expansive auxiliary stage than we have at the Theatre Upstairs. It's a nice space, the Theatre Upstairs, but it is extremely crowded.

MR. HOWARTH: I think the intimacy of the house has always been an asset. You don't want to leave a house which allows you that intimacy. But at the same time, it has a sort of grand feeling as well. If one does an epic play, one can get away with it, but one can also do a very intimate play because the space is appropriate.

MR. EIGSTI: It has a marvelous scale. I think the house is about three-quarters size, actually. It seems scaled down because you do have the feeling that you are in a kind of tiered hat-box theatre; yet it is all a bit smaller than that.

MR. HOWARTH: And there's always the romantic association that it was Harley Granville Barker's theatre, and Bernard Shaw directed his own

196

plays there; it's a writers' theatre, and there is a literary heritage and all that.[27] Although one may mock it and say that the Court isn't that, there is a literary tradition which writers touch their cap to every now and then.

MR. GASKILL: George Devine always said that reverence for the past is a lot of rubbish.

MR. HOWARTH: I know that's what he said. But why didn't he move?

MS. CLANCY: Don't you believe that buildings have some kind of geist of their own?

MR. HALLIFAX: What I think is worth remembering about the Court is that when we went there in 1956, Chelsea was just a backwater. It wasn't the swinging sixties; it was sort of the fading fifties. There were no restaurants, no life there. There was a huge, very expensive shop, which is still there, called Peter Jones, on the opposite side of Sloane Square.

It was a very barren area with absolutely no passing trade because nobody walked in Chelsea. No one ever seemed to go anywhere, and if he did, he went to the tube and scuttled down or came out and disappeared as quickly as possible.

It really was a desert then, wasn't it? When working in and around the West End, one used to say, "Oh, good, we're in Shaftsbury Avenue, so when it rains people will come in from the street to see this play that nobody else is coming to see." But in Chelsea even when it rained there was no hope.

It's also worth remembering that we did have our own workshops so that we actually built all of our designs. One of our electric meter readers found this place, a builder's yard in Park Walk, and said, "Well, he's got a first floor that is vacant." And we rushed down and rented it from him for all the time that I was there, three years or so. Everything was made there. It was on the first floor, but luckily there was a large doorway so we could move production materials in and out of it easily. We made all of the scenery, and we painted it. And the paint shop, I think, appeared in the film of—

MR. GASKILL: *A Taste of Honey.*

27. Harley Granville Barker and John Vedrenne produced thirty-two plays at the Royal Court Theatre between 1904 and 1907. The mainstay of the theatre during this time was George Bernard Shaw, who directed eleven of his own plays there (Brockett, *History of the Theatre,* 558).

MR. HALLIFAX: Yes. And we made all the costumes down there.

MR. BURGE: This may sound strange, but the existence of a permanent workshop at the National Theatre is a quite important asset, actually. I really tried very hard to reestablish that at the Court. I was shouted down always. I think when one designs one show after another, it is rather hard contracting out as we do now.

MR. EIGSTI: There is no permanent workshop?

MR. BURGE: No, but I think in any theatre organization it is a quite valuable asset.

MS. CLANCY: It makes an enormous difference.

MR. EIGSTI: What is the process then?

MR. BURGE: Every theatre that I have ever worked in where there has been a workshop always had a special atmosphere and, actually, a much more consistent style.

MR. EIGSTI: What is the process now of getting scenery? It is sent out for bids to various shops?

MR. BURGE: Yes, one goes to specialists for things used over a period of time. There is a storage where some bits and pieces are kept, but often when you get there, you find the pieces are rotten.

MS. CLANCY: They get damp and mildewed.

MR. EIGSTI: Is there a large properties room somewhere?

MR. BURGE: Only under the stage.

MR. EIGSTI: Well, do you bid out the shows then? Are there scenic suppliers in London?

MR. GASKILL: We often have them made by a man who was our stage carpenter for many years and who eventually set up his own firm. Very often, he still makes our scenery and actually quotes a very good price; so there is a sort of continuity there.

OBSERVER: I was just wondering if a thrust was ever used. Why were you locked necessarily into a proscenium?

MR. GASKILL: It is absolutely a proscenium theatre. If you had a thrust, there would be no audience left.

MR. EIGSTI: Are there any questions from the audience?

OBSERVER: In the Bond play *Saved,* Gaskill mentioned a boat appearing. Was the shifting done in the dark?

MR. GASKILL: I'm afraid so because in what I call an epic play, you have to cut at the end of the scene. You need to break it, and we never got into the convention of the half curtain.

MS. CLANCY: But the half curtain was about four feet high.

MR. GASKILL: When people ask how do we change the scenery, I say it's never a question of changing the scenery. Changing scenery is really quite easy, if you can fly things in and out. You can have periaktoi. You can truck things. You can do all sorts of things. What you can't get in and out is furniture, and if you have to go from a café which has twelve chairs and three tables to a sitting room with a couch, table, and a chair, in a tiny theatre, it is a nightmare. So my worst experiences are plays like *Saved,* which demand changes of furniture.

MS. CLANCY: Or the *Three Sisters.*

MR. GASKILL: You can do a play in which you fly in the flats as quickly as you like, but the problems are always the things that have to be carried on to the stage when you haven't got the revolve or wings large enough to truck a whole set.

MR. EIGSTI: One of the key differences in the Berliner Ensemble is the fact that the proscenium opening is not very wide, but the backstage is huge.

MR. GASKILL: The wings aren't that enormous but the depth is.

MR. BURGE: The Theater-am-Schiffbauerdamm has this wonderfully sized proscenium with a large revolve; small scenes could be revolved around. They still remain small scenes in epic space.

MR. EIGSTI: I am curious to know what the playwrights feel about the designs.

MR. HAMPTON [speaking from the audience]: I have always been very conscious that if you write the plays in a series of short scenes, and I'm afraid we do, it is very hard to solve problems which you set up in that particular theatre.

I am actually at the mercy of designers because I'm poor at reading sets; therefore, I have been very happy with the designers that I have worked with, John Gunter and Jocelyn, and I have generally been very pleased with their solutions. I have had very little to do with that side of it.

MR. EIGSTI: There is no sense that the theatre is limiting when you are visualizing your play being done there?

MR. HAMPTON: I'm used to it, and you just sit there and you don't fuss much.

MR. WARDLE [speaking from the audience]: Christopher's play *The Philanthropist* required in the opening scene that a character's brains be blown across the back wall.

MS. CLANCY: Yes. It was brilliantly done.

MR. HAMPTON: Yes, in fact, we had to hire someone from Shepperton Studios. He put a compressed gas cylinder on the back of the chair and stuffed Divex with a mixture of rice and red stuff.

MS. CLANCY: They're called rubbers here. They used Campbell's tomato rice soup, someone told me.

MR. HAMPTON: And when the character shot himself, the effects exploded on impact.

MR. EIGSTI: A problem is that writers are writing for films. Does anybody think that in the Court a specific theatrical tradition exists or do you think that there has been a kind of carryover, an influence from films?

MR. GASKILL: Well, I think writers have become terribly slapdash and lazy. They write short scenes which are set on a seashore, and then one is set in a bus and they say, "It's got to be a real bus."

And then they are in the living room. They have written television plays, and they are asking you to put them on the stage. It is the most uncraftsmanlike work.

MR. BURGE: Especially in the fringe. You see them all in the Warehouse, don't you? And possibly in the regional theatre, and when the play is done by the Court, it's a nightmare.

MR. GASKILL: Well, it's nightmare in the studio theatre, too.

MR. EIGSTI: I had a script once where I had to point out to the writer that there was not only a scene change, but that the character was in a totally different costume and attitude from the scene which immediately preceded it.

MR. GASKILL: And he probably said, "I meant that to happen."

OBSERVER: Since Caryl Churchill and Stephen Lowe and Nicholas Wright are here also, would they respond to the questions that were asked of Christopher?

MR. LOWE [speaking from the audience]: I have very little difficulty with the designers.

MS. CHURCHILL [speaking from the audience]: My first play at the Court was a play with more than one scene and lots of furniture, and it was a terrible problem because the Theatre Upstairs has even less space than downstairs. I learned from Max Stafford-Clark not to do it, and I set my next play in one place.

OBSERVER: Are there problems either directly or indirectly built into the writing of the plays which are commissioned by the Court? Do the writers say, "I'm not going to do this" sometimes?

MS. CHURCHILL: It's hard to say. I don't know if anyone else has this problem. Does it actually influence the kind of play you write by knowing that a proscenium stage is there? With *Cloud Nine,* which was a Joint Stock play, we made a decision so that it could be presented within the Royal Court proscenium. In the second act there were a lot of monologues, and one of the things that struck us most strongly was that on a proscenium stage like that, it was very difficult. The play would actually have worked better in a small space, such as a studio situation.

MR. EIGSTI: In many Royal Court plays, it seems an advantage, a positive thing, when the script reflects the author's awareness of the specific space he is writing for. I think the plays that writers conceive of in a theatrical space, as opposed to a great movie in the sky, which is in their minds, are infinitely better. And the fact that the Royal Court exists as a constant throughout must influence the writer's work.

MR. WILSON [speaking from the audience]: I wrote a play for the Court's main stage, and I had a set of blueprints, and I realized that it would not fit the scenic space. The play needed multispaces and would have been incredibly difficult to do on that stage.

There were spaces I could have gone easily to and where the play could have been done, but they were not spaces that gave an author the opportunities he would get at the Royal Court. It wasn't that I was visualizing in the sky. It was that after you work on material it begins to take on some physical reality. There seemed no way that I could tell the story in the normal fashion and put it on the stage successfully.

MR. EIGSTI: But in actual fact, in a way, you are conscious of the space limitations, which actually is a force, is it not?

MR. WILSON: Certainly. I don't take commissions until I actually see what space the story is limited to, and then I try to flow with it.

MR. WRIGHT: I think a playwright need not have characters get in a car, close the door, and drive off. You have to use whatever you have, a couple of chairs, or the top of a table, to serve as a car.

MR. GASKILL: That is leaning, though, to a kind of mannerism which has a very limited life.

MR. EIGSTI: Like Thornton Wilder.

MR. GASKILL: Also like Peter Gill's *Small Change,*[28] which was an ex-

28. Written and directed by Peter Gill, *Small Change* opened July 8, 1976.

201

quisite production. But there comes a point where you want the feel of objects having a period, a color, an identity, or an atmosphere, and if you don't have that, you do end up your own asshole because you cannot go on doing plays like that. The eye demands at some point some poetry. You can't create poetry without that. Peter Gill has done it, unquestionably. In his own work he *has* done it. But when you see it imposed on another writer who wants the smell of the life of the characters, I think it becomes dry and arid. It will not have a life. Jocelyn used to capture so wonderfully the actual life and feel of people in social situations.

MR. EIGSTI: Of the designers that I have admired, Jocelyn Herbert is certainly one. I think one of the incredible things that she was able to do was to achieve a difference from one production to the next so that one didn't have the feeling that it was all a vast panorama of the same work; there was a visual evocation somehow unique to that play, and the play that followed it was not of the same thing that had gone before. One can get into a very difficult trap when he starts working with the physical realities of something. It may work for one thing, but then the play that follows may seem like an extended version of what went before. And Jocelyn was able to make that difference. In her designs for each play she has created a unique visualization.

MR. GASKILL: I think that one of the great tragedies at the moment is that there isn't a designer attached to the theatre. Jocelyn's dedication to the work of that theatre, of that space, that organization, those writers, was absolute and persisted and still does persist, because she still continues to work there occasionally and still has a guiding eye on it.

But I think we have all become far too defocused. We work with different designers. There is very little real sense of a Court designer, at the moment, or a Court style because of that. That is a terrible pity.

MR. EIGSTI: Yes, I ran across a little notebook from the Planchon production *Gilles de Rais* in which the designer's notes about the production seemed unique to me because he wasn't talking about entrances and exits. He was talking about philosophy and ideas. And then somehow, when one saw the pictures of the production, there the ideas were. It was quite obvious that here was a real marriage of artists who were working together, and it is something that I long for.

MR. BURGE: I think that there is a lot to be said for the innovative concept of objects in open space at the Royal Court. The detail exploited

202

within that space sticks in memory. All of the productions that I have seen there had germs of that concept, had been successfully designed in terms of that.

MR. EIGSTI: The space breathes.

MR. BURGE: Yes. I remember a play by Howard Barker there.[29] It was a completely different kind of design, but it contained still that concept of a deserted space into which details of scenes are used.

MR. EIGSTI: That seems to give an apt final picture. The Court style, if it's anything, is open space with the imagery very precisely defined—in a sense what theatre began with—the focus on the specifics surrounded by open space.

29. Barker's *Stripwell*, directed by Chris Parr and designed by Bob Ringwood, was produced on October 14, 1975.

VII

Critics Talk: Respect for Writers

PARTICIPANTS: *Oscar Brockett, University of Texas*
Martin Esslin, Stanford University
Irving Wardle, The Times, *London*

SPEAKING FROM THE AUDIENCE:
Stuart Burge
Ann Jellicoe
Max Stafford-Clark

MR. BROCKETT: Since we have already heard from many people from the Royal Court that critics are not very welcome, we are here at some peril, I suppose.

Both Mr. Esslin and Mr. Wardle were practicing critics in London throughout most of the years between 1956 and 1981; they have viewed many of the productions and are prepared to make comments about the directions of the Royal Court, the defining of itself in particular ways, its relationship with the audiences, and other matters of that kind. Let me begin by asking Mr. Esslin if he has some observations.

MR. ESSLIN: I would like to relate an experience I had just after the first night of one of the great Edward Bond plays that I attended. I can't quite remember whether it was *The Sea* or *The Fool*.[1] As I was passing with the other people out of the theatre, I recognized in the crowd one of the leading German directors, who obviously had come because he was going to do the play in his own theatre, and I heard him say to his lady, "Gott sei Dank, Alles ist nach vor uns. Sie haben nur den Text gespielt," which means: "Thank God. Everything is still to be done. They played nothing but the text."

1. *The Sea* opened May 22, 1973, and *The Fool* opened November 18, 1975.

204

That, to my mind, is the greatest tribute that I have ever heard given to the Royal Court. Because if you see those plays in Germany, they are all done with elevators going up and down and moving staircases and the mouth of Hell opening at one side and the characters walking on sticks or stilts or whatever, and you don't recognize what it's all about.

This, also, sums up what came out of this conference: this is a theatre that really does have respect for the writers and doesn't go in for one of the great diseases of the theatre in our period, namely, the so-called director's theatre, where the director has some concept which he imposes and thinks of the script as little more than raw material.

I also want to add, having sat through this conference and absorbed all the fascinating material facts: when all this is published, it will be a gold mine for generations of dissertation writers!

I have strong feelings about some matters because of my own central European background. To me the Court represents a turntable on which a number of very difficult influences got focused in England and then amplified themselves again in other directions to other parts of England and to the world. I do believe that it is essential to recognize the genealogy of the Court.

One has to go back from the Court to the Old Vic and Young Vic, which was a tripartite organization that grew up after the war in which George Devine and Michel Saint-Denis and Glen Byam Shaw and other good people worked together. One goes from that, if we trace it backward, to the Compagnie des Quinze, which George and Michel Saint-Denis were concerned with. And from the Compagnie des Quinze to Copeau and the Vieux Colombier. That is one line of genealogy which leads into the great period of the French theatre at the beginning of this century. Copeau was part of a movement to which also belonged Dullin and the Pitoëff family, which had influences from Russia and from Chekhov and Stanislavski.[2]

Also, there is a line of influence through the close relationship George Devine had with the great generation of English actors: Peggy

2. Charles Dullin (1885–1949) remained part of the Copeau's Vieux Colombier until 1922, when he formed his own company in Paris. Georges Pitoëff (1884–1939), a native Russian, moved to Paris in 1922; like Copeau, he placed primary emphasis on the text. As the son of a theatre manager, Pitoëff became familiar with Constantin Stanislavski's work while living in Moscow, and he worked for a time with Vsevelod Meyerhold.

Ashcroft, who was in the first Brecht production at the Court;[3] and Gielgud,[4] who represents the English side of that Russian influence, the Komisarzhevsky influence, which was the first to come to England.[5] I think Saint-Denis and Komisarzhevsky were the two major directors who brought to England the modern conception of director from France and from Russia. On top of that, the influence of Brecht surfaced with the encounter between Devine and the Berliner Ensemble.[6]

What happened in the Royal Court represents a breakthrough in

3. Peggy Ashcroft appeared in the title role of Bertolt Brecht's *The Good Woman of Setzuan,* which opened October 31, 1956. Devine's professional association and friendship with Peggy Ashcroft dates as early as 1931, when they were both in an OUDS production of Flecker's *Hassan.* In 1932 they appeared together as Juliet and Mercutio in another OUDS production, *Romeo and Juliet,* directed by John Gielgud. They also performed together in *Cymbeline* (1932), *The Sea Gull* (1936 and 1964), *Three Sisters* (1937), *The White Guard* (1938), *Twelfth Night* (1938), and *Hedda Gabler* (1954). Devine directed Ashcroft in *King Lear* (1955) and *Rosmersholm* (1959), as well as in *The Good Woman of Setzuan.*

4. In addition to working together in the OUDS production of *Romeo and Juliet* (1932), Gielgud directed Devine as Tubal in *The Merchant of Venice* (1932), as the Player King in *Hamlet* (1934), as Peter in *Romeo and Juliet* (1932), and as the Gardener in *Richard II* (1937). They performed together in *Three Sisters* (directed by Saint-Denis, 1938). Devine codirected with Gielgud in a revival of Gielgud's *Much Ado About Nothing* (1955). He directed Gielgud again in the title role of *King Lear* (1955), designed by Isamu Noguchi.

5. Brother of the famous Russian actress Vera Komisarzhevsky, Theodore Komisarzhevsky studied architecture before joining his sister's theatre, where he followed Vsevelod Meyerhold as her artistic director. In 1910 he opened his own theatre, and between that time and 1919, when he emigrated to the West, he headed several theatres and a training school. His association with Gielgud began when Komisarzhevsky directed him in *Three Sisters* and *Katrina* in the successful season of Russian plays in Barnes during 1925 to 1926. Gielgud credits his desire to direct to Komisarzhevsky, whose artistry in lighting, architecture, scenery, and directing made a strong impression on Gielgud and all who worked with him (see Wardle, *The Theatres of George Devine,* 19—29; John Gielgud, *An Actor and His Time* [London, 1979], 97—103).

6. In the fall and winter of 1955, before taking over the Royal Court in February, 1956, Devine toured his production of *King Lear.* During the tour in Germany, Devine met for the first time Bertolt Brecht and his wife, Helene Weigel. Devine and other members of the company also visited Brecht's Theater am Schiffbauerdamm in East Berlin, where they saw *The Caucasian Chalk Circle.* Impressed with the theatre's permanent surround, Devine attempted a similar installation for the Royal Court that was eventually discarded. Devine also admired the production's "simplicity, beauty and honesty," adjectives often used to describe the designs at the Court, especially those of Jocelyn Herbert. Devine seemed most impressed by Brecht's achievement of a theatre which is "above all a theatre of its time, of its place, and of its nation" (see Wardle, *The Theatres of George Devine,* 169—70).

the English theatre of a concept of a serious theatre which had previously also inhabited the Court during the Barker/Vedrenne management in 1904–1907, particularly with Shaw's productions. It is no coincidence that it is Shaw and Barker who wrote the first blueprint for a national theatre.

In a way, what happened at the Royal Court was the breakthrough of the Continental art theatre tradition from the Cartel [des Quatre] in France, from the art theatre in Russia, from the Berliner Ensemble, and from the German subsidized theatre into the English consciousness.[7] I strongly believe that the coming of the National Theatre and the transformation of the Royal Shakespeare Company, and all that is connected with that, radiates outward from the Royal Court experience. When the National Theatre was opened in 1963, Bill Gaskill, John Dexter, and numerous actors, from Colin Blakely to Bob Stevens to Joan Plowright, who had worked at the Court, became the nucleus of the company. And similarly, Royal Court artists infiltrated the Royal Shakespeare Company. Thus the Royal Court is absolutely of basic importance.

I think that a sort of worldwide openness, both to America and to the Continent, showed itself from the very beginning. One of the earliest productions, *The Good Woman of Setzuan,* was not, I think, particularly successful, because the lesson of Brecht had not quite been absorbed, although some actors of the great English tradition, like Esmé Percy, who played one of the gods, gave a wonderful Brechtian, alienating performance.

But we should note the openness, particularly of George Devine, who was so keen on and so receptive to French things. For example, in 1957 the world premiere of *Fin de Partie {Endgame}* was done at the Royal Court at a time when it was impossible to stage the play in France. And in 1961 Roger Blin was called in to direct Genet's *The Blacks*. Beckett himself brought his own production of *Waiting for*

---

7. Copeau disciples Charles Dullin and Louis Jouvet formed with Georges Pitoëff and Gaston Baty (1885–1952) a loose alliance known as the Cartel des Quatre in 1927. They agreed to common policies for their theatres similar to those of Copeau: respect for the text, simplicity and truthfulness in staging, and the search for poetic impact rather than spectacular effect. The Cartel has been viewed "as one of the chief factors in prolonging and confirming Copeau's ideas" (see Brady, *Modern French Drama,* 3; also Brockett, *History of the Theatre,* 607–609).

Godot from the Schiller Theatre into the Royal Court in 1976 as one of five plays in a Beckett festival.

In fact, the Royal Court was the home of Beckett and was also one of the earliest homes of the Absurdist theatre, with productions of Ionesco's *The Chairs* and *Rhinoceros* and N. F. Simpson's *One Way Pendulum,* which represents an English kind of absurdism.[8] *Rhinoceros* may not have been a production in the austere tradition of the Royal Court, but with Orson Welles directing and Laurence Olivier playing Berenger, it was a memorable experience and of great importance to the history of the theatre in England. Other memorable productions include Frisch's *The Fire Raiser* in 1961 and Ionesco's *Exit the King* in 1963.

The Royal Court also opened its stage to the world by bringing in the English minorities, the Pakistanis, West Indians, and Africans, with a whole series of plays. For example, among the things that I will never forget is the performance of *The Lion and the Jewel* by Wole Soyinka in 1966, which revealed this Nigerian as one of the great writers in the world today.[9] And it was at the Court that one had a chance to see a first-class performance of Soyinka's work.

And the conference has already noted the Court's openness to the American theatre: the La Mama troupe, Schumann's Bread and Puppet Theatre, and the association of Sam Shepard with the ESC. This openness to influences from all over the world, actually welcoming people in as a part of the operation, I think, is a great achievement of the Royal Court.

We have noted the vitality of such an experiment over twenty-five years. My view is that the Court has had creative crises and new beginnings each time that its main achievement was absorbed into

8. *The Chairs* opened May 14, 1957; *Rhinoceros,* April 18, 1960; and *One Way Pendulum,* December 2, 1959.

9. Soyinka received the Nobel Prize for literature in 1986. A native of Nigeria, he completed undergraduate studies at the University of Leeds, where he also began work on an M.A. degree in 1957. In the same year his play *The Lion and the Jewel* came to the attention of the Royal Court, where he became a play reader and was a member of the Writers' Group in 1957 and 1959. For a Sunday night production on November 1, 1959, he directed his unpublished play *The Invention,* together with excerpts from *The House of Banigeji* and *A Dance of the African Forests.* In 1966 Soyinka directed *The Lion and the Jewel,* which opened in the Royal Court's main theatre on December 12 (see Stephen Larsen, *A Writer and His Gods* [Stockholm, 1983]; James Gibbs, *Wole Soyinka* [New York, 1986]).

the mainstream. I think you have the first new wave with Osborne, Wesker, and Arden, which then flowered on into Olivier's National Theatre and so on.

The second new wave was the great period of Bond's plays, and at the moment we probably have got to another moment of absorption of what's gone on with the third wave; the Howard Brentons and Howard Barkers and David Hares were again absorbed into the establishment theatres through first working at the Court, then the National, and so on.

This opens the question of the future, which is probably the most important question in this conference. Where to go from here? Because obviously, the very success of an enterprise like the Royal Court always leads to the people who are produced by that success passing into the mainstream, or who are no longer the main interest of an innovative, revolutionary, and experimental theatre like that at the Court.

MR. WARDLE: The immediate quotation that springs to my mind after what Martin has said is a remark that George Devine made to me on one of the two occasions that I ever met him, in about 1962. At that particular moment, the Court was not at its zenith, and he said, "We are the spearhead here, but the problem is how do you keep sharpening the spear? Because we are at the mercy of whatever comes in." That final statement has been qualified by some of the initiatives that have been taken, not always by writers, since that time.

And from the audience's point of view, I think one of the things that has made the Royal Court Theatre the most exciting English theatre, certainly in my experience, is the sensation on certain, perhaps widely separated occasions, of the earth shifting under your feet, something hitherto unspeakable is being spoken, something private you never expressed to anybody else is being voiced on a public platform.

The two most conspicuous and historically celebrated examples of that are the arrival of John Osborne and the arrival of Edward Bond. When the first arrived, I wasn't reviewing, and when the second arrived, I made a bloody fool of myself by attacking the play; since then I have seen the error of my ways. But nevertheless, as an audience member, the experience was very real on those occasions. And in between those examples, one has the feeling that over and over again, even if the experience is not always equaled, the Court theatre is going to start off in new directions from where it seemed to have ended.

From my point of view, admitting all the Continental genealogy to which Martin has drawn attention, the Royal Court shows English society to English society, not simply in a directly reflecting way, but with some sense of moving on, showing that there are some other places you are going. It is not just a question of saying, "This is the way the bourgeoisie behave," but "This is what may happen the day after tomorrow." This is a tendency which obviously became much more pronounced with the arrival of the politicized generation, which concentrated very much on saying, "We think we should all be allowed a fascist state week after next."

Looking at the successive periods of rebirths, which, I agree with Martin Esslin, have taken place, I think the biggest watershed of all was the arrival of Bond. Prior to his arrival, the Court's productions furnished great excitement, fun, and marvelous acting, but also a curious feeling of innocence about quite a lot of it.

If one thinks of the early years of the Court as an organization that had, no matter how unexpressed or how unsystematized, a left-wing position, there was always the feeling of the decent thing to do, no matter what the class injustice happened to be. This is best summed up in that scene of the last of the Wesker plays, *Talking About Jerusalem,* where the family go to the country to earn a living by William Morris handicraft, which turns out to be impossible.[10] The husband takes a job in a factory and notices a roll of spare worn linoleum, which he takes home. Although the theft is of no significant monetary value, when it is discovered he is fired. And the feeling in the play is that he was quite right to be fired because, although it may be unjust that this squire-type figure who runs the factory has a social superiority which his money has given him, all the same, it's wrong to steal. That's one of the old-fashioned English decencies that persisted inside the Court frame, no matter what its politics, up to the arrival of the Bond generation, at which point all this comes down in flames. I think this is one reason why I and so many other people were shattered by the first night of *Saved.* In retrospect, one can see that the great English bluff has been called; there was up to that point the idea that one lives inside a society which is looked after by Nanny, who is

10. *Talking About Jerusalem* opened July 27, 1960.

assumed to be a motherly, kindly person who has your own good at heart. With the arrival of Bond, Nanny becomes a witch who will stick her knitting needles down your eardrums if you give her half a chance.

And the whole idea of England as a decent place to live, where people are kind to each other and everything is as good as it can be in the rather gray, rainy climate, gave way to the idea of a Hell on earth; it seemed at the time to be a bit of a fantasy, but the things that are happening in the world, and indeed in England itself since the arrival of Bond, have more than justified any prophecy that he had to make at the time.

I do think that the statement that the Court was a direct descendant of the Copeau tradition needs a certain amount of qualification. Michael Hallifax has noted Devine's wish for a craftsman's theatre. On the other hand, few of his Old Vic School acting students ever set foot on the Royal Court stage. Sheila Ballantine was one, Joan Plowright was another, but there weren't very many of them. Not because Devine did not want them so much as because Tony Richardson was adamantly opposed to them. Richardson described the acting style which was absorbed at the Old Vic School as a lot of sub-Copeau jumping about, not at all suitable for the type of naturalistic repertoire which was the particular discovery of the early years at the Court.

Interestingly enough, Saint-Denis always used to say, "Don't look for immediate effects. Look for the results of my work in five years, ten years." And some people feel that his reputation was extremely inflated because so much of it consisted of promises and forecasts that kept on not coming true.

On the other hand, the last phase of Saint-Denis' career was at the Juilliard School, where the acrobatic tradition, the mask work, the pantomime, and all the skills of the French commedia were being passed on to American actors. [11] And I'm told that graduates from that Juilliard School are something like 60 percent to 70 percent employed compared to the usually unemployed majority of the acting profession in this country.

MR. ESSLIN: Irving, I agree with you about that aspect of the influence of

11. With John Houseman, Saint-Denis was a founding codirector of the new Drama Division of the Juilliard School in 1961 but never actually taught there.

Copeau. I was thinking of the general attitude that Saint-Denis brought to the theatre, which I think is still absolutely vital, one of regarding the theatre as a serious art form which is a public service and a public necessity of the culture; and second, Saint-Denis' concept of style, of finding the appropriate style for each play, a lesson, I think, that has not yet begun to be absorbed. Of the utmost importance is the idea of taking the text as the basis of the play, not imposing a style. That is the influence of Saint-Denis.

I arrived in England at the age of twenty in the beginning of 1939, having just finished, a few days before Hitler occupied Vienna, my course at the Reinhardt seminar. The people who saved my life were a wonderful family, one of whose daughters is married to Alec Guinness. I had only a very short visa, and the government said I had to leave. Mr. Michael Salmon said, "Well, you won't do that. We'll give you a student status." And he took me to Saint-Denis and George Devine, who gave me a scholarship to the London Theatre Studio (which is another step in that genealogy). But my scholarship there, alas, never materialized because the studio closed when the war broke out. But I was taken by Devine and Saint-Denis to see the end-of-term performance of the school, which was in a garage in Islington. The performance consisted of Vanbrugh's one-act *The Confederacy,* which was beautifully done. And the second part was Clemance Dane's *Bramwell Bronte,* with Peter Ustinov playing Bramwell. They were showing how different the styles were for these two plays, one a nineteenth-century realistic piece and the other an eighteenth-century comedy. This is how I got to know Devine. Later I got a job at the BBC in the German section, which was located on the left-hand side of the fifth floor; on the right-hand side was the French section, of which one of the prominent members was Jacques Duchesne, alias Michel Saint-Denis. I had a close connection with him, and I do believe that his influence was not overestimated, that it is absolutely vital. Indeed, I think George Devine would be the first to say that he regarded him as his master.

MR. WARDLE: Oh, yes.

MR. ESSLIN: So anything that happens at the Royal Court also indirectly comes from Saint-Denis.

MR. WARDLE: The fact remains that Saint-Denis was around but never worked at the Court.

MR. ESSLIN: No, but as I said, they were a joint team. They were the

212

London Theatre Studio, and I can't think of any other theatre school, certainly not the Royal Academy of Dramatic Art, which has that kind of theory behind it.

MR. WARDLE: But surely, there was divergence. Once the new English repertoire got going, there was reported back the bemused reaction of Saint-Denis, "I don't remember George ever being political."

I was just reading the Shostokovitch memoirs, and he talks about the latter days of the Moscow Art Theatre when they were putting on a play about people being forced to share apartments—five, six, seven families in one apartment with split beaverboard screens in between them—and they were trying to represent this as a comedy, even though, in fact, it stood for a horrendous set of social conditions of the time. And Stanislavski sat through part of this and came up with his famous line, "I don't believe it." Because he had a house, he didn't realize that people were sharing apartments, and so it was carefully explained to Stanislavski that there were people, even in Moscow, who didn't have an apartment to themselves. He finally accepted this and said, "Well, when we put this play on, we will put a poster outside saying this is a play about people having to share apartments because otherwise, they won't believe it when they come in."

MR. ESSLIN: Saint-Denis was very political. In fact, he was a political commentator right through the war. Very left wing. He was at constant odds with the De Gaulle faction in the BBC. But, on top of that, one of the more memorable productions that Saint-Denis did at the end of his life was *Puntila* with Glenda Jackson and Patrick McGee at the Royal Shakespeare.[12] He was probably more political than Devine, curiously enough. Don't forget that he was inspector general of the Dissent Political Association in France. He created the network of regional theatres in France after the war. He went to America to work with the Juilliard as a kind of not only cultural but political missionary. So I think the view of Saint-Denis as a kind of Stanislavski withdrawn from life is quite wrong. He was very down to earth. That's why he called himself Jacques Duchesne when he was a commentator. He was a peasant, and the Copeau tradition has that in it, although Copeau was more on the religious side, but it was religious populism that Copeau represented politically.

But I would also say that curiously, George Devine was a com-

12. *Puntila* opened July 15, 1965.

pletely different kind of animal from the later Royal Court people, including Bill Gaskill, because he was a product of the OUDS. He was a chap who had a Nanny, no doubt; he had a very middle-class sort of ambience. Of course, a middle-class intellectual was a left-wing intellectual, but he shared this with the Auden-Isherwood—Stephen Spender type of left-wing intellectual; this is a different animal from the Edward Bond–type intellectual, and it's admirable that the Royal Court could evolve, through the openness that Devine instilled, into the Edward Bond and Howard Barker type of revolution reality.

MR. WARDLE: I think there were these two sides to Devine's nature and to his professional life which have gone marching on: first, the tendency to emphasize teaching and research on the one hand, and then to want to get the show on, on the other. I think that kind of polarity has gone through the company's history in a very fruitful way.

And he was very much aware that as soon as anything succeeded, it tended to get overrun by the locusts, then taken up and become trendy and die; then it became necessary to pick up sticks and go somewhere else. He said, "There must be somewhere to go for people who aren't 'with it' because they are the people who create the 'with its.'" That was what he called one of his spear-sharpening slogans. I think this has repeatedly happened. For example, when Bill Gaskill succeeded Devine in 1965, initially there was a return to the past with new plays by established Court writers, but the season really took off when the then unknown Edward Bond arrived on the scene.

We might mention also the ways in which certain things became revitalized during the Court's history, for example, the naturalism that emerged most conspicuously in the Lawrence plays. Naturalism had been held in disrepute until the Lawrence productions revitalized the style.

At the Court, in its twenty-five-year period, one of the greatest experiences for audiences was to witness these practically unknown, unstaged plays (which looked very clumsy and thick, dense, on the page) and to see these pieces breathe and live.

In the Peter Gill productions of the Lawrence plays the ordinary processes of living, walking about and washing one's hands, or lighting a lamp, became not only interesting but objects of respect and something beautiful. That, for me, was one of the big messages of the Court. Not that the work always has to represent social conflict or political issues, but simply that the spectacle of ordinary life is something of inherent dignity.

MR. ESSLIN: Yes, I think that one of the important strands that I omitted mentioning is the revival of classic plays. It was said that *The Country Wife* was produced for cynical motives, but the fact that Restoration comedy could be done as a kind of Hogarthian social statement rather than a perfumed kind of rococo revival came out of the Court, and, similarly, the absolutely brilliant Chekhov productions, notably the *Uncle Vanya* with Scofield, and the *Three Sisters* with Glenda Jackson; both were memorable experiences. [13]

As an outsider who has been observing the Court for a long time, I believe that the danger of the Court—especially in the last few years—is that it simply becomes another theatre like the Bush, the Half Moon, or any of the other noncommercial houses. I think the distinctiveness of the Court needs to be redefined. I think that the danger of the present situation in England is that it is too easy to be on the acceptable, left side politically, by saying, "That awful bitch, Mrs. Thatcher." Because the polarization is so obvious you get a lot of vituperative but not very well-written or deeply thought-out plays; this is a danger. What always happened in the history of the Court, and has continually renewed it, was the discovery of somebody like Bond or Brenton or David Hare. What it amounts to is finding the really outstanding young writers who will put over their message in a form that is in itself valuable. That is the problem, and it often is a matter of luck. But on the other hand, the luck is generated by the fact that people know that this is the *place* where that kind of work is best done.

MR. BROCKETT: I've heard it said several times since we've been here that the justification of the Royal Court continuing is that it is the only proscenium theatre devoted to this kind of work.

Is it really not more accurate to say that it is the only West End theatre that is devoted to this? Is the proscenium itself important, or is it not the fact that it is considered to be a member of a certain class of theatre rather than the fact that it's a proscenium arch theatre? It seems to me that there have not been many playwrights' theatres that have been able to maintain themselves for very long. In this country,

13. *Uncle Vanya* opened February 24, 1970; *Three Sisters* opened April 18, 1967.

La Mama is certainly devoted to the playwright, but the fact that it's an off-off-Broadway theatre means that it does not always get the kind of attention that another kind of theatre would.

MR. WARDLE: The point of the Court's being a proscenium theatre is a simple one: it is the conventional kind of building to which the broad spectrum of English playgoing audiences would go, rather than a fringe space such as the back room of a pub or an attic, which would attract a different audience. Therefore, instead of presenting a Brenton play to a fringe audience, who would automatically go along with the villainy of Mrs. Thatcher, at the Court the writer has to find ways to put that view across.

I, personally, would differ totally from the most vocal opposition to the Court, which comes from the politicized wing, for example, from John McGrath and the 7 : 84 Company, in whose view the effect of the Court's work has been to devour generation after generation of potentially radical writers and castrate and emasculate them in order to give a bourgeois public a thrill.

MR. ESSLIN: The Theatre Upstairs has the possibility of doing exactly what the Bush Theatre and all of the other pub theatres are doing. I remember memorable occasions, especially a play by Howard Brenton called *Fruit,* which had a marvelously satirical attack on Heath and was brilliantly done.[14] In the play, journalists discover that the prime minister is a homosexual and threaten an exposé but then discover the shock value is nil because the homosexuality had been known all the time. Therefore, one couldn't really blackmail anybody with it. It was a superb piece of political satire; thus that kind of thing has been and can be done in the Theatre Upstairs but probably couldn't be done in the same way on the Court's main stage.

On the other hand, Brenton's *Magnificence,* which also was a wonderful experience in the theatre, did present, with the means that were possible in a larger theatre, not just a piece of pamphleteering but the genuine exploration of a similar issue in a way that was artistically valid because both points of view were being well represented.[15] That is the essence of really good political theatre. The political theatre in which all the people with ties and suits are idiots isn't convincing because it's *part de prie.*

14. *Fruit* opened in the Theatre Upstairs September 28, 1970.
15. *Magnificence* opened June 28 1973.

MR. BROCKETT: Why is it important that the Royal Court is a proscenium theatre?

MR. STAFFORD-CLARK [speaking from the audience]: I think it's important because a proscenium really demands the examination of the work put on in it. Studio theatres are inclined to make the work intimate, to make the experience of theatregoing warmer. I think that diffuses the value of the work examined. The proscenium provides a much more rigorous test. But I think that we're not a West End theatre any more. Although the policy and the alignment were more toward the West End when the theatre was founded, since then the Court, while geographically remaining in the same place, has shifted eastward, away from the West End.

MR. BROCKETT: I really don't understand why the proscenium stage is a special asset.

MR. ESSLIN: There's a very important sociological or social factor: if a play is written for a proscenium-type theatre, it has a much larger chance of being done in other theatres because the prevailing type of theatres in our culture, whether they are in Germany or Scandinavia or, indeed, in America, is that type. This may change, but it now remains the case.

MR. BURGE [speaking from the audience]: The Court's value is not only that it's a proscenium theatre. It has, in a sense, become an established theatre. If the Court disappears, there's no established theatre that actually does new work.

MR. BROCKETT: To me that is a more satisfying answer, to say it's an established theatre. Because obviously you can do plays written for certain kinds of theatres in other kinds of theatres. Shakespeare did not write for a proscenium arch theatre, but he's done there all the time.

MR. ESSLIN: Yes, it has now become an established convention that Shakespeare's done that way. In any event, the difference is not that great, particularly since the spare style now being done is nearer the Shakespearean style.

The difficulty is that the National Theatre, for example, which does do new writers like Brenton and Hare, is under a different kind of economic constraint; they have to do plays with 90 percent ticket sales in a house holding some nine hundred people. That is a different proposition from having a 75 percent capacity and the house holding four hundred people, which is the situation at the Court.

217

OBSERVER: We have talked about the future. You've pointed out the period when Osborne was in dominance, moving on to Bond. What's happening now, and likely to happen?

MR. WARDLE: I feel that one of the important things that happened between 1975 and the present is that the Court has begun to assimilate the work of the fringe movement. In its early stages, it was difficult for new writers representing change to achieve an accommodation because the policy of the Court then was to work inside the administration for change, and not to offend the Arts Council any more than was necessary, to collect capitalist backers as energetically as possible, and to do the work, no matter how subversive, while disturbing the people with the money as little as possible.

In the view of many young theatre makers who arrived after 1968, the effect of this was to corrupt everyone or, at least, to muzzle everyone concerned in the operation no matter how excellent their intentions were in the first case.

There were these two diametrically opposite ways of pursuing radical theatre, either to operate *inside* the existing structure and manipulate it to your direction, or to go away and make something of your own.

This topic was touched on a day or two ago in relation to David Hare's association with the Court as literary director, because he was very much a product of the touring, fly-by-night fringe movement that was not really in sympathy with the early Court administration. Particularly since the arrival of Max Stafford-Clark, who also works in Joint Stock with Bill Gaskill, a much greater accommodation between the two groups now exists. Max comes out of the fringe movement, and yet he has been able to combine what he represents with what was already established at the Court. For example, we were talking about classics. Certainly one of the most illuminating classical revivals I've seen there *ever* was the modern Irish version of *The Sea Gull*, which Max directed.[16]

Meanwhile, the experimental work continues into the future. I think it is happening largely by a sort of moving away to what has been described as "the Royal Court in exile," that is, through the operation of the Joint Stock company. Although in Joint Stock the

16. The Irish version of *The Sea Gull* by Thomas Gilroy opened April 8, 1981.

218

writer remains primary (in the form of delivering the final script), there is a much greater contribution from the company, and from the directors, in deciding what projects are to be rejected or accepted, and in producing a body of preliminary research from which the final text will emerge. So, with luck, these two elements are converging without any concomitant loss.

MS. JELLICOE [speaking from the audience]: I think in a way the Royal Court Theatre's job is done. The first year, we discovered about seven playwrights, by the end of the second year, fifteen. There are now hundreds of theatres that do new work. What there are not are audiences which are being radically affected in a plastic society. I suspect there are about fifty thousand regular playgoers in Britain. But the theatre is not really touching people, and it's not fighting the plastic society and television. I think the job now is not to look for new writers; we've plenty of new writers. It is to reach people who don't go to theatre. It is to touch people with art who have no feeling for art, who have no knowledge of it. They watch television six hours a night. That should be our job now, not looking for new writers.

MR. WARDLE: Whose job?

MS. JELLICOE: The job of artists in the theatre. I think we are all living in a very precious little world where one audience is going to the National and to the Royal Shakespeare and to the Royal Court and to certain significant theatres in the provinces, but in all, it is a very small audience, and we are not touching people as a whole. We are not touching the radicals that we are all paying lip service to.

MR. ESSLIN: I'm grateful for what you have said. I come from this plastic world of radio and television. I've spent thirty-seven years with the BBC and was in charge of radio drama in England for sixteen years. I must say that the influence on the mass media of what is being presented to the fifty thousand theatregoers at theatres like the Royal Court is enormous. It is true that much of the television output is plastic, but it also presents plays by Wesker, Osborne, David Hare, Hampton, and many other writers who come out of this tradition. I know from my own experience as head of radio drama that one can get today an audience of a million people for a play by Pinter or a million people for a play by Howard Barker.

We must always keep in mind that in our civilization, the theatre is a minority, an elitist art form, which nevertheless has an enormous amplification through its indirect influence on the media. Actually, the amount of serious, socially concerned drama on the British radio and television is remarkable. I'm quite convinced over the long run it will have considerable influence on changing the social climate. It has already done so, but I think it will be even more true over the long run.

MS. JELLICOE: But my point is that television is a plastic medium. The audience is entirely passive. I think it is the duty of artists to take their art to people, not to send it through television sets.

MR. ESSLIN: Oh, no, I agree with you ideally, but if you add up all the seats in all the theatres in the British Isles, you will never get more than a 5 percent attendance.

MS. JELLICOE: I believe that it is all the more important in light of that to go to the people.

MR. BROCKETT: But couldn't you argue that what you really need now is something that's comparable to what happened with *Look Back in Anger* in 1956? At that time, you had all the people who were not going to the theatre also, didn't you? Attracting an audience that had not been going there, I thought, was one of the things which occurred at the time. Osborne brought a new kind of play, with new kinds of attitudes.

MR. ESSLIN: The sociological background to the *Look Back in Anger* explosion is that it represented a generation which was the first product of the new education act of 1945. They were people born around 1930 from working-class backgrounds who had been absorbed into a new type of middle class through that first educational system to give free access to universities. That was a new audience, but it came out of, not a theatre event, but the sociological revolution of a political revolution.

OBSERVER: But how much influence does television have in theatre?

MR. BURGE: I have to say that I was working in television at the time *Look Back in Anger* was first performed, and we regarded it as an old-fashioned play. Already television was doing extremely interesting social plays, but, of course, they weren't noticed by the bourgeois audience.

MS. JELLICOE: Would you name those shows?

MR. ESSLIN: John Arden's first play was a radio play, *The Life of Man*, which is beautiful, and it was not long before he wrote *Sergeant Musgrave's Dance*. Don't forget that Tony Richardson was working at

220

BBC television before he took up with the Royal Court, and he did some interesting things, sometimes going against the text, but certainly very socially aware.

I agree with Ann that television is a plastic medium. It has terrible drawbacks, but in the history of British television drama, over and over again, there are examples of productions that have a very real political and social influence.

Any cultural manifestation has some influence. David Hockney's painting had an influence on design at the Court. Everything is interconnected, and whatever emerges may start the ice flow to break elsewhere.

MR. BURGE: We probably should say that the Royal Court's job is never finished—the theatre's job is never finished. But, of course, it changes.

I think it would be interesting perhaps to hear a few words from Max about his views about how it *can* change.

MR. STAFFORD-CLARK: I think about it every day. Most of us who have been with Joint Stock have been on the road a number of years and it's like coming home to go into the Court. We toured enormously with Joint Stock. And there are pockets throughout the country that have been quite infected by that.

OBSERVER: Would a play like Dunbar's *The Arbor* attract a different kind of audience to the Court? And would it have a more telling effect if it were broadcast on television back into the culturally deprived area from which it came?

MR. STAFFORD-CLARK: Parts of it have been done there. But I doubt that you could have televised it. Its language and form would not be accepted for television. The audience that it attracted at the Court was a fairly typical Royal Court audience. It was done first in the Young Writers' Festival in the Theatre Upstairs and then brought downstairs and expanded for a full-length play on the main stage. We could not have done that if we had not first had the opportunity to see it in the Young Writers' Festival. This illustrates the importance of the youth theatre as only one among many resources of new writing that the Royal Court must keep expanding for the future.

Notes on Participants

OSCAR G. BROCKETT, theatre historian, has been awarded a Guggenheim fellowship and served as the Fulbright lecturer at the University of Bristol, 1963–1964. He has taught at several American universities, including Indiana and Southern California, where he held the positions of Distinguished Professor of Theatre and DeMille Professor of Drama, respectively. He served as dean of the College of Fine Arts at the University of Texas, where, as holder of the Z. T. Scott Family Chair in Drama, he now devotes full time to research and teaching. A widely known historian, Brockett has written eight books and over fifty articles on various aspects of the theatre. His book *History of the Theatre,* one of the most significant published in its field since World War II and now in its fifth edition, has been translated into Chinese and Italian.

STUART BURGE, artistic director for the English Stage Company between 1977 and 1979, began his career as an actor in the first Young Vic Company and became one of George Devine's assistants at the Old Vic Theatre School. He served as director of the Queen's Theatre, Hornchurch, and the Nottingham Playhouse. He has directed nearly one hundred plays for television, including *David Copperfield* and *Sons and Lovers.* In 1981 he returned to the Royal Court, where he appeared as Sorin in *The Sea Gull,* directed by Max Stafford-Clark. Burge recently directed *The Old Men at the Zoo* and *Much Ado About Nothing* for television, as well as Nigel Williams' *Breaking Up* and Ann Devlin's *Naming the Names.*

CARYL CHURCHILL, playwright, has written for radio, television, and the stage. She made her debut at the Royal Court as a playwright in 1972 with *Owners,* directed by Nicholas Wright, in the Theatre Upstairs. Other works of hers produced at the Court include *Objections to Sex and Violence* (directed by John Tydeman), *Traps* (directed by John Ashford), *Top Girls,* and *Serious Money* (both directed by Max Stafford-Clark). Joint Stock productions that have played at the Court are *Light Shining in Buckinghamshire, Cloud Nine* (both directed by Max Stafford-Clark), and *Fen* (directed by Les Waters).

DEIRDRE CLANCY's career encompasses well over fifty productions for theatre, opera, and film. In addition to her work for the Royal Court, she has designed many productions for the National Theatre: *Spring Awakening,*

Grand Manoeuvres, The Playboy of the Western World, Watch It Come Down, Il Campiello, Volpone, The Madras House, Lorenzaccio, A Midsummer Night's Dream, Cinderella, Golden Boy, Wild Honey, and *The Government Inspector.* She has also designed for the Royal Shakespeare Company, Edinburgh Festival, English National Opera, and in Munich, Rome, and Stratford (Ontario). At Chichester she designed the costumes for *The Way of the World* and *Annie Get Your Gun.* Her career in the United States includes designing costumes in New York for the Metropolitan Opera, for a production of *Strange Interlude,* and in Minneapolis for the Guthrie Theatre.

HARRIET CRUICKSHANK joined the ESC at the Royal Court Theatre in 1971 as assistant to the general manager; in 1973 she became manager of the Theatre Upstairs. Soon thereafter she left the Court, returning in 1977 as head of public relations, a position she held until 1981, when she resigned to start her own literary and theatrical agency.

JOHN DILLON, artistic director of the Milwaukee Repertory Theater since 1977, has directed at leading regional theatres during the last ten years. His productions include Mamet's *Lakeboat,* Gray's *Namesake,* Gogol's *Dead Souls,* Strindberg's *The Dance of Death,* and Wilder's *The Matchmaker.* Between 1970 and 1973, Dillon was a member of Joseph Chaiken's Open Theatre, touring with the company throughout North America, Europe, and the Middle East.

KARL EIGSTI, designer, studied in England on a Fulbright fellowship and received his M.A. in design from the University of Bristol in 1963. Since then he has designed many New York productions and for the leading regional theatres, including Cincinnati's Playhouse in the Park, the Long Wharf Theatre, and, especially, Arena Stage, where he has designed many productions over the last twenty years. In addition to his work as a professional designer, he has for several years taught design, first at the New York University School of the Arts, and now at Brandeis University.

MARTIN ESSLIN, professor of drama at Stanford University, served as head of radio drama at the BBC from 1963 until he retired in 1977 after thirty-seven years of service. His many publications include *The Theatre of the Absurd; The Work of Harold Pinter; Brecht: A Choice of Evils; Reflections: Essays on Modern Drama; An Anatomy of Drama; Mediation: Essays on Brecht, Beckett, and the Media,* published by the Louisiana State University Press in 1980; *The Age of Television;* and, most recently, *The Field of Drama: How the Signs of Drama Create Meaning on Stage and Screen.*

GERALD FREEDMAN, artistic director for the Great Lakes Theater Festival, has served as the artistic director of the New York Shakespeare Festival and the American Shakespeare Theater and was former codirector of the Acting Company. He staged the original New York productions of *Hair, The Robber Bridegroom,* and *The Gay Life,* the 1980 Broadway revival of *West Side Story,* which he codirected with Jerome Robbins, and New York City Opera revivals of *Brigadoon* and *South Pacific*.

WILLIAM GASKILL began directing at the Royal Court in 1957 and served as artistic director for the ESC between 1965 and 1972, following two years with the National Theatre as associate director. Among the many productions he has directed at the Court are *A Resounding Tinkle*, *Epitaph for George Dillon*, *One Way Pendulum*, *The Happy Haven*, *Macbeth*, *Three Sisters*, *Saved*, *Early Morning*, *The Sea*, *Lear*, and *Man Is Man*. In 1979 he returned to the Court to direct Nicholas Wright's *The Gorky Brigade*, in 1981 to direct Stephen Lowe's *Tibetan Inroads*, and in 1986 to direct *Women Beware Women* by Thomas Middleton and Howard Barker.

AMLIN GRAY, for many years resident dramatist at the Milwaukee Repertory Theater, now artistic associate of the organization, won the Obie Award in 1981 for his play *How I Got That Story*. His other plays include *Outlanders*, *The Fantod*, *Namesake*, and *Kingdom Come*.

MICHAEL HALLIFAX is an associate of the National Theatre of Great Britain, which company, under its first director, Sir Laurence Olivier, he joined in 1966. For several years he served as stage manager for many productions in London's West End. George Devine, artistic director of the newly formed English Stage Company, appointed him stage director, and he remained with that company from its first day in the Royal Court Theatre in January, 1956, to the end of February, 1959. After eighteen months as manager of the Comedy Theatre, he joined the Royal Shakespeare Company, first as manager and licensee of the Royal Shakespeare Theatre, Stratford-upon-Avon, for three and a half years and then as London manager at the Aldwych Theatre. During the first four months of 1986 he undertook a lecture tour in America visiting universities and colleges to talk about the British theatre.

CHRISTOPHER HAMPTON, the first resident dramatist at the Court, made his debut at the Court as a playwright with *When Did You Last See My Mother?* in 1966. Other works by Hampton staged at the Court include *Total Eclipse*, *The Philanthropist*, *Savages*, and *Treats*. He also has translated and adapted such classics as *Uncle Vanya*, *Hedda Gabler*, *A Doll's House*, *Don Juan*, *Tales from the Vienna Woods*, *The Wild Duck*, *Ghosts*, and *Tartuffe*. In the spring of 1981, David Hare directed a revival of *Total Eclipse* at the Lyric Hammersmith, London. Hampton's recent plays include *Tales from Hollywood*, premiered at the Mark Taper Forum in 1982 and subsequently performed at the National Theatre, and *Les Liaisons Dangereuses* for the Royal Shakespeare Company, which transferred to the Ambassadors Theatre in October, 1986, and to New York in 1987. His screenplays include *The Honorary Consul* (1983), *Wolf at the Door* (1986), and *The Good Father* (1986). Most recently he has worked on a film based on Joseph Conrad's *Nostromo*, which is to be produced by Steven Spielberg and directed by David Lean.

225

DAVID HARE, playwright, is the author of ten full-length plays, which include *Slag, Plenty, Fanshen,* and *A Map of the World,* all of which have been seen in both London and New York. His last play, *Pravda,* written with Howard Brenton, ran for eighteen months at the National Theatre, and he has also presented a double bill, *The Bay at Nice,* at the National Theatre. His first feature film, *Wetherby,* which he wrote and directed, won the Golden Bear at Berlin in 1985.

DONALD HOWARTH, director and playwright, had his first play, *Sugar in the Morning,* directed in 1959 by William Gaskill at the Royal Court, where he subsequently served as literary manager for two years. His other plays produced at the Court include OGODIVELEFTTHEGASON and *Three Months Gone.* In addition to writing plays, he also directs. At the Court he has directed Mustapha Matura's *Play Mas* and *Rum 'an Coca-Cola* and Jemi Ajibade's *Parcel Post;* for the Market Theatre in Johannesburg, *Mama Is Terry Home for Good?* by the American writer James Edward Shannon. Four of his plays were premiered in South Africa, including *Othello Sleges Blankes.* While working at The Space in Cape Town, Howarth saw John Kani and Winston Ntshona performing for the first time in *Sizwe Bansi Is Dead.* Eight years later, the three joined forces to work on *Waiting for Godot* at the Baxter Theatre, University of Cape Town. During 1980–1981 they took the production to the United States and London.

ANN JELLICOE, playwright and director, has had a number of plays produced at the Royal Court Theatre: *The Sport of My Mad Mother* (directed by George Devine and Ann Jellicoe); *The Knack* (directed by Jellicoe); *The Rising Generation* (directed by Jane Howell); and *Shelley* (directed by Jellicoe). Her translations include *Rosmersholm* and *The Sea Gull,* and her children's plays are *Clever Elsie, Smiling Peter, Silent John* and *A Good Thing or a Bad Thing* (both directed by Jellicoe). She has directed a number of plays at the Royal Court and is the author of eight other plays and translations that were first produced elsewhere. She served as literary manager of the Royal Court between 1972 and 1974. After she moved to the West of England, she was chiefly involved in discovering and developing the principle of setting up very large plays using the talent and resources of whole towns, built around a small core of professional theatre artists. To pursue this work she founded the Colway Theatre Trust in 1979 for which she produced ten plays.

BROOKS JONES, a pioneer in America's regional theatre movement, was producer of the McCarter Theatre, formed the Playhouse in the Park in Cincinnati, and has guest directed at several of the leading regional houses in the country. Since the early 1980s he has directed major arts festivals in New York and other parts of the country and is currently organizing festivals in Mexico City and in the Philippines.

STEPHEN LOWE, playwright, joined Alan Ayckbourne's company in Scarborough

226

and was commissioned to write a double bill, *Comic Pictures*, which Ayckbourne directed there in 1976. His later plays include an adaptation of *Ragged Trousered Philanthropists* for Joint Stock in 1978 and two television plays. He is currently playwright-in-residence at Dartington College of Arts. His plays produced at the Court include *Touched, Glasshouses,* and *Tibetan Inroads,* directed by William Gaskill.

MICHAEL MURRAY was producing director of the Cincinnati Playhouse in the Park for nine years, artistic director of the Charles Playhouse in Boston for eleven years, and has directed at many regional theatres. He is currently director of the theatre arts program at Brandeis University.

ROB RITCHIE was literary manager, then associate director, at the Court between 1979 and 1984. Since then he has worked as script associate for Channel Four Television and completed two books on British theatre: *The Joint Stock Book* and *Writing for the Theatre.* He now divides his time between writing and free-lance dramaturgy. In 1986 he returned to the Court as an associate director.

JOEL SCHECHTER is an associate professor of dramatic criticism at the Yale School of Drama and the editor of *Theater* magazine. He is also dramaturg and associate director for special projects at the Yale Repertory Theatre. His most recent book is *Durov's Pig: Clowns, Politics and Theatre.*

ANTONY SHER, actor, has appeared in a number of Court productions, including David Hare's *Teeth 'n' Smiles; Prayer for My Daughter,* directed by Max Stafford-Clark; Snoo Wilson's *The Glad Hand;* and Caryl Churchill's *Cloud Nine.* At the National Theatre he starred in Sam Shepard's *True West.* He is an associate artist of the Royal Shakespeare Company, where he has played leading roles in David Edgar's *Maydays,* Peter Barnes's *Red Noses,* Bulgakov's *Molière,* and Molière's *Tartuffe* (the latter two both recorded by RKO Films), as well as the Fool in Adrian Noble's production of *King Lear.* He also performed the title role in Bill Alexander's production of *Richard III,* for which he won five major awards including the London Standard's Best Actor Award (1985) and the Laurence Olivier Best Actor Award (1985), which was also given for his performance in Harvey Fierstein's *Torch Song Trilogy* in London's West End. His television credits include *The History Man;* his films include *Shadey* (screenplay by Snoo Wilson). He is author of the book *Year of the King.*

ALEXANDER SPEER is administrative director of the Actors Theatre of Louisville. His responsibilities include coordination of all financial aspects of the organization and serving as liaison between the board of directors and the theatre's administrative staff. Speer has been with Actors Theatre since 1965.

MAX STAFFORD-CLARK, artistic director of the ESC since 1979, also served as artistic director at the Traverse in Edinburgh in 1968–1969. He directed several productions at the Court before becoming its artistic director, including David Hare's *Slag* and Howard Brenton's *Magnificence,* and has directed many significant plays since then. Caryl Churchill's *Cloud Nine* and *Serious Money* were both directed by Stafford-Clark, and in 1988 he staged Farquhar's *The Recruiting Officer* and Timberlake Wertenbaker's new play, *Our Country's Good,* offering them in repertoire.

IRVING WARDLE has served as drama critic for *The Times* since 1963. Before that, he was a subeditor for *The Times Educational Supplement* and critic for the *Observer.* His publications include *The Theatres of George Devine* and *Shaw: The Plays.* His plays include *The Houseboy* (Open Space Theatre) and *Dolls,* which appeared at the Soho Poly Theatre in July, 1986.

SNOO WILSON was one of seven authors of two collective scripts produced at the Court, *Lay By* and *England's Ireland,* both of which he directed, the latter in conjunction with David Hare. Other plays by Wilson produced at the Court include *The Pleasure Principle,* directed by David Hare, and *The Glad Hand,* directed by Max Stafford-Clark. His plays produced elsewhere include *The Beast, The Everest Hotel,* and *Flaming Bodies.*

NICHOLAS WRIGHT, joint artistic director of the Royal Court with Robert Kidd, 1975–1977, joined the Royal Court as casting director in 1967. He served as director of the Theatre Upstairs, 1969–1971 and 1972–1974. Among the works he has directed at the Court are *AC/DC, The Great Caper,* and Caryl Churchill's *Owners.* Several of his own plays have been produced at the Court, including *The Gorky Brigade,* directed by William Gaskill. In 1980 his play *One Fine Day* appeared at the Riverside Studios, London. *The Custom of the Country* and *The Desert Air* were produced by the Royal Shakespeare Company in 1983 and 1984, respectively; Joint Stock produced *The Crimes of Vautrin* in 1983. He is an associate director of the National Theatre of Great Britain, with special responsibility for new writing.

Bibliography

Manuscript Sources

Minutes, correspondence, and other documents are in the personal collection of Oscar Lewenstein, resident in England. Copies of the minutes and correspondence are in the possession of the editors.

Anderson, Lindsay, Jocelyn Herbert, Ann Jellicoe, Anthony Page, David Storey, and Nicholas Wright to the ESC Council, December 19, 1973.

Bond, Edward, to the English Stage Company Council, January 21, 1977.

Field, Tony, to Greville Poke, November 26, 1976.

Kidd, Robert, to the English Stage Company Council, January 10, 1977.

Kidd, Robert, to Greville Poke, January 10, 1977.

Lewenstein, Oscar, to Greville Poke, January 24, 1977.

Lewenstein, Oscar. Artistic Report to the ESC Council, July 22, 1975.

————. "Suggested Structure for Artistic Direction in the Event of the English Stage Company Taking Over the Old Vic," November 27, 1973.

Minutes of Meetings of the ESC Council, January 24, 1973; July 22, August 12, 1975; May 27, 1976.

Minutes of Meetings of the ESC Management Committee, December 30, 1975; January 15, April 22, May 5, June 8, August 11, October 20, November 17, 1976; May 16, June 27, 1977.

Stafford-Clark, Max. Royal Court Policy Statement, March 18, 1980.

Wardle, Irving, to Billy J. Harbin, March 4, 1984.

Books

Biner, Pierre. *The Living Theatre: A History Without Myths.* New York, 1972.

Bradby, David. *Modern French Drama, 1940–1980.* Cambridge, 1984.

Brockett, Oscar G. *History of the Theatre.* 5th ed. Boston, 1987.

Browne, Terry. *Playwrights' Theatre.* London, 1975.

Carpenter, Humphrey. *O.U.D.S.* Oxford, 1985.

Duncan, Ronald. *How to Make Enemies.* London, 1968.

Findlater, Richard, ed. *At the Royal Court: Twenty-five Years of the English Stage Company.* Ambergate, 1981.

Gibbs, James. *Wole Soyinka.* New York, 1986.

Gielgud, John. *An Actor and His Time.* London, 1979.

Johnstone, Keith. *Impro: Improvisation and the Theatre.* London, 1981.

Kureishi, Hanif. *Borderline.* London, 1981.

Lahr, John, ed. *The Orton Diaries.* London, 1986.

Lahr, John. *Prick Up Your Ears.* London, 1978.

Larsen, Stephen. *A Writer and His Gods.* Stockholm, 1983.

Leeming, Glenda. *Wesker the Playwright.* London, 1983.

Roberts, Philip. *The Royal Court Theatre, 1965–1972.* London, 1986.

Wardle, Irving. *The Theatres of George Devine.* London, 1978.

Articles

Burian, Jarka M. "Contemporary British Scenography, Part I." *Theatre Design and Technology,* XIX (Spring, 1983), 4–12.

———. "Contemporary British Scenography, Part II." *Theatre Design and Technology,* XIX (Fall, 1983), 4–13.

Gaskill, William. "Glorious Riches Spring from Talents in Turmoil." *The Times,* January 13, 1986.

Gussow, Mel. "Profiles (Peggy Ramsay)." *New Yorker,* May 23, 1988, pp. 35–60.

Khan, Naseem. "The Fringe." *Drama,* CXLIX (Autumn, 1983), 8–10.

Lohr, Steve. "Cash Woes of Britain's Theaters." *New York Times,* November 10, 1986.

Morley, Sheridan. "Stuart Burge's Loyalty to the Royal Court." *The Times,* April 15, 1981.

———. "Transatlantic Tributes." *The Times,* August 15, 1985.

Myerson, Jonathan. "David Hare: Fringe Graduate." *Drama,* CXLIX (Autumn, 1983), 26–28.

Schumann, Peter. "Bread and Puppets." *The Drama Review,* XIV, No. 3 (1970), 35.

Tynan, Kenneth. Review of *Lady on the Barometer, Observer,* December 8, 1958.

Wesker, Arnold. "The Strange Affair of the Actors' Revolt." *Sunday Times Weekly Review,* August 30, 1981.

Wright, Nicholas. To the Editor. *Time Out,* February 7, 1980.

Dissertation

Bolar, Gordan. "The Sunday Night Productions Without Decor at the Royal Court Theatre, 1957–1975." Ph.D. dissertation, Louisiana State University, 1984.

Index